书山有路勤为径，优质资源伴你行
注册世纪波学院会员，享精品图书增值服务

EASILY PASS NPDP EXAM
WITH 1000 PRACTICE QUESTIONS

NPDP考试
轻松通关1000题

楼 政 著

电子工业出版社
Publishing House of Electronics Industry
北京·BEIJING

未经许可，不得以任何方式复制或抄袭本书之部分或全部内容。

版权所有，侵权必究。

图书在版编目（CIP）数据

NPDP 考试轻松通关 1000 题 / 楼政著. —北京：电子工业出版社，2024.3
ISBN 978-7-121-47161-2

Ⅰ.①N… Ⅱ.①楼… Ⅲ.①企业管理－产品管理－产品质量认证－习题集 Ⅳ.①F273.2-44

中国国家版本馆 CIP 数据核字（2024）第 014226 号

责任编辑：袁桂春
印　　刷：涿州市京南印刷厂
装　　订：涿州市京南印刷厂
出版发行：电子工业出版社
　　　　　北京市海淀区万寿路 173 信箱　邮编 100036
开　　本：880×1230　1/16　印张：17.75　字数：415 千字
版　　次：2024 年 3 月第 1 版
印　　次：2024 年 3 月第 1 次印刷
定　　价：88.00 元

凡所购买电子工业出版社图书有缺损问题，请向购买书店调换。若书店售缺，请与本社发行部联系，联系及邮购电话：(010) 88254888，88258888。

质量投诉请发邮件至 zlts@phei.com.cn，盗版侵权举报请发邮件至 dbqq@phei.com.cn。

本书咨询联系方式：(010) 88254199，sjb@phei.com.cn。

序

本书为希望顺利通过 NPDP 认证考试的考生而写。

作为一名专业培训师和咨询顾问，在长期的专业认证培训（如 NPDP、PMP、ACP 等）中，我发现很多学员在学习过程中有三个普遍的痛点。为了帮助学员消除痛点，提高学习效果和答题水平，我采取了相应的对策。

第一个痛点是学员看书的积极性和效率不高，效果也一般。不过，学员做题的积极性却很高。有学员问我，能否通过做题来学习。这倒是一条途径。于是，我开发了一些和教材[①]章节完全同步的试题，学员上完课或看完教材后就可以同步做试题，一旦做错了题，就回到教材上找出处，并延伸阅读考点相关内容。通过对照、澄清、纠错、查漏和补缺，学员可以有效地增补和巩固知识。这种找准痛点下手，针对性极强的方法显著提升了学员的学习效率和效果，受到了学员的欢迎。

第二个痛点是在备考过程中，学员对自己的知识掌握程度和答题水平不甚了解。经过一段时间的培训后，学员学习了大量知识、方法和工具，迫切需要用一套综合试题来测量自己的当前水平，同时提前熟悉真实考试情境。于是，我开发了一套期中综合试题，帮助学员进行当前水平评估并熟悉真实考试情境。这套综合试题完全按照真实考试的要素进行设计，包括考试内容、题型、占比等，能够较好地检测学员的综合水平。

第三个痛点是一些学员临考前信心不足，甚至有些焦虑。学员第一次参加 NPDP 考试，难免存在一些因未知带来的不安。一些学员因为工作繁忙，平时投入学习中的有效时间不多，临考前有些焦虑。为了消除这个痛点，给予学员更多的信心，我开发了两套考前冲刺试题。这些试题可以帮助学员全面复习考点，练习应试技巧，熟悉真实考试情境，提供改进机会，减轻考试压力。

---

① 教材指《产品经理认证（NPDP）知识体系指南（第 2 版）》。

为了提高这些试题的质量和效果，我研究了 PDMA（Product Development Management Association，NPDP 颁证机构）公布的所有试题，在总结提炼出其中的规律后，开发了这本试题集。本书的特点有三：一是试题完全按照 NPDP 考试真题的方式设计，包括试题类型、内容、占比，以及题干、问题和选项等；二是完全覆盖了考点和知识点。这些试题将教材中的知识点和考点进行了全面覆盖，同时突出了考试重点；三是解析详尽，每道题的解析都细化到了章、节、小节，直至页和行，便于学员迅速、准确地找到知识点所在位置，进行有针对性的学习。

我将这些试题应用到教学实践中，邀请学员使用、验证和反馈。为了紧贴最新的考试，我不断对这些试题进行修订、更新和完善。

总之，这 1000 道试题形成了一个有机结合的整体，帮助学员由点到面，由易到难，由浅入深，全面掌握知识点和考点，学练结合，帮助学生提高应试能力，并为真实考试做好充分准备，从而顺利通过考试。

用好这些试题，将为你实现以下价值。

1. 发现错误或疑问：到与试题对应的教材中的章节去查阅相关知识点，进行澄清、纠错、查漏、补缺，最终掌握知识点，从而提高答题正确率。

2. 练习应试技巧：提前熟悉真实考试情境，掌握应对考试的技巧和策略。通过模拟考试，提高时间管理能力。

3. 提供反馈和改进机会：提供及时的反馈和评估，了解自己的优势和不足之处。通过分析考试结果，发现自己在知识、技巧或策略上存在的问题，并有针对性地进行改进和提升。

4. 提高答题技巧和应变能力，培养"题感"，从而更好地应对考试。

5. 检验知识水平：评估自己对所学知识的理解和掌握程度。发现自己在各个知识点上的薄弱环节，及时进行补充和巩固，提高学习效果。

6. 减轻考试压力：让自己提前适应考试环境和紧张氛围，减轻在真实考试中的紧张感和压力。通过模拟考试，增强信心，培养良好的应对压力和控制情绪的能力。

7. 预测考试成绩：通过考前冲刺试题，较好地预测自己在真实考试中的成绩，从而进行目标设定和规划备考策略。

导读

——如何用好本书帮助你顺利通过 NPDP 认证考试

本书结构

本书按照学员的学习过程进行编排。书中试题分为三部分。

- 第一部分是分章同步试题，共 400 道题，涵盖了所有知识点和考点。分章同步试题的特点有三：一是分章同步试题中的知识点是按照从教材第一页到最后一页的顺序编排的，换句话说，分章同步试题是引领学员从头到尾完整看一遍教材的"抓手"；二是分章同步试题全面覆盖了教材中的知识点和考点，在真实考试中，绝大部分考点都来源于教材；三是分章同步试题难度适中，比较适合刚开始学习的学员。分章同步试题的优点有二：一是学员由分章同步试题带动阅读教材，错了再学，印象更深刻，效果也更好；二是学员将所有知识点从头到尾进行扫描式学习，基础更扎实，掌握更全面。
- 第二部分是一套期中综合试题，共 200 道题，覆盖了重要的知识点和考点。期中综合试题的特点有三：一是完全按照真实考试的考题数量、内容分布比例和出题形式，将 200 道题和各章考点随机组合而成；二是难度比分章同步试题要大些，与真实考试难度相仿；三是可以帮助学员初步掌握解题技巧和时间控制方法。期中综合试题的优点也有二：一是可以帮助学员提前熟悉真实考试情境，做到心中有数；二是对自己的期中学习成果进行检验，以便制定下一步的学习目标。

- 第三部分是两套考前冲刺试题，共 400 道题，覆盖了重要的知识点和考点。考前冲刺试题的特点有三：一是反映了新版试题的新内容和新方向；二是与真实考试试题的内容和难度高度相似，通过冲刺成绩基本就能够预测真实考试成绩；三是覆盖面广，包含了几乎所有重要考点。考前冲刺试题的优点有三：一是让学员提前进入真实考试状态；二是减轻学员的考试紧张感和压力，考前冲刺试题的成绩与真实考试成绩的相关性很高，通过考前冲刺，提前知道自己的成绩，掌握更多的已知信息可以帮助学员消除紧张感；三是切实帮助学员提高考试通过率。这些试题都是经过教学实践验证、筛选过的高质量试题。

如何使用本书

1. 备考前期，做分章同步试题。学完一章就做该章的同步试题。通过做分章同步试题，发现自己的知识盲区，再结合学习教材内容，进行巩固。

2. 备考中期，做期中综合试题。集中用 3.5 小时做这套题，测试自己的综合知识水平，并对自己考前知识掌握程度进行摸底。

3. 备考后期，如考试前两周，做考前冲刺试题。每周集中用 3.5 小时做一套冲刺试题。熟悉真实考试的情境，找到自己的薄弱环节，查漏补缺。

需要强调的是，在做题时不要只做题而不分析总结。要特别留意做错的题目，下面通过举例进行说明。

以下哪个是正确的战略层级？

A. 愿景、使命、经营战略、公司战略、创新战略、职能战略
B. 愿景、使命、公司战略、经营战略、创新战略、职能战略
C. 愿景、使命、公司战略、经营战略、职能战略、创新战略
D. 愿景、使命、经营战略、公司战略、职能战略、创新战略

如果你的答案是 A，在查阅试题答案与解析后发现正确答案是 C，解析中说明了该考点出自教材第 5 页图 1.1 和图 1.2，你就可以按图索骥，在教材中找到这两张图并进行学习。找出自己选错的原因，马上用红笔对错误之处进行标记，并将该错题整理汇总到一个专门的错题集中，便于考前集中高效温习。

总之，将该书与教材联合使用，才能达到最佳效果，通过做题温书，温书再做题，你的知识面一定会越来越广，对知识的掌握会越来越扎实，答题正确率也会越来越高，这样就能顺利通过考试。

做题须知

- 集中时间做题，答完后到教材上找考点出处，在教材上标记，总结分析错题。**楼老师金句：宁愿分析一道题，也不快刷十道题。**
- 将错题记录下来，多做几次，直到都做对为止。**楼老师金句：弄懂是关键，强化才入心。**
- 树立信心后，再做下一套试题。直到把所有试题全部做完。高质量的试题做 1000 道完全够了。不要搞题海战术。**楼老师金句：信心为王者，方法数第一。**
- 把所有错题汇总到一个文档中，将教材里缺、漏、错知识点也汇总到一个文档中。考试前将两个文档过一遍。**楼老师金句：抓住重点是关键，缺漏错中有黄金。**
- 把冲刺考试当作真实考试，测试自己的时间控制、解题方法和正确率。**楼老师金句：用好模拟考，真考才有底。**
- 总结和优化方法。真实考试前几天把错题和缺、漏、错知识点全看一遍，再上考场。**楼老师金句：巧干刻苦加努力，必过拿证不费力！**

联系作者

因篇幅和呈现方式所限，未能将解题技巧、错题分析、弱点诊断、更多高质量试题和解析视频放入本书。如果你想获得更多最新真题和更详尽的试题解析视频，可以联系楼政老师的助理，手机和微信：18681113109。

楼政老师的项目管理、产品管理和创新方法实战训练营更具实效，也更精彩。

目录

NPDP 分章同步测试 1

 教材第 1 章 "战略" 分章同步试题 2
 试题答案与解析 13
 教材第 2 章 "组合管理" 分章同步试题 17
 试题答案与解析 23
 教材第 3 章 "产品创新流程" 分章同步试题 25
 试题答案与解析 35
 教材第 4 章 "产品设计与开发工具" 分章同步试题 38
 试题答案与解析 46
 教材第 5 章 "产品创新中的市场调研" 分章同步试题 49
 试题答案与解析 55
 教材第 6 章 "文化、团队与领导力" 分章同步试题 57
 试题答案与解析 63
 教材第 7 章 "产品创新管理" 分章同步试题 65
 试题答案与解析 77

NPDP 期中测试 81

 NPDP 期中综合试题 82
 试题答案与解析 111

NPDP 考前冲刺 120
    考前冲刺试题一 121
    试题答案与解析 185
    考前冲刺试题二 194
    试题答案与解析 263

作者介绍 273

NPDP 分章同步测试

教材第 1 章 "战略" 分章同步试题

1. 以下哪个不是产品创新中的关键因素？
   A. 独特的定位　　　　　　　　　　B. 能力和资源的利用
   C. 竞争优势　　　　　　　　　　　D. 良好的自然环境

2. 以下哪个是正确的战略层级？
   A. 愿景、使命、经营战略、公司战略、创新战略、职能战略
   B. 愿景、使命、公司战略、经营战略、创新战略、职能战略
   C. 愿景、使命、公司战略、经营战略、职能战略、创新战略
   D. 愿景、使命、经营战略、公司战略、职能战略、创新战略

3. 新产品战略的制定始于_____。
   A. 最大化利用外部机会和内部资源　　B. 清晰的高层级管理目标
   C. 推动产品创新技术进步　　　　　　D. 愿景

4. "作为一个组织，我们是谁？"这句话是指以下哪个？
   A. 愿景　　　　　　　　　　　　　B. 使命
   C. 组织身份　　　　　　　　　　　D. 价值观

5. 以下关于愿景的正确描述是哪个？
   A. 永不改变　　　　　　　　　　　B. 企业目标
   C. 对未来的具体化和可视化展望　　D. 有时包含该组织价值观的信息

6. 以下关于组织使命的正确描述是哪个？
   A. 组织所遵循的价值主张　　　　　B. 对组织期望的未来状态的描述
   C. 关于公司经营哲学和经营原则的说明　D. 以上皆对

7. 使命提供了什么？
   A. 集聚的人员、资源和行动　　　　B. 产品创新团队的长期目标

C. 组织愿景　　　　　　　　　　　　D. 最新战略

8. 一个组织的价值观是什么？
   A. 个人或组织坚守的精神准则　　　　B. 对组织期望的未来状态的描述
   C. 有关公司经营理念和经营原则的声明　D. 以上皆对

9. 以下哪个不是经营战略？
   A. 指导并决定组织性质和方向的框架
   B. 选择所提供的产品（或服务）及市场
   C. 选择一套完整的行动并提供独特的价值，核心就是为企业选定的市场交付这些价值
   D. 多元化组织的总体战略

10. 以下关于公司战略的正确描述是哪个？
    A. 多元化组织的总体战略
    B. 回答"我们应该在哪些业务领域进行竞争"和"如何将不同的业务协同起来，从而提升整个组织的竞争优势"
    C. A 和 B
    D. 与经营战略没有区别

11. 从经营战略落实到产品创新的步骤，第一步是制定经营目标，第二步是明确产品创新的作用，第三步是什么？
    A. 制定公司战略　　　　　　　　　　B. 制定愿景和使命
    C. 明确产品创新战略重点，制订"进攻计划"　D. 项目组合选择和资源配置

12. 通常在何时使用 SWOT 分析？
    A. 制定企业战略时　　　　　　　　　B. 审查新产品开发目标时
    C. 进行市场机会分析时　　　　　　　D. 在确定客户会购买哪些特性时

13. 以下哪个更为全面地考虑了产品创新环境？
    A. 技术、生产、营销、财务
    B. 企业本身、企业所在行业、更为广泛的区域乃至全球环境
    C. 行业结构、行业规模、行业增速、技术水平、市场、竞争、政府支持、资源
    D. 文化、社会、技术、资源、实体环境、法律、经济、政策

14. 在PESTLE分析中，人口增长率、教育水平、年龄分布以及生活方式等要素属于哪一类？

    A. 环境　　　　　B. 经济　　　　　C. 社会　　　　　D. 技术

15. 在制定战略时会用到德尔菲技术。使用德尔菲技术时通常会邀请谁参加？

    A. 普通用户　　　B. 大众消费者　　C. 非专业人士　　D. 主题专家

16. 商业模式画布的内容有哪些？

    A. 战略、组合、流程、工具、团队、市场调研、创新管理
    B. 客户细分、价值主张、渠道通路、客户关系、收入来源、关键业务、核心资源、重要合作、成本结构
    C. 价值主张、整体解决方案、市场细分、定位目标市场、抢滩战略、渠道选择、促销计划、沟通信息
    D. 市场潜力、财务潜力、技术能力、营销能力、制造能力、知识产权、法规影响、投资需求

17. 在制定商业模式画布时，团队策划并回答以下问题："需要与每个客户群建立什么样的关系？客户的期望是什么？如何建立客户关系？"这些问题属于以下哪个方面？

    A. 客户细分　　　B. 价值主张　　　C. 渠道通路　　　D. 客户关系

18. 在制定商业模式画布中的关键业务时，要考虑什么？

    A. 需要通过哪些研发、营销、制造和渠道活动来实现价值主张
    B. 谁是重要合作方或关键供应商
    C. 需要哪些实物资源、智力资源、人力资源和资金
    D. 最重要的成本驱动因素是什么

19. 良好创新战略的特征不包括以下哪项内容？

    A. 反复尝试新事物，吸取教训，然后重新对工作优先级进行排序
    B. 拥抱变化
    C. 率先上市就一定会成功
    D. 尽可能并尽早邀请客户参与

20. 在里夫斯提出的信息优势创新战略中，不包括以下哪项内容？

    A. 管理复杂性

B. 了解竞争对手正在做什么和提供了什么

C. 决定在哪里竞争

D. 具体项目的范围、进度、成本和质量都是有价值的战略信息

21. 波特竞争战略没有提及以下哪个？

    A. 成本领先战略   B. 差异化战略

    C. 率先上市战略   D. 细分市场战略

22. 波特成本领先战略的特点是什么？

    A. 专注于产品质量   B. 专注于产品性能

    C. 专注于达到最低的生产和销售成本   D. 专注于率先上市的价值

23. 以下哪个不是波特差异化战略的特点？

    A. 通过吸引价格敏感型客户从而提升公司的市场份额

    B. 应用于"宽市场范围"

    C. 通过交付独特、优质的产品和建立客户忠诚度来获取市场份额

    D. 客户通常更关注产品质量和特性

24. 波特差异化战略的优势有哪些？

    A. 有利于建立客户忠诚度

    B. 具有差异化的产品特性可以带来更高的利润率

    C. 在研发上的投入非常有限

    D. A 和 B

25. 波特细分市场战略的劣势是什么？

    A. 持续降低成本会影响产品质量

    B. 过于依赖单一狭窄的市场可能导致风险

    C. 公司必须持续创新，开发出新的产品特性，才能吸引客户

    D. 未能开发出符合价值定位的产品特性会导致市场份额大幅下降

26. 迈尔斯和斯诺对探索者的定义是什么？

    A. 率先进入市场者

    B. 迫于强大压力才做出回应者

C. 在市场发生变化时只是简单做出回应者

D. 定位于稳定的产品或服务领域，守住一个安全的小众市场者

27. 在迈尔斯和斯诺战略框架中，探索者主要侧重于以下什么指标？

    A. 新产品销售额占比
    B. 内部收益率和投资回报率
    C. 市场份额
    D. 客户满意度

28. 在迈尔斯和斯诺战略框架中，防御者是指什么样的公司？

    A. 开发新产品特性的公司
    B. 开展大量产品创新项目但从未推出任何新产品的公司
    C. 利用价格作为主要防御武器来击败新产品的公司
    D. 产品占据了某个市场，用非产品创新手段保护该市场的公司

29. 在迈尔斯和斯诺战略框架中，分析者战略有何特点？

    A. 往往使用世界级新技术
    B. 很少率先进入市场
    C. 始终守住自己的利基市场
    D. 率先进入市场

30. 分析者也称模仿者或快速跟随者，其目标是什么？

    A. 仿制产品的特性或功能更具市场价值
    B. 从探索者手中抢到最多50%的市场份额
    C. 降低成本，分析者认为成本才是最重要的
    D. 获得利基市场的份额

31. 在市场变化时，没有明确的产品开发计划或市场进入计划。这是哪种战略类型？

    A. 探索者
    B. 率先进入市场者
    C. 回应者
    D. 防御者

32. 克里斯坦森对延续式和颠覆式技术的阐述是什么？

    A. 这两种技术有类似的客户利益
    B. 延续式技术很少有利可图
    C. 颠覆式技术引入了新的商业模式，创造了新市场或新价值网络
    D. 颠覆式技术应用于快速增长的市场中

33. 颠覆式创新往往始于满足什么市场对性能的需求？

    A. 低端市场　　　　　　　　　　B. 高端市场

    C. 中高端市场　　　　　　　　　D. 以上皆错

34. 颠覆式创新的特点包括以下哪个？

    A. 新产品或新服务聚焦于满足现有产品或市场中细分市场的需求

    B. 新产品为细分市场中的客户提供了他们看重的独有特性，这些客户能够引领或极大地影响整体市场的需求

    C. 新产品的整体特性被改进到一定程度后，越来越多的客户被转化。此时，该产品新特性带来的价值远远超过了所有负面特性或性能不足所造成的影响

    D. 以上皆对

35. 在皮萨诺创新景观图中，创新有哪四种类型？

    A. 常规型创新、颠覆型创新、激进型创新、架构型创新

    B. 开放型创新、特殊型创新、整合型创新、封闭型创新

    C. 被动型创新、主动型创新、战略型创新、优化型创新

    D. 初始级创新、改进级创新、成功级创新、领先级创新

36. 需要新商业模式而不是新技术，这在皮萨诺创新景观图中属于哪种类型？

    A. 常规型创新　　　　　　　　　B. 颠覆型创新

    C. 激进型创新　　　　　　　　　D. 架构型创新

37. 在皮萨诺创新景观图中，激进型创新的特点是什么？

    A. 开发新技术　　　　　　　　　B. 开创新商业模式

    C. 开拓新市场　　　　　　　　　D. 制定新的客户价值主张

38. 产品平台的构成包括哪些内容？

    A. 区分和定义技术　　　　　　　B. 产品战略的基础

    C. 基本要素清晰　　　　　　　　D. 以上皆对

39. 产品平台战略的优势包括哪些？

    A. 大幅提升运营效率　　　　　　B. 快速、连续地推出一系列产品

    C. 从长期视角制定产品战略　　　D. 以上皆对

40. Sun 公司开发的 Java 以及微软公司开发的.NET 框架是哪方面的例子？
    A. 产品平台
    B. 共享文化
    C. 共享价值观
    D. 共同目标

41. 技术战略涉及什么？
    A. 开发和维持技术从而获得竞争优势
    B. 决定组织该如何利用当前的技术
    C. 研究、开发和发布产品创新流程
    D. 开发一个特定的技术平台

42. 用于技术预测的工具是以下哪个？
    A. 专利分析
    B. 趋势分析
    C. 德尔菲技术
    D. 以上皆对

43. 技术驱动型组织通过什么方法获得竞争优势？
    A. 新颖的、开创性的技术
    B. 注重满足客户需求
    C. 注重满足市场需求
    D. 注重满足社会需求

44. 大多数技术生命周期可以用什么曲线来描述？
    A. 正态分布曲线
    B. S 曲线
    C. 指数曲线
    D. 贝塔分布曲线

45. 当越来越多的风险规避型组织都开始考虑应用某一新技术时，说明此时该新技术进入了哪个阶段？
    A. 引入阶段
    B. 成长阶段
    C. 成熟阶段
    D. 衰退阶段

46. 为什么知识产权对产品创新而言非常重要？
    A. 它有利于建立产品开发经理的声誉
    B. 它可以为实现收益奠定基础
    C. 它提升了创造力
    D. 它是创新流程的良好指标

47. 以下哪个不是知识产权？
    A. 专利
    B. 植物品种权
    C. 科学定理
    D. 商标

48. 知识产权管理方法有哪几种？

    A. 常规型创新、颠覆型创新、激进型创新、架构型创新

    B. 开放型创新、特殊型创新、整合型创新、封闭型创新

    C. 被动型、主动型、战略型、优化型

    D. 初始级、改进级、成功级、领先级

49. 在产品研发和创新流程中事后才考虑知识产权，这是哪种知识产权管理方法？

    A. 主动型　　　　B. 战略型　　　　C. 被动型　　　　D. 优化型

50. 如何使具有知识产权的新产品实现价值？

    A. 用公司品牌来营销产品　　　　　　B. 把知识产权卖给另一家公司

    C. 把知识产权授权给另一家公司　　　D. 以上皆对

51. 在制定营销战略时，组织应该怎么做？

    A. 由营销部门独立制定　　　　　　　B. 制定时符合总体经营战略

    C. 每五年制定一次　　　　　　　　　D. 制定时无须考虑总体经营战略

52. 市场营销组合定义是以下哪个？

    A. 在同一时间销售一套产品　　　　　B. 产品、价格、促销和地点

    C. 参与营销产品的群体　　　　　　　D. 营销战略和计划的组合

53. 产品分为哪三个层次？

    A. 声望、质量和售后　　　　　　　　B. 权力、品牌和售后服务

    C. 精神、物质和心理　　　　　　　　D. 核心利益、有形特性和增强特性

54. 以下哪个是产品增强特性的例子？

    A. 产品在冰箱中的保质期延长　　　　B. 增加压缩机性能的化学添加剂

    C. 具有多个清洁附件的吸尘器　　　　D. 免费售后服务

55. 产品的有形特性包括什么？

    A. 特性、风格、包装、质量和品牌　　B. 安装、信用、售后服务和质保

    C. 价格和促销　　　　　　　　　　　D. 以上皆对

56. 产品的核心利益是什么？

   A. 真正驱使人们购买和复购某产品的收益　　B. 产品的基本技术

   C. 产品的工作原理　　　　　　　　　　　　D. 产品生命周期

57. 在波士顿矩阵中，有瘦狗、现金牛、问题和明星四个象限。低市场增长率和低市场份额的是哪类产品？

   A. 瘦狗　　　　B. 现金牛　　　　C. 问题　　　　D. 明星

58. 在波士顿矩阵中，有瘦狗、现金牛、问题和明星四个象限。高市场增长率和高市场份额的是哪类产品？

   A. 瘦狗　　　　B. 现金牛　　　　C. 问题　　　　D. 明星

59. "现金牛"产品的定义是什么？

   A. 具有显著未来市场潜力的产品

   B. 奶制品

   C. 销售下滑的产品

   D. 在整体增长缓慢的市场中具有较高市场份额的产品

60. 什么是核心竞争力？

   A. 技能、知识和才能的综合

   B. 在为客户创造和交付价值的过程中，为组织提供一个或多个竞争优势的能力

   C. 组织为综合利用其资源（实物资源、人力资源和资金）所开展的活动和提供的职能

   D. 行为胜任力包含认知和个性特质，技术胜任力则包含通过学习获得的专业知识，如项目管理

61. 制定产品创新能力战略时，首先要做什么？

   A. 识别所需能力与现有能力之间的差距

   B. 进行"能力盘点"，对组织当前资源和优势做到心中有数

   C. 进行 SWOT 分析，重点分析组织利用机会和应对威胁的能力

   D. 明确组织使命、目标、经营战略和创新战略

62. 能力战略层级的最下面一层是以下哪个？

   A. 战略　　　　B. 竞争优势　　　　C. 组织职能　　　　D. 资源

63. 数字化战略的重点是利用技术来提高经营绩效。它为组织指明了什么？
    A. 通过市场开创竞争优势的方向，以及如何实现这些变化的方法
    B. 通过商业模式开创竞争优势的方向，以及如何实现这些变化的方法
    C. 通过数字技术开创竞争优势的方向，以及如何实现这些变化的方法
    D. 通过大客户开创竞争优势的方向，以及如何实现这些变化的方法

64. 数字化产品创新的关键变化体现在以下哪个关键绩效指标上？
    A. 关系管理   B. 活力指数   C. 研发投入   D. 专利数量

65. 数字化时代产品的一个核心特点是什么？
    A. 便宜   B. 定期更新和升级产品
    C. 高质量   D. 以上皆错

66. 在制定数字化战略框架时，会收集市场数据，并采用分析工具，最后输出什么？
    A. 公司数据   B. 政策
    C. 管理报告   D. 商业智能工具

67. 数字化战略制定流程包括识别、排序、设计、实施和什么？
    A. 监督   B. 改进   C. 控制   D. 发布

68. 一家公司每季度对数字化战略进行反馈、评审、改进和增强，这表明处于数字化战略流程的哪个阶段？
    A. 排序   B. 实施   C. 改进   D. 设计

69. 开放式创新可以通过很多方式来实现，但不推荐以下哪种方式？
    A. 联盟   B. 只内部开发   C. 合作   D. 签约

70. 以下哪个是开放式创新的收益？
    A. 无法产生独特能力，更难形成差异化优势
    B. 外部研发方会成为竞争对手
    C. 降低与内部研发相关的成本和不确定性，挖掘研发深度，拓宽研发广度
    D. 在筛选数以千计的创意时，评估成本通常很高

71. 开放式创新有哪四种类型？

   A. 开放型创新、特殊型创新、整合型创新、封闭型创新
   B. 常规型创新、颠覆型创新、激进型创新、架构型创新
   C. 被动型创新、主动型创新、战略型创新、优化型创新
   D. 初始级创新、改进级创新、成功级创新、领先级创新

72. 开放型创新者的关键成功因素是什么？

   A. 技术、服务、时间和其他
   B. 技术导向
   C. 质量、服务、时间、品牌和其他
   D. 质量、服务、时间、品牌、技术和其他

73. 一家企业的开放式创新参与机制为外包、联盟、并购、风险投资或授权许可，该企业属于什么类型？

   A. 寻求者   B. 提供者   C. 中介者   D. 开放者

74. 可持续经营也被称作什么？

   A. 可持续发展
   B. 可持续创新
   C. 可持续设计
   D. 绿色经营

75. 制定可持续经营战略的第一步是什么？

   A. 在组织使命中纳入可持续性
   B. 评估问题并明确目标
   C. 制定可持续经营战略
   D. 以上皆错

76. 制定可持续经营战略的第二步是什么？

   A. 制定可持续经营战略
   B. 评估问题并明确目标
   C. 在组织使命中纳入可持续性
   D. 以上皆错

77. "既满足当代发展需要，又不损害后代满足自身需要能力的发展模式"是指以下哪个概念？

   A. 可持续发展
   B. 可持续产品创新
   C. 可持续经营
   D. 可持续经济

78. 碳定价是衡量温室气体排放的外部性方法。以下哪个不是企业使用碳定价的原因？

   A. 准备应对政府关于碳定价的政策和公开承诺

B. 以财务形式表现气候变化问题

C. 在组合管理的财务要素中，公平比较可持续（不可持续）项目

D. 不考虑环保因素

79. 可持续性成熟度模型有哪几个级别？

    A. 常规型创新、颠覆型创新、激进型创新、架构型创新

    B. 初始级、改进级、成功级、领先级

    C. 被动型、主动型、战略型、优化型

    D. 开放型创新、特殊型创新、整合型创新、封闭型创新

80. 循环经济的目标是在产品生命周期中创造闭环。哪个不是其中的原理？

    A. 通过控制有限的存量和对可再生资源的流动进行平衡，从而保护并增加自然资源

    B. 通过公众认知推动循环经济

    C. 通过循环利用产品、零部件和原材料，优化资源产出，并在技术和生物周期中保持资源利用率最大化

    D. 通过发现并消除外部负面影响来提升系统效率

试题答案与解析

序号	答案	知识点	教材页码
1	D	产品创新关键因素	P4 第 7 行
2	B	战略层级	P5 图 1.1 和 P6 图 1.2
3	D	创新和战略决策层级	P6 图 1.2
4	C	组织身份	P6 倒数第 7 行
5	C	愿景	P7 第 4 行
6	C	使命	P7 第 10 行
7	A	使命	P7 第 11 行
8	A	价值观	P7 倒数第 7 行
9	D	经营战略	P8 倒数第 6 行和倒数第 4 行
10	C	公司战略	P9 倒数第 2 行和倒数第 1 行
11	C	从经营战略到产品创新	P10 图 1.3

序号	答案	知识点	教材页码
12	A	SWOT 分析	P11 倒数第 7 行
13	B	产品创新环境	P12 图 1.5
14	C	PESTLE 分析	P13 图 1.7
15	D	德尔菲技术	P13 倒数第 2 行
16	B	商业模式画布内容	P15 第 12 行
17	D	商业模式画布客户关系	P16 倒数第 5 行
18	A	商业模式画布关键业务	P17 第 4 行
19	C	良好创新战略的特征	P18 第 9 行
20	D	信息优势创新战略	P19 第 3 行
21	C	波特竞争战略	P20 图 1.9
22	C	波特成本领先战略	P21 第 5 行
23	A	波特差异化战略特点	P21 倒数第 3 行
24	D	波特差异化战略优势	P22 第 2 行
25	B	波特细分市场战略劣势	P23 第 3 行
26	A	迈尔斯和斯诺探索者战略	P23 图 1.10
27	C	迈尔斯和斯诺探索者战略	P24 第 1 行
28	D	迈尔斯和斯诺防御者战略	P24 倒数第 10 行
29	B	迈尔斯和斯诺分析者战略	P24 倒数第 9 行
30	A	迈尔斯和斯诺分析者战略	P24 第 14 行
31	C	迈尔斯和斯诺回应者战略	P24 倒数第 2 行
32	C	克里斯坦森颠覆式创新定义	P25 第 6 行和第 9 行
33	A	克里斯坦森延续式与颠覆式创新对比	P25 图 1.11
34	D	克里斯坦森颠覆式创新特点	P26 第 4 行
35	A	皮萨诺创新景观图	P27 图 1.12
36	B	皮萨诺创新景观图颠覆型创新	P27 倒数第 7 行
37	A	皮萨诺创新景观图激进型创新	P27 倒数第 4 行
38	D	产品平台的构成	P28 倒数第 7 行
39	D	产品平台战略的优势	P28 倒数第 3 行
40	A	产品平台战略的示例	P29 倒数第 8 行
41	A	技术战略	P30 第 4 行
42	D	技术预测的工具	P30 倒数第 3 行

序号	答案	知识点	教材页码
43	A	技术驱动型组织特点	P31 第 4 行
44	B	技术 S 曲线	P32 图 1.14
45	B	技术 S 曲线阶段	P32 第 5 行
46	B	知识产权重要性	P33 第 10 行
47	C	知识产权类型	P33 倒数第 9 行
48	C	知识产权管理方法	P34 第 5 行
49	C	知识产权管理方法被动型	P34 图 1.16
50	D	知识产权管理优化方法	P35 图 1.17
51	B	营销战略	P35 倒数第 8 行
52	B	市场营销组合	P36 第 7 行
53	D	产品三个层次	P37 图 1.20
54	D	产品层次中的增强特性	P37 图 1.20
55	A	产品层次中的有形特性	P37 图 1.20
56	A	产品层次中的核心利益	P37 倒数第 2 行
57	A	波士顿矩阵瘦狗产品	P39 倒数第 2 行
58	D	波士顿矩阵明星产品	P38 倒数第 2 行
59	D	波士顿矩阵现金牛产品	P39 第 1 行
60	B	核心竞争力	P40 第 7 行
61	D	制定产品创新能力战略的步骤	P40 倒数第 2 行
62	D	能力战略层级	P41 图 1.22
63	C	数字化战略作用	P42 第 1 行
64	A	数字化产品创新关键特征	P43 第 4 行
65	B	数字化时代产品特点	P44 第 13 行
66	C	制定数字化战略框架	P45 图 1.23
67	B	数字化战略制定流程	P45 图 1.24
68	C	数字化战略流程的改进阶段	P46 倒数第 5 行
69	B	开放式创新基础	P47 第 3 行
70	C	开放式创新收益和挑战	P47 图 1.25
71	A	开放式创新类型	P48 图 1.26
72	B	开放式创新的关键成功因素	P48 图 1.27
73	D	开放式创新的参与机制	P49 图 1.28

序号	答案	知识点	教材页码
74	D	可持续经营	P50 第3行
75	B	制定可持续经营战略第一步	P51 倒数第2行
76	C	制定可持续经营战略第二步	P52 倒数第9行
77	A	可持续发展定义	P53 倒数第3行
78	D	使用碳定价原因	P54 倒数第1行
79	B	可持续性成熟度模型	P55 图1.29
80	B	循环经济原理	P56 第8行

教材第 2 章 "组合管理" 分章同步试题

1. 什么是产品组合？

    A. 用来销售的所有商品、服务或知识

    B. 为创造独特的产品、服务或成果而进行的临时性工作

    C. 组织正在投资并进行战略权衡的一组项目或产品

    D. 各种类型产品的集合

2. 组合管理的任务是什么？

    A. 实施战略
    B. 完成使命
    C. 正确地做项目
    D. 做正确的项目

3. 组合管理要实现的目标有哪些？

    A. 价值最大、项目平衡、战略一致、管道平衡、盈利充分

    B. 范围正好、准时交付、预算之内、质量达标、客户满意

    C. 投资合理、风险适度、回报丰厚、人员胜任、股东满意

    D. 技术先进、市场拓展、模式新颖、资源优化、持续增长

4. 组合管理包括两种活动，分别是什么？

    A. 组合选择和组合评审
    B. 组合启动和组合完成
    C. 资源配置和组合支持
    D. 市场营销和技术要求

5. 组合管理的关键特征不包括以下哪个？

    A. 处于动态环境中的决策过程需要持续评审

    B. 每个项目会有不同的完成期

    C. 旨在提高组合中项目或产品的总体成功率

    D. 资源不会受到限制，可以随时满足要求

6. 组合中包含哪些项目类型？

    A. 突破型项目　　B. 平台型项目　　C. 衍生型项目　　D. 以上皆对

7. 突破型项目有何特点？
   A. 本质上是延续式创新
   B. 与现有实践相比有着显著差异
   C. 增强了现有产品线
   D. 以上皆对

8. 平台型项目有何特点？
   A. 高风险
   B. 开发一组子系统及接口，将其组成一个共用架构，继而在该共用架构上高效地开发和制造出一系列衍生产品
   C. 产品族中的一个产品
   D. 以上皆对

9. 在项目组合中，哪种类型的项目可以填补现有产品线空缺？
   A. 突破型项目
   B. 平台型项目
   C. 衍生型项目
   D. 支持型项目

10. 哪种类型的项目风险最低？
    A. 突破型项目
    B. 平台型项目
    C. 衍生型项目
    D. 支持型项目

11. 库珀提出，在组合管理中实现战略一致包含三个目标，以下哪个不是？
    A. 管道平衡
    B. 战略匹配
    C. 战略贡献
    D. 战略优先级

12. 库珀建议用于项目选择和组合评审的三种方法不包括以下哪种？
    A. 自上而下法
    B. 自下而上法
    C. 头脑风暴
    D. 二者结合法

13. 在组合选择中，自上而下法的第一步是什么？
    A. 制定愿景和战略
    B. 记录可用资源
    C. 安排研发预算
    D. 与自下而上法进行对比

14. 在组合管理中，自下而上法的步骤包括以下哪个？
    A. 识别潜在项目

B. 制定战略选择标准，用于评估项目

C. 按照选择标准对每个潜在项目进行评估

D. 以上皆对

15. 以下哪个不是组合管理中二者结合法的步骤？

    A. 列出事业部或产品类别所需资金和战略优先级

    B. 制定产品创新流程

    C. 按照战略标准和资金对每个潜在项目进行估算和排序

    D. 不但考虑每个项目的优先级与预算，而且考虑事业部或产品类别的优先级，最后将项目分配到相应的"战略桶"中

16. 通过分析当前产品组合，可以发现以下哪个机会？

    A. 新市场机会，找出可以开拓的新市场

    B. 新技术机会，找出可以开发的新技术

    C. 新产品机会，找出可以进行产品改进或产品线延伸的领域

    D. 新商业模式机会，找出可以建立的新商业模式

17. 新产品成功因素不包括以下哪个？

    A. 组织拥有独特、出色的产品，该产品有别于竞争对手的产品，能够为客户提供独特收益和显著价值

    B. 聚焦于一个有吸引力的市场，该市场规模较大且在不断增长，利润率高，竞争不激烈且竞争压力小

    C. 善于利用组织内部优势。组织能够利用自身在营销和技术方面的优势、能力及经验开发出相应的产品和项目

    D. 产品开发团队人数众多

18. 选择项目时应考虑可持续性。组合管理可持续性方面的标准不包括以下哪个？

    A "三重底线"和碳排放   B. 符合ISO生命周期评估要求

    C. 可制造性   D. 资源再利用或再循环

19. 关于通过/失败法，以下哪个说法是错误的？

    A. 是定量化评估方法

    B. 要采用一些标准对每个创意进行评估

C. 只有符合所有标准要求的创意才能进入下一关

D. 在进行评估时，最好邀请跨职能部门（如营销、技术和制造部门等）的代表

20. 应由谁来给新产品机会进行评分？

    A. 跨职能团队　　　　　　　　　B. 市场营销经理

    C. 产品经理　　　　　　　　　　D. 首席执行官

21. 公司有三个候选项目。大家对优先做哪个项目争论不已。产品经理准备用评分法对这三个项目进行评分。评出的结果如下，应该优先做哪个项目？

项目	销售潜力	技术先进性	产品竞争力
	权重系数		
	（10）	（7.5）	（5）
1	8	6	8
2	8	9	7
3	6	6	8
4	5	6	5

A. 项目 1　　　B. 项目 2　　　C. 项目 3　　　D. 项目 4

22. 在组合选择中，以下哪个不是定量评估方法？

    A. 净现值　　　　　　　　　　　B. 内部收益率

    C. 投资回收期　　　　　　　　　D. 战略一致性

23. 新产品机会的范围和比例取决于什么？

    A. 首席执行官的偏好

    B. 盈利

    C. 市场需求

    D. 公司战略或经营战略，并与创新战略保持一致

24. 以下除了哪个，其他都是实现平衡组合应考虑的内容？

    A. 明确组合维度和关键标准

    B. 应用组合维度和关键标准，实现组合中产品创新机会的最佳平衡，并确保与战略保持一致

    C. 建立价值观

    D. 持续进行组合管理，在整个开发管道和产品生命周期中，始终进行组合管理，确保合理选择

项目和项目平衡

25. 在汇报时，将产品组合可视化非常重要。以下哪个是最常用的组合可视化工具？
    A. 气泡图					B. 思维导图
    C. 亲和图					D. 用户体验地图

26. 在可视化组合平衡气泡图中，哪对变量不常用？
    A. 风险和回报				B. 净现值和内部收益率
    C. 市场风险和技术风险			D. 市场新颖度和技术新颖度

27. 以下哪个显示了良好的组合管理？
    A. 同一时间段内项目数量太多		B. 糟糕的项目计划和实施
    C. 项目选择和资源配置合理		D. 产品创新项目经常与其他业务争夺优先权

28. 在组合管理中，合理的资源配置带来的益处不包含以下哪个？
    A. 更有效的项目流程			B. 更多的成果输出
    C. 更高的员工满意度			D. 更多的市场需求

29. 库珀提出的资源配置方法包括以下哪个？
    A. 自上而下法和自下而上法		B. 基于项目资源需求和基于新经营目标
    C. 气泡图和资源工作表			D. 定量方法和定性方法

30. 在配置资源时，一开始就按现有项目在清单中的优先级，从高到低对项目进行排序。这是什么资源配置方法？
    A. 基于资源限制条件			B. 基于项目资源需求
    C. 基于新经营目标			D. 基于技术要求

31. 在配置资源时，一开始就问"希望从新产品中获得多少回报或利润"，这是什么资源配置方法？
    A. 基于资源限制条件			B. 基于项目资源需求
    C. 基于新经营目标			D. 基于技术要求

32. 资源规划与配置中有哪四个重要角色？
    A. 项目经理、资源负责人、资源规划者、产品规划者

B. 项目经理、资源负责人、资源规划者、产品经理

C. 项目经理、资源负责人、资源经理、产品经理

D. 项目经理、项目发起人、资源规划者、产品经理

33. 在资源配置时，将项目资源需求换算为全职人力工时数并将其分配到项目中，这是谁的工作？

    A. 项目经理　　　　　　　　　　B. 资源负责人
    C. 资源规划者　　　　　　　　　D. 项目发起人

34. 在配置资源时，资源负责人通常使用什么工具来收集项目团队所需的资源？

    A. 产品创新章程　　　　　　　　B. 产品路线图
    C. 用户画像　　　　　　　　　　D. 资源需求表

35. 当资源利用率高于100%时，说明该资源存在什么情况？

    A. 负荷正常　　　　　　　　　　B. 资源过载
    C. 负荷不足　　　　　　　　　　D. 以上皆错

36. 以下哪个不属于组合管理复杂性的内容？

    A. 项目间资源争夺成为常态　　　B. 可用资源的类型和数量因时而异
    C. 项目可能被意外取消　　　　　D. 文化和氛围因组织而异

37. 在建立组合管理系统时，应采取循序渐进的原则。资源管理可以从资源需求的粗略估算到较为详细的资源用时估算。以下哪个是最详细的评估方法？

    A. 资源供需（低、中、高）　　　B. 量化资源
    C. 资源分解结构　　　　　　　　D. 资源用时

38. 在做出取消项目的决策时会受到一些强制因素的影响，这些因素是指以下哪个？

    A. 对外承诺、上级指示、沉没成本效应或不想打击团队积极性
    B. 心理惯性、预算支出、团队承诺和情感
    C. 流程、方法、工具和技术
    D. 范围、进度、成本和质量

39. 在敏捷团队中，阻碍项目组合管理进程的因素主要是以下哪个？

    A. 团队成员无法进行自我管理

B. 敏捷教练不胜任工作

C. 很难从敏捷团队中获得资源信息，也存在资源数据丢失或提供资源数据迟缓的问题

D. 迭代周期太短

40. 通常而言，组合绩效度量指标不包括什么？

A. 战略价值
B. 财务价值
C. 确定性水平
D. 技术水平

试题答案与解析

序号	答案	知识点	教材页码
1	C	产品组合定义	P67 第 2 行
2	D	组合管理特点	P67 第 9 行
3	A	组合管理 5 个目标	P67 第 10 行
4	A	组合管理内容	P68 第 3 行
5	D	组合管理关键特征	P68 倒数第 2 行
6	D	组合中项目类型	P69 第 7 行
7	B	突破型项目特点	P69 第 11 行
8	B	平台型项目特点	P69 倒数第 9 行
9	C	衍生型项目特点	P69 倒数第 5 行
10	D	支持型项目特点	P69 倒数第 1 行
11	A	组合管理与战略一致 3 个目标	P70 第 5 行
12	C	项目选择和评审 3 种方法	P70 倒数第 5 行
13	A	自上而下法步骤	P71 第 7 行
14	D	自下而上法步骤	P71 倒数第 2 行
15	B	二者结合法步骤	P72 第 7 行
16	C	新产品机会来源	P72 倒数第 7 行
17	D	新产品成功因素	P73 第 5 行
18	C	组合管理可持续性标准	P74 倒数第 9 行
19	A	通过/失败法	P75 第 2 行
20	A	新产品机会评估者	P75 第 6 行

序号	答案	知识点	教材页码
21	B	评分法	P76 图2.4。项目1为165分，项目2为182.5分，项目3为145分，项目4为120分
22	D	定量评估方法	P77 倒数第9行
23	D	平衡组合概述	P78 第7行
24	C	实现平衡组合	P78 倒数第3行
25	A	气泡图	P79 第8行
26	B	气泡图常用维度	P80 3张图
27	C	好的组合管理特点	P81 第2行
28	D	资源配置合理的益处	P81 倒数第7行
29	B	资源配置方法	P82 第2行
30	B	基于项目资源需求的资源配置	P82 倒数第6行
31	C	基于新经营目标的资源配置	P83 第5行
32	A	资源规划与配置中的角色	P83 图2.10
33	B	资源配置流程与角色	P82 图2.10
34	D	配置资源工具	P84 倒数第2行
35	B	资源利用率	P85 第2行
36	D	组合管理复杂性	P85 倒数第3行
37	D	组合管理复杂性的变化	P86 图2.14
38	A	组合管理准则之变更管理	P87 第6行
39	C	项目组合管理的障碍	P88 倒数第6行
40	D	组合绩效度量指标	P90 图2.17

教材第 3 章 "产品创新流程" 分章同步试题

1. 关于产品创新流程的定义，以下哪个是错误的？
   A. 一系列的活动、工具和技术，包括产品线规划、战略制定、概念生成、概念筛选和研究，最终为客户交付成功的成果——产品
   B. 一组经过严格定义的任务和步骤，通过规范且适用的方法，组织可以不断地将创意转化为可销售的产品或服务
   C. 用于开发新产品或改进现有产品的结构化和规范化方法，组织接受这些方法并达成共识
   D. 指导并决定组织性质和方向的框架，即选择所提供的产品（或服务）及市场

2. 在 2012 年的 PDMA 研究报告中，最佳公司和其他公司的新产品成功率有着显著差异。在该报告中，阐述了什么结论？
   A. 产品创新流程可以帮助提升新产品成功率
   B. 产品创新流程无法提升新产品成功率
   C. 绝大多数最佳公司都不采用产品创新流程
   D. 绝大多数其他公司都采用了产品创新流程

3. 在产品创新生命周期中，以下哪个参数在开始时低，在结束时达到峰值？
   A. 干系人的影响力   B. 风险
   C. 项目累积成本   D. 不确定性水平

4. 在产品创新生命周期中，以下哪个参数在开始时高，在结束时降到谷底？
   A. 项目累积工时   B. 变更成本
   C. 项目累积成本   D. 项目风险和不确定性水平

5. 在标准决策框架中，第一步应该做什么？
   A. 收集信息   B. 识别问题或机会
   C. 分析情况   D. 提出多个解决方案

6. 关于模糊前端，以下哪种说法是正确的？

   A. 生成可进一步被评估为新产品概念创意时的不确定性

   B. 产品创新时期起始阶段，总体状态较为混沌，产品概念也非常模糊

   C. 市场机会分析的下一步

   D. 和产品开发阶段一样

7. 什么是产品创新章程？

   A. 一份被用于获得内部支持的介绍文案，篇幅通常为 1~2 页

   B. 一份规范和管理产品创新团队的指导书

   C. 一份关于新产品具体概念的商业论证书

   D. 一份关键的战略文件，是组织对新产品进行商业化的核心

8. 除了包含背景、聚焦领域、总体目标和具体目标以及特别准则等内容，产品创新章程还应包含什么内容？

   A. 公司愿景和使命   B. 公司战略和经营战略
   C. 可持续性   D. 组织身份

9. 在产品创新章程中，背景除了包含项目目的、项目范围、项目团队在实现项目目标中的角色、项目制约因素、现有及未来的关键技术、项目（产品）收益，还包括什么？

   A. 项目具体目标   B. 外部机构参与
   C. 环境、行业和市场分析 D. 目标市场

10. 在产品创新章程中，聚焦领域包含关键技术和营销方法、核心竞争力、企业优势和什么？

    A. 目标市场   B. 产品创新流程
    C. 上市周期   D. 平台战略

11. 在产品创新章程中，总体目标和具体目标包括什么？

    A. 新产品盈利目标   B. 新产品上市时间
    C. 新产品开发成功率   D. 以上皆对

12. 在产品创新章程中，特别准则不包括什么？
    A. 预算支出责任　　　　　　　　B. 项目背景
    C. 外部机构的参与　　　　　　　D. 项目治理和领导力

13. 以下哪个是产品创新章程中可持续性方面的内容？
    A. 加班　　　　　　　　　　　　B. 利润最大化
    C. 强调减少、再利用和再循环因素　　D. 漂绿

14. 博思、艾伦和汉密尔顿提出的产品创新流程有何特点？
    A. 分为6个基本阶段，但没有独立的关口　　B. 迭代的流程
    C. 以人为本　　　　　　　　　　D. 快速试错和低成本试错

15. 在20世纪80年代早期，分阶段产品创新流程的一个飞跃是以下哪个？
    A. 博思、艾伦和汉密尔顿的六个基本阶段流程
    B. 产品开发三部曲
    C. 库珀的门径流程
    D. NASA的阶段评估流程

16. 门径流程的主要阶段包括发现、筛选、商业论证、开发、测试与确认，以及什么？
    A. 试销　　　　　　　　　　　　B. 量产
    C. 上市　　　　　　　　　　　　D. 产品使用测试

17. 在门径流程中，阶段数量不取决于以下哪个因素？
    A. 团队氛围
    B. 新产品上市的紧迫性
    C. 与新产品不确定性或风险水平相关的技术和市场领域的知识储备
    D. 不确定性水平

18. 以下哪个不是门径阶段的主要内容？
    A. 活动　　　　　　　　　　　　B. 综合分析
    C. 可交付成果　　　　　　　　　D. 关口标准

19. 在门径流程中的关口处，常用的决策标准是以下哪个？

　　A. 战略一致　　　B. 技术指标　　　C. 风险与回报　　　D. 以上皆对

20. 门径流程的缺点是什么？

　　A. 强调高质量的决策

　　B. 对所有参与者保持公开透明

　　C. 如未得到充分理解，就会变得僵化和成本高昂

　　D. 适用于各类组织

21. 敏捷门径流程的优点有什么？

　　A. 产品设计更为灵活　　　　　　B. 产品上市速度更快

　　C. 应对市场变化的能力更强　　　D. 以上皆对

22. 数字化产品创新流程有何特点？

　　A. 串行和线性　　　　　　　　　B. 没有尽头和非线性

　　C. 移情和以人为本　　　　　　　D. 感性和新颖

23. 什么是集成产品开发？

　　A. 系统地运用由多功能学科集成而得的团队成果，有效果、有效率地开发新产品，以满足客户需求的一种理念

　　B. 一种系统化、协作式的方法，用来识别问题并创造性地解决问题

　　C. 在合作环境下，由自治式团队进行产品迭代开发的一种方法

　　D. 以上皆错

24. 关于并行工程定义的正确描述是哪个？

　　A. 集成、并行设计产品及其相关过程的系统方法，包括制造和支持

　　B. 同一时间完成阿尔法测试和贝塔测试

　　C. 持续开发工程产品

　　D. 不适用于复杂产品开发

25. 瀑布模型分哪几个阶段？

　　A. 发现、筛选、商业论证、开发、测试与确认、上市

　　B. 需求、设计、实施、验证、维护

C. 探索、筛选、商业评估、开发、测试、商业化

D. 概念、计划、合同、开发和质量、上市、生命周期

26. 在经典瀑布模型中，验证阶段可以被描述成什么？

    A. 根据项目需求写代码

    B. 确保产品符合客户期望

    C. 通过客户来识别产品缺点

    D. 根据具体需要来发现项目完成所需的软件和硬件

27. 在集成产品开发中，有哪几个决策点？

    A. 概念阶段决策点　　　　　　　　B. 计划阶段决策点

    C. 产品准备上市阶段决策点　　　　D. 以上皆对

28. 集成产品开发体系的组织实践等级分几级？

    A. 4 级　　　　B. 3 级　　　　C. 5 级　　　　D. 以上皆错

29. 集成产品开发的优点是以下哪个？

    A. 在产品创新项目中，通过有效协同多功能团队可以将技能和能力聚焦到共同目标上

    B. 需要在开发阶段早期明确客户需求，以便为后续阶段创造和实现价值提供依据，而要做到这些必须有干系人的积极参与

    C. 如果团队无法有效协作和共同创造，那么干系人协作会遇到障碍并会导致问题复杂化

    D. 需要对前端创新和设计控制进行适当平衡，这对项目成功而言至关重要，否则会导致效率低下，最终会延误产品交付

30. 集成产品开发的缺点是什么？

    A. 在流程中，所有人员和技能都要较好地胜任工作

    B. 高质量、主动的风险管理及对客户需求的关注，确保了准确交付价值

    C. 在产品创新项目中，通过有效协同多功能团队（包括内部和外部）可以将技能和能力聚焦到共同目标上

    D. 将效率的提升转化为成本管理的改善和盈利能力的提高

31. 精益产品创新方法的核心概念和原则不包括以下哪个？

    A. 消除浪费　　　　　　　　　　　B. 拥抱变化

C. 预先收集尽可能多的信息和知识　　D. 不断和不懈地学习，寻找改进机会

32. 精益产品创新方法的理念包括哪些？
    A. 知识增长　　　　　　　　　　　B. 精益流
    C. 管理、改进和持续学习　　　　　D. 以上皆对

33. 以下哪个是精益产品创新方法13项原则中的一项？
    A. 明确由消费者定义的价值，将增值与浪费区分开来
    B. 通过项目管理最小化风险
    C. 商业论证是驱动力
    D. 高级管理者参与整个流程

34. 以下哪个是精益产品创新方法的优点？
    A. 需要专职且经验丰富的人员，这样才能为系统改进提出建议，并对系统变化做出积极响应
    B. 需要强有力的供应商管理。若要使用精益产品创新方法或实现准时交付，就要与供应商进行良好的沟通和协同
    C. 适用于各种规模的项目
    D. 组织有意愿且有能力接受项目目标和方向上的变化

35. 以下哪个是精益产品创新方法的缺点？
    A. 流程的重点在于信息的顺畅流动，而非严格的治理
    B. 通过均衡驱动的方法简化合作和优化设计
    C. 需要改变组织结构和文化
    D. 用简单和可视化工具获取知识、追踪进度、进行优先级排序和解决问题

36. 在敏捷软件开发宣言中，更为重视个体和互动、可工作的软件、客户合作以及什么？
    A. 详尽的文档　　　　　　　　　　B. 合同谈判
    C. 流程与工具　　　　　　　　　　D. 响应变化

37. Scrum敏捷框架中的3个角色是什么？
    A. 程序员、测试员、UI设计师
    B. 产品负责人、敏捷教练、敏捷团队
    C. 流程倡导者、流程负责人、流程经理

D. 项目经理、资源经理、发起人

38. 在 Scrum 实践中，不推荐以下哪种做法？

   A. 冲刺规划会议是每次冲刺的起点

   B. 在冲刺规划会议上，产品负责人和敏捷团队商讨并确定本次冲刺所要完成的工作

   C. 冲刺周期由敏捷教练决定

   D. 冲刺开始后，产品负责人带领敏捷团队交付产品成果

39. 在 Scrum 框架中，哪项不是敏捷教练的工作？

   A. 管理敏捷团队

   B. 实时更新团队进展信息，确保各方都被知会

   C. 激发团队创造力，并给团队授权

   D. 清除团队和产品负责人之间的障碍

40. 在敏捷中的每日站会上，不推荐开展哪项工作？

   A. 汇报已经完成的成果   B. 解决问题

   C. 汇报尚未完成的成果   D. 汇报下一步要做的工作

41. 以下哪个不符合敏捷 12 项原则？

   A. 首要任务是通过尽早和持续交付有价值的软件来满足客户

   B. 开发团队里最省时有效的信息传递方式是电子邮件

   C. 即使在开发后期，也欢迎需求变更

   D. 只有自组织团队才能做出最好的架构和设计

42. 敏捷方法的优点是什么？

   A. 需要有经验的团队成员

   B. 任何一个团队成员的缺席都会对项目开发产生较大的负面影响

   C. 由于冲刺周期短，反馈及时，团队更容易应对变化

   D. 范围容易蔓延

43. 敏捷方法的缺点是什么？

   A. 任何一个团队成员的缺席都会对项目开发产生较大的负面影响

   B. 可用于很难提供业务需求文件或很难对项目进行量化时

C. 可在大量变化中进行前瞻性开发，也可以快速进行编码和测试

D. 在流程和管理上投入的费用非常少，可以更快、更省地交付成果

44. 什么是系统工程？

   A. 将系统思维与系统流程模型结合起来，通过系统、集成化的设计流程及项目管理方法和工具开发出解决方案

   B. 系统地运用由多功能学科集成而得的团队成果，有效果、有效率地开发新产品，以满足客户需求的一种方法

   C. 一整套人员、工具、技术和流程的集合。通过制订项目目标和计划，并实现项目目标所需的所有工作，领导项目，支持团队，监控进度，确保项目圆满完成

   D. 在产品设计和制造流程中，采用跨职能团队同时协同展开而不是按单个职能顺序展开的方式进行开发

45. 在系统工程设计框架中，最后一个步骤是什么？

   A. 构建功能结构
   B. 选择合理的解决方案组合
   C. 确定原理解
   D. 评估原理解

46. 系统工程的特点是什么？

   A. 预先、有目的和深入的设计思考
   B. 通过从一般分析到具体分析来界定问题
   C. 跨学科
   D. 以上皆对

47. 系统工程的优点是以下哪个？

   A. 对问题的过度分析和过多的预设细节会造成延迟风险
   B. 当产品创新过程进入尾声时，有效应对变化的能力会越来越弱
   C. 多系统优势明显且极具价值
   D. 长期计划或开发风险会造成解决方案过时

48. 以下哪个是系统工程的缺点？

   A. 多系统优势明显且极具价值
   B. 与设计相关的决策非常详细，并可在客户深度参与下提前做出决策
   C. 在项目早期就有学习机会，可将知识传播给所有干系人

D. 随着项目进展，需求可能过时，变得不再合适或需要

49. 一种创造性的问题解决方法，或者一种系统化、协作式的方法，用来识别问题并创造性地解决问题，这种方法被称作什么？

   A. 集成产品开发　　　　　　　　　B. 设计思维
   C. 敏捷方法　　　　　　　　　　　D. 精益产品创新方法

50. 设计思维框架分为哪两大部分？

   A. 识别问题和解决问题　　　　　　B. 提出方案和验证方案
   C. 制作原型和测试原型　　　　　　D. 设计和优化

51. 精益创业的核心特点是什么？

   A. 严谨的流程和框架
   B. 自组织团队
   C. 快速试错或低成本试错
   D. 综合考虑项目或系统的所有方面，并将这些方面整合到一起

52. 以下哪个是精益创业中的典型方法？

   A. 开发—测量—学习循环
   B. 自组织团队、冲刺、产品增量
   C. 知识增长、人员参与、持续学习、精益流
   D. 阶段、关口、把关者、关口会议

53. 精益创业中的学习计划包括哪四个要素？

   A. 产品、市场、技术、营销　　　　B. 市场、组织、商业、技术
   C. 管理、技术、市场、收益　　　　D. 个人、团队、事业部、公司

54. 精益创业中的创业三阶段不包括以下哪个？

   A. 开发人员与产品匹配　　　　　　B. 问题和解决方案匹配
   C. 产品与市场匹配　　　　　　　　D. 规模化

55. 最小可行产品是什么？

   A. 尺寸较小但功能完善的产品
   B. 具备恰好满足早期客户所需功能，并为未来开发提供反馈的产品

C. 简陋且无法使用的早期产品

D. 以上皆错

56. 在精益创业中，将产品的某一功能转型为整个产品，这是什么转型方式？

    A. 放大式转型 B. 缩小式转型
    C. 价值获取转型 D. 商业架构转型

57. 关于敏捷方法和精益方法，以下哪个说法不妥当？

    A. 精益方法旨在减少浪费，提高运营效率
    B. 敏捷方法旨在对变化做出迅速响应
    C. 精益方法可以完全替代敏捷方法
    D. 敏捷方法不可以完全替代精益方法

58. 关于敏捷方法与门径流程，以下哪个说法是错误的？

    A. 门径流程注重微观规划，敏捷方法注重宏观规划
    B. 门径流程适用于开发硬件产品，而敏捷方法适用于开发软件产品
    C. 敏捷方法与门径流程不能互相取代
    D. 门径流程的组织跨度比敏捷方法的组织跨度大

59. 谁应承担产品创新流程治理和控制的责任？

    A. 产品经理 B. 项目经理
    C. 项目团队 D. 高级管理者或管理团队

60. 以下哪种做法是组织拥有成熟产品创新流程的标志？

    A. 在整个产品创新流程中，将干系人和高级管理层相结合
    B. 使用迭代和风险管理步骤促进有效和高效的产品创新
    C. 持续在产品管道中补充新产品
    D. 基于各种模型和经验开发自己的最佳实践

试题答案与解析

序号	答案	知识点	教材页码
1	D	产品创新流程的定义	P99 第7行
2	A	流程与新产品成功率的关系	P100 第10行
3	C	产品创新成本投入水平	P101 图3.1
4	D	产品创新生命期中的不确定性	P101 图3.2
5	B	决策流程	P102 图3.3
6	B	模糊前端的特点	P103 第3行
7	D	产品创新章程特点	P103 倒数第3行
8	C	产品创新章程内容	P104 第12行
9	C	产品创新章程中的背景	P104 倒数第3行
10	A	产品创新章程中的聚焦领域	P105 第4行
11	D	产品创新章程中的目标	P105 第13行
12	B	产品创新章程中的特别准则	P105 倒数第5行
13	C	产品创新章程中的可持续性	P106 第9行
14	A	博思、艾伦和汉密尔顿流程	P107 第10行
15	C	门径流程	P107 倒数第4行
16	C	门径流程主要阶段	P108 图3.4
17	A	门径流程阶段数量的决定因素	P109 第6行
18	D	门径流程阶段内容	P110 第1行
19	D	门径流程关口决策标准	P110 倒数第11行
20	C	门径流程缺点	P111 第3行
21	D	敏捷门径流程优点	P112 第4行
22	B	数字化产品创新流程特点	P113 第9行
23	A	集成产品开发定义	P114 第9行
24	A	并行工程定义	P114 第12行
25	B	瀑布模型五阶段	P115 第1行
26	B	瀑布模型验证阶段	P115 第6行
27	D	集成产品开发模型	P115 图3.7

序号	答案	知识点	教材页码
28	C	集成产品开发实践等级	P116 图 3.8
29	A	集成产品开发优点	P117 第 3 行
30	A	集成产品开发缺点	P117 第 11 行
31	B	精益产品创新方法特点	P118 第 3 行
32	D	精益产品创新方法的理念	P118 图 3.9
33	A	精益产品创新方法 13 项原则	P119 第 10 行
34	C	精益产品创新方法优点	P120 第 8 行
35	C	精益产品创新方法缺点	P120 倒数第 10 行
36	D	敏捷软件开发宣言	P121 第 10 行
37	B	Scrum 中的 3 个角色	P122 第 1、第 2 和第 3 行
38	D	Scrum 实践做法	P123 倒数第 8 行
39	A	敏捷教练职责	P124 第 2 行
40	B	敏捷每日站会	P125 第 3 行
41	B	敏捷 12 项原则	P126 第 3、第 4 和第 5 行
42	C	敏捷优点	P126 倒数第 3 行
43	A	敏捷缺点	P127 倒数第 9 行
44	A	系统工程定义	P127 倒数第 4 行
45	D	系统工程步骤	P128 倒数第 7 行
46	D	系统工程特点	P128 倒数第 4 行
47	C	系统工程优点	P129 倒数第 10 行
48	D	系统工程缺点	P129 倒数第 2 行
49	B	设计思维定义	P130 倒数第 3 行
50	A	设计思维框架	P131 图 3.12
51	C	精益创业特点	P132 倒数第 7 行
52	A	精益创业中的 BML	P133 第 6 行
53	B	精益创业中的学习计划	P134 图 3.14
54	A	精益创业中的创业三阶段	P135 倒数第 3 行
55	B	最小可行产品定义	P136 倒数第 8 行
56	A	精益创业中的转型方式	P137 第 10 行
57	C	敏捷和精益区别	P138 倒数第 10 行
58	A	敏捷与门径流程区别	P140 图 3.17

序号	答案	知识点	教材页码
59	D	产品创新流程治理责任者	P141 第 8 行
60	D	成熟产品创新流程的标志	P142 倒数第 2 行

教材第 4 章 "产品设计与开发工具" 分章同步试题

1. 在设计流程中，需要考虑什么因素？

    A. 消费者的需要和需求

    B. 材料和部件可得性

    C. 成本与消费者愿意或能够支付的价格

    D. 以上皆对

2. 在创意生成中，包含哪两种思维方式？

    A. 发散思维和收敛思维　　　　B. 定性方法和定量方法

    C. 一级方法和二级方法　　　　D. 家中方法和家外方法

3. SCAMPER 法中的"C"代表什么方法？

    A. Cut（切除）　　　　　　　B. Converse（逆向）

    C. Combine（合并）　　　　　D. Control（控制）

4. 头脑风暴的规则不包含以下哪个？

    A. 不对创意进行评判

    B. 鼓励疯狂的创意，也可以在别人的创意上再生成创意

    C. 一次只专注于一个主题

    D. 重视创意质量而不是数量

5. 讲述消费者使用产品和体验的故事，目的是更好地理解有关具体产品设计属性或新需求的问题或话题。这是什么创意生成工具？

    A. 思维导图　　　　　　　　　B. 故事板

    C. 头脑书写法　　　　　　　　D. 用户画像

6. 象征创造力，寻找新的创意、可能性和解决方案，这是六项思考帽中的哪顶？

    A. 蓝色　　　　B. 黄色　　　　C. 绿色　　　　D. 白色

7. 通过观察用户在一天中所从事的个人活动、遭遇的问题和产生的情绪，了解用户在体验产品或服务时的举动、行为和环境。这是什么创意生成工具？

   A. 故事板　　　　　　　　　　　　B. 生命中的一天
   C. 用户画像　　　　　　　　　　　D. 情感分析

8. 与客户进行深入沟通，了解客户并与客户建立直接的情感联系。设计者需要将自己置身于客户的世界中，了解客户的问题，并从客户的角度提出解决方案。这是什么创意生成工具？

   A. 移情分析　　　　　　　　　　　B. 情感分析
   C. 生命中的一天　　　　　　　　　D. 感性工学

9. 对用户群体进行客观和直接观察，然后设计出虚构角色，这是什么创意生成工具？

   A. 用户画像　　　　　　　　　　　B. 用户体验地图
   C. 用户故事　　　　　　　　　　　D. 焦点小组

10. 以下关于用户体验地图的正确描述是哪个？

    A. 消费者使用产品或服务时的行动和行为流程图
    B. 对用户群体进行客观和直接观察后所设计的虚构角色
    C. 通过向专家组发送问卷，然后根据专家匿名回复的结果进行预测的方法
    D. 鼓励团队成员将思维方式分成六种明确的功能和角色的一种工具

11. 在概念设计阶段，合理的步骤是什么？

    A. 产品设计规格—概念说明—技术规格
    B. 概念说明—产品设计规格—技术规格
    C. 概念说明—技术规格—产品设计规格
    D. 产品设计规格—技术规格—概念说明

12. 概念工程的第一个阶段是什么？

    A. 生成概念　　　　　　　　　　　B. 用专业方法进行落实
    C. 将对客户的了解转化为需求　　　D. 了解客户环境

13. 卡诺模型将产品需求分为哪三类？

    A. 功能需求、美观需求、精神需求　B. 本能、行为、反思

C. 基本需求、期望需求、兴奋需求　　D. 核心利益、有形特性、增强特性

14. 产品创新团队正在运用卡诺模型将产品属性进行分类。团队发现某项产品属性和满意度之间呈比例关系，该功能越强，客户满意度就越高。该属性是以下哪个？
    A. 魅力属性　　　　　　　　　　　B. 期望属性
    C. 必备属性　　　　　　　　　　　D. 无差异属性

15. 创建一个图，图的水平方向为要素或维度，在每个要素下有一连串的概念或创意。然后将每个要素下的创意组合起来，形成解决方案后进入产品设计阶段。这是什么概念设计工具？
    A. 联合分析　　　　　　　　　　　B. 概念场景
    C. 形态分析　　　　　　　　　　　D. 概念工程

16. 以下哪个是关于概念场景的正确说法？
    A. 以客户为中心的流程，明确了产品创新流程的"模糊前端"，目的是开发产品概念
    B. 生成满足潜在用户需求和期望的系统解决方案，其目的是识别若干解决方案（或设计参数）中的共同要素
    C. 基于逻辑、数据而非直觉的问题解决方法
    D. 产品设计团队收集草图、插图、照片和活动描述，然后设计客户体验场景。场景详细描述了实际参与者、环境、参与者的目标及参与者实现目标的方法

17. TRIZ 的特点是什么？
    A. 基于逻辑和数据　　　　　　　　B. 依靠直觉和灵感
    C. 选项 A 和 B　　　　　　　　　D. 无法重复也无法预测

18. 以下哪个是最常使用的 TRIZ 工具？
    A. 头脑书写法　　　　　　　　　　B. 阿奇舒勒 40 个发明原理
    C. 克罗斯比 7 顶思考帽　　　　　　D. 科学方法

19. 用带盖子的玻璃杯装巧克力。吃完巧克力后，可用玻璃杯盛水。该设计应用了 TRIZ 中的什么发明原理？
    A. 分割　　　B. 局部质量　　　C. 多用性　　　D. 空间维度变化

20. 一个好的产品概念说明应该包含什么内容？

    A. 功能需求、美观需求、精神需求
    B. 本能、行为、反思
    C. 基本需求、期望需求、兴奋需求
    D. 核心利益、有形特性、增强特性

21. 在黄貂鱼产品概念说明案例中，"无线接收器配有一根铜质天线，可以放在急救人员的背心中"，这是关于产品什么方面的描述？

    A. 核心利益   B. 有形特性   C. 增强特性   D. 设计规格

22. 在黄貂鱼产品概念说明案例中，"提供7天24小时支持服务"，这是关于产品什么方面的描述？

    A. 核心利益   B. 有形特性   C. 增强特性   D. 设计规格

23. 在黄貂鱼产品概念说明案例中，"电池容量≥2500mAh"，这是关于产品什么方面的描述？

    A. 核心利益   B. 概念说明   C. 增强特性   D. 设计规格

24. 联合分析的第一步是什么？

    A. 识别用户关注的所有产品属性
    B. 将属性量化为等级
    C. 制定基本偏好模型
    D. 确定将属性进行建模的方式

25. 在功能分析中，不常用的功能分类是以下哪个？

    A. 基本功能和次要功能
    B. 物质功能和非物质功能
    C. 外部功能和内部功能
    D. 使用功能和美学功能

26. 以下哪个不是FAST技术图的特点？

    A. 按照"如何—为什么"（How-Why）的逻辑构建，将功能从左到右进行排列
    B. 从左到右进行分析时，要回答一个问题：该功能是如何实现的
    C. 通常与非补偿模型结合使用
    D. 当从右到左进行分析时，则要回答另一个问题：为什么需要该功能

27. Halo 公司的产品开发团队通过对竞争对手的产品进行拆解来识别其中的功能。Halo 公司的开发团队不做任何改变，只通过复制竞争对手的组件来实现 Halo 公司产品的功能。这是什么类型的逆向工程方法？

    A. 模仿型逆向工程
    B. 研究型逆向工程
    C. 低成本型逆向工程
    D. 率先进入市场型逆向工程

28. 以下哪个不属于功能性设计中的内容？

    A. 安全性设计
    B. 简单化设计（平台设计）
    C. 重新设计（改进型产品或衍生产品）
    D. 可装配性设计

29. 可生产性设计的目的是什么？

    A. 决定产品的最终性能
    B. 在确保质量标准的同时，尽量减少产品成本和生产时间
    C. 简化产品设计，降低制造流程中的装配成本
    D. 考虑维护、修理和零部件更换

30. 设计者考虑零部件组装、生产成本及质量，从而简化产品设计，降低制造流程中的装配成本。这是什么设计方法？

    A. 可生产性设计
    B. 可回收性设计
    C. 可维护性设计
    D. 可装配性设计

31. 可维护性设计中的注意事项不包括以下哪个？

    A. 尽可能使用定制件
    B. 在可拆卸性设计时，要考虑零件易获得性
    C. 应用模块化架构
    D. 系统可以自我调整

32. 强调产品、零部件、材料可再利用和可再加工的是什么设计方法？

    A. 可用性设计
    B. 可回收性设计
    C. 可维护性设计
    D. 可服务性设计

33. 设计时考虑用户如何与产品（或用户界面）进行交互，如何使用产品，都有哪些行为等，这是什么设计方法？

    A. 可用性设计
    B. 可回收性设计
    C. 可维护性设计
    D. 可服务性设计

34. 以下关于可服务性设计的描述正确的是哪个？

   A. 重点是提升在维修和排除故障时诊断、拆卸或更换产品的零件、部件、子组件或组件的能力

   B. 有助于产品在工作和运行中迅速进入正常状态，达到规格要求，且不会出故障

   C. 采用可回收再利用或可再加工的材料、零部件和产品

   D. 可服务性总成本包括故障诊断、物流、运输成本及实际服务时间

35. 什么是质量功能展开？

   A. 一种确保产品制造质量的方法

   B. 一种生产高质量、高购买量产品的计划和方法

   C. 一种把市场需求翻译成技术需求的方法

   D. 一种把创新融入产品设计的方法

36. 在质量功能展开中，最常见的工具是以下哪个？

   A. 控制图　　B. 质量屋　　C. 流程图　　D. 散点图

37. 产品经理在使用质量功能展开时，第一步需要做什么？

   A. 识别客户需求　　　　　　　B. 识别设计属性或需求

   C. 连接客户需求和设计属性　　D. 评估竞争产品

38. 如果一个设计属性与任何一个客户需求都不是强相关的，那么在对该设计属性的处理方法中，以下哪个是不恰当的？

   A. 有可能是不需要的　　　　　B. 直接忽略或删除

   C. 有可能是多余的　　　　　　D. 有可能是遗漏了客户需求

39. 质量屋的屋顶表达了什么？

   A. 客户需求　　　　　　　　　B. 设计属性之间的相关性

   C. 竞争对手的设计属性　　　　D. 评分结果

40. 在运用质量功能部署中，识别设计属性时不需要重点关注的是哪个？

   A. 与客户需求强相关的设计属性　　B. 缺乏竞争力之处

   C. 十分吸引人的卖点　　　　　　　D. 常规属性

41. 稳健设计的核心特点是什么？

    A. 使产品或流程对变异不敏感

    B. 激发消费者的情绪和感受，创造出良好的情感联想，让消费者对产品产生信任感

    C. 和可服务性设计类似

    D. 和可回收性设计类似

42. 根据用户产生情感的程度对情感进行分类，并将信息处理分为三种水平。其中哪个水平最低？

    A. 反思　　　　　　B. 本能　　　　　　C. 行为　　　　　　D. 以上皆错

43. 有助于设计者评估情感化设计对用户偏好和购买意向的影响的方法不包括以下哪个？

    A. 感性工学　　　　　　　　　　　　B. 情感分析
    C. 概念工程　　　　　　　　　　　　D. 神经网络法

44. 有声思维梯度法、数量化理论Ⅰ、偏最小二乘法及用于估算目的的遗传算法和模糊逻辑是以下哪个方法中用到的？

    A. 突发情绪法　　　　　　　　　　　B. 微软反应卡
    C. 神经网络法　　　　　　　　　　　D. 感性工学

45. 以下关于原型法的描述正确的是哪个？

    A. 模仿竞争对手产品的一种方法

    B. 将产品概念转为实物模型的一种设计方法

    C. 通常指阿尔法原型和贝塔原型

    D. 以上皆错

46. 对原型进行分类，常用哪两个维度？

    A. 实物/分析　　　　　　　　　　　　B. 单一/综合
    C. A和B选项　　　　　　　　　　　　D. 风险与回报

47. 以下哪个不是产品原型？

    A. 纸质原型　　　　　　　　　　　　B. 阿尔法原型
    C. 市场上的产品　　　　　　　　　　D. 贝塔原型

48. 以下哪个是功能原型法？

   A. 制作原型来测试产品如何工作并交付预期功能

   B. 制作原型来评估所设计的外观、感觉、功能和界面是否满足消费者需求

   C. 制作原型并用结构化的方式来描述不同交付阶段的产品或服务，以及产品和用户间的互动

   D. 制作原型来验证系统集成及技术实现方式

49. 以下哪个是阿尔法原型？

   A. 用于在试生产阶段之前对产品进行评估的完整功能版本产品

   B. 用于测试的虚拟原型

   C. 用于确定零件和部件规格的最终版产品

   D. 用于测试目的的非完整功能版本产品

50. 虚拟原型法可用于做什么？

   A. 形态和形状分析
   B. 零部件配合关系
   C. 渲染和装配分析
   D. 以上皆对

51. 快速原型法也称实体自由成形技术，其核心优势是什么？

   A. 缩短产品开发周期和上市时间
   B. 提高产品质量
   C. 有利于循环经济
   D. 提高盈利能力

52. 快速原型法经常采用什么技术？

   A. 纸质原型
   B. 3D 动画
   C. 3D 打印
   D. 油泥模型

53. 六西格玛设计的目标是什么？

   A. 高效利用资源和高产出
   B. 通过稳健性设计减少流程变异
   C. A 和 B 选项
   D. 盈利最大化

54. IDOV 是用于新产品和服务设计的六西格玛设计方法。它由哪几个阶段构成？

   A. 识别（Identify）、设计（Design）、优化（Optimize）、验证（Validate）

   B. 定义（Define）、测量（Measure）、分析（Analyze）、改进（Improve）、控制（Control）

   C. 识别（Identify）、定义（Define）、优化（Optimize）、验证（Validate）

   D. 调查（Investigate）、设计（Design）、优化（Optimize）、验证（Validate）

55. 以下哪个不属于可持续性设计的要求？
    A. 利润、人类和地球
    B. 经济、社会和环境
    C. 三重底线
    D. 核心利益、有形特性和增强特性

56. 可持续性方法中有哪些指导原则？
    A. SPSD 框架（可持续产品和服务开发）
    B. ARPI 框架（分析、报告、排序和改进）
    C. MDE 框架（材料、设计和生态）
    D. 以上皆对

57. 以下哪个不属于产品可持续性指数？
    A. 产品功能数量
    B. 水资源利用和效率
    C. 健康影响
    D. 可再制造或再利用

58. 生命周期评估流程分为四个阶段，第一个阶段是什么？
    A. 对结果进行说明并采取措施
    B. 列出产品生命周期清单
    C. 明确生命周期评估的目标与范围
    D. 生命周期影响评估

59. 有一种方法综合了质量功能展开、对标和生命周期评估，研究产品及其组成部分对环境产生的影响。这是什么方法？
    A. 质量功能展开
    B. 环境质量功能展开
    C. 生命周期评估
    D. 以上皆错

60. 生命周期成本可通过什么形式进行估算？
    A. 传统成本法
    B. 环境成本法
    C. 社会成本法
    D. 以上皆对

试题答案与解析

序号	答案	知识点	教材页码
1	D	设计流程考虑因素	P156 第 3 行
2	A	创意生成的两种思维方式	P157 第 3 行

序号	答案	知识点	教材页码
3	C	SCAMPER 法内容	P157 倒数第 8 行
4	D	头脑风暴规则	P158 第 4 行
5	B	故事板定义	P158 第 10 行
6	C	六顶思考帽中绿色帽子	P159 第 2 行
7	B	生命中的一天定义	P159 倒数第 9 行
8	A	移情分析定义	P159 倒数第 6 行
9	A	用户画像定义	P159 倒数第 3 行
10	A	用户体验地图定义	P160 第 4 行
11	B	设计流程步骤	P160 图 4.1
12	D	概念工程步骤	P161 第 8 行
13	C	卡诺模型三种需求	P162 倒数第 5 行
14	B	卡诺模型四种质量要素	P163 第 5 行
15	C	形态分析步骤	P164 第 8 行
16	D	概念场景定义	P165 第 2 行
17	A	TRIZ 特点	P165 倒数第 7 行
18	B	常用的 TRIZ 工具	P167 第 6 行
19	C	TRIZ 40 个发明原理	P168 图 4.5
20	D	产品概念说明的内容	P169 第 2 行
21	B	产品概念说明的有形特性	P170 第 7 行
22	C	产品概念说明的增强特性	P171 倒数第 10 行
23	D	设计规格示例	P172 图 4.7
24	A	联合分析步骤	P173 倒数第 2 行
25	B	功能分析中的功能分类	P174 倒数第 10 行
26	C	FAST 技术图特点	P175 第 5 行
27	A	逆向工程类型	P175 倒数第 3 行
28	D	功能性设计内容	P176 第 10 行
29	B	可生产性设计目的	P176 倒数第 8 行
30	D	可装配性设计目的	P177 第 6 行
31	A	可维护性设计注意事项	P178 倒数第 4 行
32	B	可回收性设计定义	P179 第 4 行
33	A	可用性设计定义	P179 第 10 行

序号	答案	知识点	教材页码
34	C	可服务性设计特点	P179 倒数第 7 行
35	C	质量功能展开定义	P180 倒数第 6 行
36	B	质量功能展开中的质量屋	P180 倒数第 5 行
37	A	质量功能展开第 1 步	P181 倒数第 3 行
38	B	质量功能展开第 3 步	P183 倒数第 2 行
39	B	质量屋的屋顶	P182 倒数第 5 行 P184 图 4.12
40	D	质量功能展开第 6 步	P185 第 3 行
41	A	稳健设计特点	P186 第 11 行
42	B	信息处理三种水平	P187 第 3 行
43	C	情感化设计中的方法	P187 第 8 行
44	D	感性工学中的方法	P187 倒数第 11 行
45	B	原型法定义	P188 倒数第 10 行
46	C	原型分类维度	P189 图 4.15
47	C	原型种类	P189 图 4.15
48	A	功能原型法定义	P190 第 7 行
49	D	阿尔法原型定义	P190 倒数第 4 行
50	D	虚拟原型法应用	P191 倒数第 8 行
51	A	快速原型法优势	P192 第 3 行
52	C	快速原型法 3D 打印	P192 第 7 行
53	C	六西格玛设计目标	P193 第 2 行
54	A	六西格玛设计方法 IDOV	P194 第 2 行
55	D	可持续性设计要求	P195 第 3 行
56	D	可持续性方法中的指导原则	P196 第 3 行
57	A	产品可持续性指数	P197 图 4.18
58	C	生命周期评估流程四个阶段	P198 第 2 行
59	B	环境质量功能展开定义	P199 第 2 行
60	D	生命周期成本三种估算方法	P200 第 3 行

教材第5章"产品创新中的市场调研"分章同步试题

1. 在产品创新中,市场调研有何作用?
   A. 了解并满足相关方和客户需求
   B. 获取产品创新决策所需的信息
   C. 减少不确定性并将风险最小化,从而提高新产品成功率
   D. 以上皆对

2. 客户之声是什么?
   A. 引导客户经历一系列情境并通过结构化深度访谈提炼出客户需求的过程
   B. 潜在客户对新产品概念的看法
   C. 通过市场调研出的特性集合
   D. 由工程师开发出的规格文件

3. 开展市场调研工作要采取六个关键步骤。第一个步骤是什么?
   A. 定义结果的准确度   B. 定义问题
   C. 收集数据   D. 分析与解读数据

4. 一级市场调研包括什么方法?
   A. 问卷调查、深度访谈、焦点小组   B. 历史数据研究
   C. 环境扫描式研究   D. 互联网文章

5. 以下哪个是二级市场调研的数据和信息来源?
   A. 辛迪加数据(Syndicated Data)   B. 焦点小组
   C. 客户现场访问   D. 以上皆对

6. 定性市场调研有何特点?
   A. 对少数受访者进行调研
   B. 获得客户的信念、动机、看法和观点
   C. 调研结果不代表整体市场
   D. 以上皆对

7. 关于样本量，以下哪个说法是错误的？

    A. 置信区间越小，所需样本量越大

    B. 置信度越高，所需样本量越大

    C. 调研中总体方差越大，所需样本量越大

    D. 调查结果准确度和置信度与样本量无关

8. 以下哪个不是概率抽样类型？

    A. 系统抽样　　　B. 分层抽样　　　C. 判断抽样　　　D. 整群抽样

9. 以下哪个是焦点小组的优点？

    A. 小组人员间的互动能引发讨论，也能提供新的洞察并促进深度了解

    B. 可公开参与者的评论

    C. 调查结果不适用于焦点小组之外的人群，即结果不可预测

    D. 调查结果的质量在很大程度上受到主持人技能的影响

10. 以下哪个是焦点小组的缺点？

    A. 通过小组人员间的讨论提供新洞察

    B. 群体动力会抑制某些个体的贡献

    C. 迅速从客户处获得反馈

    D. 参与者的行为可以被观察到

11. 以下哪个是深度访谈的优点？

    A. 必须由受过访谈技巧和主题内容专业训练的专业人士进行

    B. 会有偏见和主观解读

    C. 更轻松、更个人化、更私密和更安全

    D. 无法预测也不具备普遍性

12. 人种学方法分为哪两种方法？

    A. 未经训练的测评组和训练有素的测评组

    B. 家外调研法和家中调研法

    C. 定量方法和定性方法

    D. 一级方法和二级方法

13. 以下哪个是人种学方法的优点？

    A. 耗时长，尤其是当调研者想要调研目标市场中众多受访者时

    B. 取决于调研者对所观察内容的解读

    C. 提供了一个独特的机会，可以识别客户真正重视的特性、功能和状态，并发现未识别的不满意之处或隐藏的问题

    D. 在统计可靠性上缺乏依据

14. 客户现场访问是哪类企业用得最多的市场调研方法？

    A. B2B　　　　B. B2C　　　　C. C2C　　　　D. O2O

15. 在客户现场访问时，应该注意什么？

    A. 务必知会销售代表并获得其支持

    B. 尽可能在会议室外进行访谈，要直接观看产品使用情况，以便能够获得第一手信息

    C. 要求客户识别问题

    D. 以上皆对

16. 以下哪个情境不可以运用社交媒体？

    A. 制定公司战略

    B. 在创意生成和设计阶段

    C. 在产品创新的商业化和上市阶段

    D. 了解用户需求

17. 社交媒体有何缺点？

    A. 可以与现有及潜在市场进行直接、即时的联系

    B. 通过甄选，可与某些特定客户建立联系

    C. 使用和参与某一特定社交媒体的人可能持有主观偏见

    D. 有机会与忠诚的支持者或领先用户进行互动

18. 关于问卷调查，以下哪个描述是正确的？

    A. 向受访者提出一系列设定的问题

    B. 采用足够大的样本用于调查，选择具有某些特征的样本

    C. 可以是定性方法，也可以是定量方法

    D. 以上皆对

19. 消费者测评组分为哪两种？

    A. 未经训练的测评组和训练有素的测评组
    B. 家外调研法和家中调研法
    C. 定量方法和定性方法
    D. 一级方法和二级方法

20. 消费者测评组不具备什么价值？

    A. 可以很好地了解消费者对产品的喜爱程度及偏好
    B. 可以提供大数据，供决策参考
    C. 消费者测评组对获得产品更新或改进的创意方面非常有价值
    D. 训练有素的测评组可以成为客观测量的"仪器"

21. 概念测试和概念分类是用来做什么的？

    A. 启发客户需求
    B. 评估客户对新产品或服务创意的接受程度
    C. 验证规格
    D. 确认营销计划

22. 通过功能性磁共振成像技术、脑电图、心电图、面部编码分析等工具来收集数据，从而调研客户需求，这是什么市场调研方法？

    A. 眼动追踪
    B. 感官检验
    C. 概念测试与概念分类
    D. 生物特征反馈

23. 什么是大数据？

    A. 是在采集、存储、共享、分析和可视化过程中，用不同装置收集的大量复杂数据
    B. 具有大量、高速和多样等特征的数据
    C. A 和 B 选项
    D. 容量很大的数据包

24. 大数据应用在市场调研中的优点不包括以下哪个？

    A. 大数据具有成本效益性，提高了客户的间接参与度
    B. 大数据让管理者只能获取客户的显性需求
    C. 数据采集是实时的，生成数据的速度要比传统调研方法快得多

D. 可以将重心从以产品为中心的内部创新转移到围绕客户体验的创新上

25. 乐高公司建了一个专门网站，成为其粉丝及用户开展产品创意和对创意进行投票的平台。乐高公司所采用的这个方法被称作什么？

    A. 大数据　　　B. 外包　　　C. 众包　　　D. 众筹

26. 因子分析的主要应用是什么？

    A. 减少变量的数量并找出变量之间关系的结构

    B. 对关键变量进行排序和分组

    C. 深入用户家中，进行长期跟踪，找到和需求相关的因子

    D. A 和 B 选项

27. 产品经理詹姆斯将相似的产品放在一起进行分析，根据产品在多维空间中的分布推断出消费者认为的重要维度。通过该分析，他还发现了市场中的空白。詹姆斯采用了哪种分析方法？

    A. 多维尺度分析　　　　　　B. 因子分析

    C. TURF 分析　　　　　　　D. 联合分析

28. 联合分析的目的是什么？

    A. 识别市场空白

    B. 明确最能影响客户选择或决策的属性组合

    C. 发现产品缺陷

    D. 明确哪个版本更优

29. A/B 测试不适用于对什么类型的产品概念进行深入洞察？

    A. 世界级新产品　　　　　　B. 增强型新产品

    C. 产品线延伸　　　　　　　D. 衍生型新产品

30. TURF 分析适用于什么情境？

    A. 在产品生命周期涉及多个方案和重复购买时

    B. 能最大限度地发挥产品线和产品平台的市场潜力时

    C. 在评估和优化产品组合，吸引数量最多和重复购买意愿最高的客户时

    D. 以上皆对

31. 在产品上市前测试产品能否满足消费者的需求和要求，应该用什么方法？
    A. 产品使用测试　　　　　　　　　B. 试销
    C. 市场测试　　　　　　　　　　　D. 设计验证测试

32. 贝塔测试常在何种情境中进行？
    A. 在实验室中　　　　　　　　　　B. 在真实的使用情境中
    C. 在开发团队中　　　　　　　　　D. 在公司内部

33. 关于增强现实和虚拟现实，以下哪个说法是错误的？
    A. 虚拟现实用一个完全独立的虚拟现实取代了参与者的真实世界
    B. 增强现实将新的现实要素嵌入参与者的当前环境中
    C. 虚拟现实和增强现实完全一样
    D. 增强现实有时被称为混合现实

34. 市场测试不包含以下哪个具体方法？
    A. 销售波调研　　　　　　　　　　B. 模拟试销
    C. 产品使用测试　　　　　　　　　D. 受控试销

35. 以下哪个是试销的优点？
    A. 极大地降低了因市场拓展失败而浪费资金和其他资源的概率
    B. 可以测试和验证分销和营销计划中的所有要素
    C. 让竞争对手提前察觉己方的市场计划，从而让他们拥有更充足的时间来应对竞争
    D. A 和 B 选项

36. 在机会识别与评估阶段，通常使用哪种市场调研方法？
    A. 阿尔法测试和贝塔测试　　　　　B. 市场测试和问卷调查
    C. 焦点小组和贝塔测试　　　　　　D. 二级市场调研和客户现场访问

37. 通常用于概念开发与测试阶段的市场调研方法是什么？
    A. 焦点小组和阿尔法测试
    B. 客户现场访问和贝塔测试
    C. 焦点小组、领先用户小组、线上论坛和客户网站访问
    D. 阿尔法测试和贝塔测试

38. 通常在原型与产品使用测试阶段采用的市场调研方法是什么？

    A. 伽马测试　　　　　　　　　　　B. 贝塔测试

    C. 市场测试　　　　　　　　　　　D. 焦点小组、客户现场访问和问卷调查

39. 通常在上市前产品与市场测试阶段采用的市场调研方法是什么？

    A. 客户现场访问　　　　　　　　　B. 焦点小组和概念测试

    C. 贝塔测试和市场测试　　　　　　D. 二级市场调研

40. 以下哪个是常用的产品创新和管理度量指标？

    A. 获客投入　　　　　　　　　　　B. 净推荐值

    C. 付费意愿　　　　　　　　　　　D. 以上皆对

试题答案与解析

序号	答案	知识点	教材页码
1	D	市场调研作用	P210 第 7 行
2	A	客户之声定义	P211 第 11 行
3	B	市场调研六个步骤	P212 第 5 行
4	A	一级市场调研方法	P213 第 7 行
5	A	二级市场调研方法	P214 第 3 行
6	D	定性市场调研定义	P215 第 8 行
7	D	样本量特点	P216 第 9 行
8	C	概率和非概率抽样方法	P216 倒数第 4 行和 P217 第 6 行
9	A	焦点小组优点	P218 倒数第 4 行
10	B	焦点小组缺点	P219 第 2 行
11	C	深度访谈优点	P220 第 10 行
12	B	两种人种学方法	P221 倒数第 3 行
13	C	人种学方法优点	P222 第 10 行
14	A	客户现场访问适用情境	P223 第 9 行
15	D	客户现场访问注意事项	P224 第 7 行
16	A	社交媒体适用情境	P225 第 5 行

序号	答案	知识点	教材页码
17	C	社交媒体缺点	P226 第 8 行
18	D	问卷调查内容	P227 倒数第 6 行
19	A	两种消费者测评组	P228 倒数第 11 行
20	B	消费者测评组价值	P229 倒数第 8 行
21	B	概念测试和概念分类的用途	P230 第 2 行
22	D	生物特征反馈用到的工具	P231 倒数第 4 行
23	C	大数据定义	P232 第 11 行和倒数第 6 行
24	B	大数据优点	P233 倒数第 6 行
25	C	众包示例	P234 倒数第 10 行
26	D	因子分析的主要应用	P235 倒数第 5 行
27	A	多维尺度分析用途	P236 第 3 行
28	B	联合分析目的	P237 第 2 行
29	A	A/B 测试适用情境	P238 第 8 行
30	D	TURF 分析适用情境	P239 第 4 行
31	A	产品使用测试适用情境	P240 第 9 行
32	B	贝塔测试适用情境	P241 第 3 行
33	C	增强现实和虚拟现实区别	P241 倒数第 7 行
34	C	市场测试三种方法	P242 倒数第 8 行
35	D	试销优点	P243 第 5 行
36	D	机会识别与评估阶段的市场调研方法	P244 第 6 行和 P247 图 5.3
37	C	概念开发与测试阶段的市场调研方法	P245 第 5 行和 P247 图 5.3
38	D	原型与产品使用测试阶段的市场调研方法	P247 图 5.3
39	C	上市前产品与市场测试阶段的市场调研方法	P247 图 5.3
40	D	产品创新和管理度量指标	P248 第 4 行

教材第6章"文化、团队与领导力"分章同步试题

1. 关于文化和氛围，以下哪个说法是正确的？
   A. 文化是组织中人们拥有的共同信念、核心价值观、行为和期望的集合
   B. 氛围则是在特定工作环境中的一些局部特征
   C. 虽然文化无法用语言来表述，但是可以从组织的日常活动和行为中体现出来
   D. 以上皆对

2. 成功的创新文化与氛围的共同要素不包含以下哪个？
   A. 创新是天才们从事的活动，所以要招募天才
   B. 将战略和创新目标清晰地传达到组织各个层级
   C. 合理的失败被认为是学习机会，不会受到责罚
   D. 个人和团队在实现创新目标方面取得的成效会得到适当的认可和奖励

3. 高级管理层在产品创新战略中的角色是什么？
   A. 制定愿景、使命和方向
   B. 提供足够的资源以及支持系统
   C. 支持产品创新流程
   D. 以上皆对

4. 产品战略由谁来制定？
   A. 高级管理层
   B. 高级产品管理者
   C. 职能经理
   D. 项目经理

5. 流程负责人负责什么？
   A. 战略成果
   B. 流程产出量和输出质量
   C. 组织内各级人员的参与
   D. 以上皆对

6. 流程经理承担什么责任？
   A. 推出成功的新产品
   B. 确保资源合理配置
   C. 确保产品创新流程的成功实施
   D. 确保所有项目经理都按进度表实施项目

7. 理想的跨职能团队的特征不包括以下哪个？
   A. 包含全部应有的职能代表者
   B. 树立清晰的项目和团队目标及预期绩效结果
   C. 人数不超过 7 人
   D. 体现职能工作、项目工作与职业发展的一致性

8. 职能型团队适用于什么样的产品创新情境？
   A. 开展基础研究，以便在一系列产品线中进行部署，其中职能专长和知识对开发而言至关重要
   B. 在资源较少的创业型企业和小企业中，同时开展的项目较少
   C. 在采用防御者战略进行产品增量改进的组织中，对职能能力的要求多过对多学科活动的要求
   D. 以上皆对

9. 以下哪个团队类型常用于增量型产品开发？
   A. 重量型团队　　　　　　　　　B. 轻量型团队
   C. 老虎团队　　　　　　　　　　D. 职能型团队

10. 当采用重量型团队结构时，重量型团队领导者的权力和职能领导者相比如何？
    A. 权力取决于本组织使用的矩阵结构
    B. 重量型团队领导者和职能领导者拥有相同的权力
    C. 职能领导者的权力更大
    D. 重量型团队领导者的权力更大

11. 项目团队位于同一地点，项目领导者是每个团队成员在团队中贡献的唯一评估者。这是什么类型的团队？
    A. 重量型团队　　　　　　　　　B. 轻量型团队
    C. 自治型团队　　　　　　　　　D. 职能型团队

12. 致力于共同目标的一小群人，通过努力来实现共担责任的目标。这被称作什么？
    A. 团队　　　　B. 工作组　　　　C. 矩阵　　　　D. 职能

13. 以下哪个说法是正确的？
    A. 职能型团队结构的优点是资源最大化利用，专业性高，有深度，具有规模经济，责任清晰，职业发展路径明晰

B. 重量型团队结构的缺点是项目领导力和项目聚焦度不足，团队成员会有沮丧感

C. 轻量型团队结构的优点是更高的项目聚焦度、承诺与责任，集成化的解决方案

D. 自治型团队结构的缺点是能够打破部门壁垒

14. 以下哪个要素对高绩效团队而言很重要？

    A. 共同目标、领导力和开放式沟通

    B. 授权、互信和冲突管理

    C. 自尊、高效流程与多元化

    D. 所有这些要素对高绩效团队而言都重要

15. 在塔克曼团队发展模型中，在形成阶段、震荡阶段之后是什么阶段？

    A. 解散阶段　　　　B. 规范阶段　　　　C. 成熟阶段　　　　D. 改进阶段

16. 在塔克曼团队发展模型中，成熟阶段有何特点？

    A. 大家努力工作，没有人际摩擦

    B. 团队结构和流程运行良好，大家合力实现团队目标

    C. 项目工作完成很快，团队成员学习水平也很高

    D. 以上皆对

17. 与迈尔斯-布里格斯或五大人格特质相比，DISC工作评估工具有何优点？

    A. 反映了团队成员在职业环境中的行为，而不仅仅是单个人个性的反映

    B. 更有效

    C. 历史上更著名

    D. 以上皆错

18. 在团队中，有种人喜欢快节奏的工作，做决策很快，并以行动为导向。在DISC工作评估工具中，这种人属于什么类型？

    A. 支配型　　　　B. 影响型　　　　C. 稳健型　　　　D. 谨慎型

19. 在团队中，有种人精力充沛且非常健谈，也会被其他人认为是"只说不做"的人。这种人属于什么类型？

    A. 支配型　　　　B. 影响型　　　　C. 稳健型　　　　D. 谨慎型

20. 在 DISC 工作评估工具中，谨慎型的人有什么行为特点？
    A. 喜欢快节奏的工作，决策很快
    B. 具有平和、冷静、有价值的特质
    C. 非感性的，只热衷于精确和细致的工作
    D. 很容易建立社会关系，并喜欢接触新人

21. 在创新 Z 模型中，开创者的专注点通常是什么？
    A. 可能性　　　B. 互动　　　C. 分析　　　D. 实施

22. 在创新 Z 模型中，谁倾向于通过采取行动来实现目标？
    A. 开创者　　　B. 推进者　　　C. 执行者　　　D. 规划者

23. 导致创新团队冲突的潜在原因有哪些？
    A. 人力资源和资金
    B. 技术观点
    C. 职能部门优先级
    D. 以上皆对

24. 托马斯冲突管理模型中的两个维度是什么？
    A. 合作与自信
    B. 自我与他人
    C. 情感特质与思维倾向
    D. 概率与影响

25. 在托马斯冲突管理模型中，合作水平高但自信水平低是哪种冲突管理方法？
    A. 竞争　　　B. 包容　　　C. 折中　　　D. 合作

26. 团队领导者的角色不包括以下哪个？
    A. 提出目标
    B. 微观管理，严密监控团队成员的工作
    C. 充分发挥团队成员的潜能
    D. 鼓励和激励团队成员

27. 团队绩效不受下述哪个沟通因素的影响？
    A. 组织的文化和环境，包含鼓励高绩效的价值观和行为
    B. 组织结构，包括各职能间的角色和关系
    C. 制定了促进和提高团队绩效的流程
    D. 产品经理的业余爱好

28. 在情商中，以下哪个是位列第一的自我管理要素？
    A. 自我调节　　　　　　　　　　B. 移情和社交技能
    C. 自我认知　　　　　　　　　　D. 激励

29. 自我调节是高情商领导者的特质，它是一种什么样的能力？
    A. 控制情绪冲动
    B. 将不良情绪转化为正能量
    C. A 和 B 选项
    D. 认知并尊重他人的感受，理解如何以及何时提供反馈

30. 虚拟团队的适用情境是哪个？
    A. 团队成员在不同地点办公
    B. 团队成员在线共同协作
    C. 团队成员可以获得遍布全球各地的本地市场信息
    D. 以上皆对

31. 在虚拟团队模式中，启动与组建团队活动不包括以下哪个？
    A. 经验教训　　　　　　　　　　B. 招聘合适的人
    C. 个人领导力　　　　　　　　　D. 共同目标

32. 在虚拟团队模式中，语言和习俗是一项实践活动，它属于哪个要素？
    A. 会议　　　　B. 领导力　　　　C. 沟通　　　　D. 知识管理

33. 在虚拟团队模式中，会议要素中的实践活动不包括以下哪个？
    A. 会议形式　　　B. 系统工程　　　C. 严格的计划　　　D. 质量标准

34. 在虚拟团队模式中，知识管理是一个关键要素。以下哪个是其中的实践活动？
    A. 鼓励多元化　　B. 经验教训　　　C. 现场访问　　　D. 80/20 倾听

35. 在虚拟团队模式中，以下哪个是领导力实践活动？
    A. 经验教训　　　B. 协作工具　　　C. 系统工程　　　D. 80/20 倾听

36. 团队与领导力中的可持续性体现在很多方面，以下哪个不属于该范畴？

   A. 在商业论证中，将财务收益放在首位，可持续性作为可选项

   B. 获得高级管理层的承诺

   C. 在构建可持续创新和资源能力上进行投资，并充分利用现有能力

   D. 将可持续性纳入现有的创新项目和创新流程中

37. 为开放性、创造性的工作设计激励制度，应该秉承什么理念？

   A. 鼓励工作人员探索、利用新颖或独特的机会

   B. A 和 C 选项

   C. 容忍早期失败

   D. 重视短期绩效

38. 在制订创新激励方案时，不建议采取以下哪个措施？

   A. 设计长期可行权的股票期权，以鼓励创新专业人士在新产品开发中进行长期研究

   B. 建立一种接受风险的文化，鼓励创新团队在创新中接受风险

   C. 对错误和失败零容忍

   D. 主动设计一些试验，以便能够在失败中学习

39. 有效的培训对高效创新而言至关重要。以下哪个通常不是培训计划中采用的度量指标？

   A. 专利数量

   B. 培训人数数量

   C. 学习创新方法的产品创新员工占比

   D. 创新培训计划制订

40. 创新健康状况评估通常涵盖哪些方面？

   A. 财务、客户、内部流程、学习与成长

   B. 战略一致性、产品组合管理、产品创新流程、生命周期与产品管理、团队与领导、产品创新工具与市场调研

   C. 培训计划、文化、战略、客户

   D. 价值最大、项目平衡、战略一致、管道平衡、盈利充分

试题答案与解析

序号	答案	知识点	教材页码
1	D	文化和氛围定义	P258 第 2 行和第 8 行
2	A	创新文化与氛围的成功要素	P259 倒数第 6 行
3	D	高级管理层在产品创新战略中的角色	P260 倒数第 10 行
4	B	产品战略制定者	P261 第 4 行
5	D	流程负责人的职责	P262 第 2 行
6	C	流程经理的职责	P262 第 4 行
7	C	理想的跨职能团队的特征	P263 第 5 行
8	D	职能型团队适用情境	P264 第 2 行
9	B	轻量型团队适用情境	P265 第 1 行
10	D	重量型团队特点	P266 第 1 行
11	C	自治型团队特点	P267 第 3 行
12	A	团队定义	P268 倒数第 8 行
13	A	团队结构比较	P268 图 6.6
14	D	高绩效团队特点	P269 图 6.7
15	B	塔克曼团队发展模型阶段	P270 第 8 行
16	D	塔克曼团队发展模型成熟阶段	P271 第 1 行
17	A	DISC 优点	P271 倒数第 2 行
18	A	DISC 支配型	P272 第 1 行
19	B	DISC 影响型	P272 第 3 行
20	C	DISC 谨慎型	P272 第 11 行
21	A	创新 Z 模型开创者	P273 图 6.8
22	C	创新 Z 模型执行者	P273 倒数第 2 行
23	D	冲突原因	P274 倒数第 8 行
24	A	托马斯冲突管理模型维度	P275 图 6.9
25	B	托马斯冲突管理模型包容	P275 倒数第 12 行
26	B	团队领导者的角色	P276 倒数第 11 行
27	D	沟通因素影响团队绩效	P277 第 2 行

序号	答案	知识点	教材页码
28	C	情商中的自我认知	P278 第 2 行
29	C	情商中的自我调节	P278 第 8 行
30	D	虚拟团队适用情境	P279 第 4 行
31	A	虚拟团队模式中的启动与组建团队	P279 图 6.12 和 P280 第 4 行
32	C	虚拟团队模式中的沟通	P279 图 6.12 和 P281 第 11 行
33	B	虚拟团队模式中的会议	P279 图 6.12 和 P282 第 1 行
34	B	虚拟团队模式中的知识管理	P279 图 6.12 和 P283 第 8 行
35	D	虚拟团队模式中的领导力	P279 图 6.12 和 P283 倒数第 9 行
36	A	团队与领导力中的可持续性	P284 倒数第 2 行
37	B	创新激励特点	P286 倒数第 1 行
38	C	创新激励措施	P287 第 1 行、第 9 行和倒数第 9 行
39	A	平衡计分卡中的培训计划	P288 第 1 行
40	B	创新健康状况评估	P289 第 2 行

教材第7章"产品创新管理"分章同步试题

1. 以下哪个是产品创新中的可控因素？
   A. 公司战略　　　B. 竞争对手　　　C. 政府政策　　　D. 国际环境

2. 以下哪个不属于产品创新的关键成功因素？
   A. 较早、清晰和明确的产品定义　　　B. 高级管理层支持
   C. 不允许错误和失败　　　D. 瞄准有吸引力的市场

3. 产品开发与管理协会（PDMA）开展的比较绩效评价研究总结了产品创新最佳公司所具备的独特因素，都有哪些？
   A. 重视创新并承担风险　　　B. 采用"率先上市"战略
   C. 应用专业的组合管理工具　　　D. 以上皆对

4. 最佳公司非常重视创新模糊前端，以下哪个是模糊前端的实践？
   A. 广泛使用市场调研工具
   B. 经常使用工程设计工具
   C. 在了解客户需求上投入更多的精力
   D. 使用正式的度量指标来衡量和报告新产品绩效

5. 马丁·埃里克森将产品管理的范围定义为_____。
   A. 技术、产品与管理的交汇点　　　B. 技术、产品与市场的交汇点
   C. 经营、用户体验和技术的交汇点　　　D. 技术、商业模式与市场的交汇点

6. 产品经理的职责不包括以下哪个？
   A. 了解客户体验　　　B. 完成项目中的具体工作包
   C. 制定产品价格和定位战略　　　D. 推动产品上市

7. 产品经理的技能包括以下哪些？
   A. 了解产品，理解客户需求　　　B. 拥有市场知识

C. 具有战略思维　　　　　　　　　　D. 以上皆对

8. 关于产品经理和项目经理，以下哪个说法是错误的？

   A. 项目经理负责产品开发

   B. 项目经理制定产品战略，从零开始，参与产品创意生成和开发，直至产品完全退市为止

   C. 产品经理对市场成功负责

   D. 项目经理跟踪进度，组织协调资源并按时完成项目

9. 关于产品和项目，以下哪个说法是错误的？

   A. 项目是创造产品或服务的过程

   B. 产品是解决客户问题和满足市场需求的产物

   C. 项目就是产品，产品就是项目

   D. 项目是为创造独特的产品、服务或成果而进行的临时性工作

10. 关于产品管理和项目管理，以下哪个说法是正确的？

    A. 项目管理以战略为主，产品管理以开发为主

    B. 项目管理以行业知识为主，产品管理以技术为主

    C. 项目管理以经营为导向，产品管理以团队为导向

    D. 项目管理以预算为主，产品管理以利润为主

11. 产品经理要想成功，必须专注在哪些关键方面？

    A. 树立愿景，制订计划，实现愿景　　B. 指导产品开发

    C. 将产品商业化　　　　　　　　　　D. 以上皆对

12. 产品战略三角是什么？

    A. 市场需求、价值主张、经营需求　　B. 范围、进度、成本

    C. 地球、人类、利润　　　　　　　　D. 技术、产品、市场

13. 产品生命周期包括哪些阶段？

    A. 开发阶段、引入阶段、成长阶段、成熟阶段、衰退阶段

    B. 引入阶段、开发阶段、成长阶段、成熟阶段、衰退阶段

    C. 引入阶段、成长阶段、开发阶段、成熟阶段、衰退阶段

    D. 引入阶段、开发阶段、成长阶段、衰退阶段、退市阶段

14. 产品生命周期正在变得越来越短,主要原因是什么?

    A. 开发者为了更多盈利,获得领导地位,满足客户需求

    B. 客户要求越来越多,竞争加剧,技术持续进步和变化,全球化交流增多

    C. 产品复杂度越来越高,技术越来越新颖

    D. 开发人员流动快

15. 关于产品生命周期中的成熟阶段,以下哪个说法是正确的?

    A. 由于市场饱和,销售开始趋于平稳。由于激烈的竞争、替代产品的出现和消费者喜好变化,保持盈利变得困难

    B. 是产品创意由概念转为实际开发的转折点,且该创意已经成熟,可以进行开发

    C. 描述了在产品生命周期中,公司应开始制定新的开发理念的节点

    D. 在该阶段,用户还在使用该产品会被认为是老套的消费者

16. 产品开发阶段的现金流有何特点?

    A. 为正数　　　B. 为负数　　　C. 为零　　　D. 不确定

17. 产品上市后,通常在产品生命周期哪一阶段不会产生利润?

    A. 引入阶段　　　B. 成长阶段　　　C. 成熟阶段　　　D. 衰退阶段

18. 在产品生命周期中,通常哪一阶段的销量会迅速下降?

    A. 引入阶段　　　B. 成长阶段　　　C. 成熟阶段　　　D. 衰退阶段

19. 在产品生命周期中,引入阶段的价格策略是什么?

    A. 通过降低成本进行收割。持续提供产品,但要面向具有忠诚度的利基市场

    B. 采用低价位的渗透定价法以获取市场份额,或者采取高价位的撇脂定价法以尽快收回开发成本

    C. 保持定价,此时的市场竞争较少,公司持续满足不断增长的需求

    D. 由于出现了新的竞争者,价格会有所下降

20. 在产品生命周期中,成长阶段的分销策略是什么?

    A. 对销售渠道进行选择,直到客户接受并认可该产品

    B. 销售渠道要随着需求及购买产品的客户数量增长而增加

    C. 加强分销渠道,给分销商更多激励,从而扩大客户购买产品的机会

D. 产品退市，清理存货，或者将该产品卖给别的公司

21. 在产品生命周期中，成熟阶段的促销策略是什么？

    A. 应瞄准早期采用者，通过有效沟通让客户了解产品，教育早期潜在客户

    B. 向为数更多的客户群进行推广

    C. 强调产品差异化和增加新产品特性

    D. 让产品退出市场，仅保留部分存货，或者将该产品卖给别的公司

22. 产品生命周期进入衰退阶段，应该采取什么产品策略？

    A. 维持产品，通过增加新特性或发现新用途重新激活产品

    B. 增加产品特性，通过产品差异化与竞争对手开展竞争

    C. 保持产品质量并增加产品特性和服务支持

    D. 建立起品牌与质量标准，并对专利和商标等知识产权进行保护

23. 在产品生命周期中，产品组合管理应注意哪些方面？

    A. 除了实现产品种类平衡，还应确保产品生命周期中的产品数量平衡

    B. 在引入阶段或上市阶段的产品数量不宜过多

    C. 在衰退阶段的产品数量不宜过多

    D. 以上皆对

24. 产品经理在产品生命周期中都扮演了什么角色？

    A. 开创者、推进者、规划者、执行者

    B. 支配者、影响者、稳健者、谨慎者

    C. 洞察专家、增长黑客、留存大师、方案达人

    D. 寻求者、提供者、中介者、开放者

25. 在产品引入阶段，产品经理的重点工作是什么？

    A. 倾听市场和客户的意见

    B. 根据需求推动组织进行调整

    C. 通过合理定价刺激市场需求，加快产品推广

    D. 以上皆对

26. 产品经理的工作重点为扩大客户触达面，优化产品以满足更多的客户，这说明产品经理处在产品生命周期的哪个阶段？

   A. 引入阶段　　　B. 成长阶段　　　C. 成熟阶段　　　D. 衰退阶段

27. 产品经理在成熟阶段的工作重点是什么？

   A. 关注并听取客户反馈，同时向开发和工程团队提供有价值的信息
   B. 确保产品从引入阶段到成长早期的过渡中成功跨越鸿沟
   C. 关注经营数据，精心管理产品成本、营销和销售成本等，延长成熟产品的寿命
   D. 有效地管理产品退市并顺利转移到下一个产品中

28. 产品经理在衰退阶段的角色是什么？

   A. 方案达人　　　B. 洞察专家　　　C. 增长黑客　　　D. 留存大师

29. 在杰弗里·摩尔的跨越鸿沟模型中，鸿沟通常位于哪个位置？

   A. 早期采用者和早期大众之间　　　B. 早期大众和后期大众之间
   C. 创新者和早期采用者之间　　　　D. 后期大众和落后者之间

30. 跨越鸿沟的应对措施有哪些？

   A. 可衡量的优势和可见的结果　　　B. 一致性
   C. 简单性和易试性　　　　　　　　D. 以上皆对

31. 新式走向市场战略和老式走向市场战略有何区别？

   A. 新式走向市场战略是迭代式的，事后考虑"到哪里促销"
   B. 新式走向市场战略是迭代式的，事先考虑"到哪里促销"
   C. 老式走向市场战略是迭代式的，事先考虑"到哪里促销"
   D. 老式走向市场战略是线性化的，事先考虑"到哪里促销"

32. 一份简短、清晰且简单的说明，说明一个产品概念将如何及在哪些方面为潜在客户提供价值。这是以下哪个概念？

   A. 价值主张　　　B. 产品定位　　　C. 市场细分　　　D. 产品规格

33. 整体解决方案主要包含什么内容？

   A. 产品性能　　　　　　　　　　　B. 产品售后服务

C. 核心利益、有形特性和增强特性　　　　D. 产品规格

34. 在新式走向市场战略中,在考虑"出售给谁"时,应该关注什么?

   A. 细分市场　　B. 市场规模　　C. 市场份额　　D. 产品定价

35. 在新式走向市场战略中,准确定位目标市场是指什么?

   A. 明确产品优势

   B. 对市场进行细分

   C. 将产品主要收益与每个细分市场的需求进行对比

   D. 划分产品类别

36. 以下关于抢滩战略的正确描述是哪个?

   A. 用最快的速度占领市场

   B. 用最小的代价占领市场

   C. 杠杆式的市场推广方法,先选出最具潜力的细分市场作为产品首次上市地点。在该市场获得成功后,再陆续将产品投放到其他细分市场

   D. 用最优质的资源占领市场

37. 在新式走向市场战略中,将产品推向目标市场的渠道有很多。在选择渠道时,要考虑以下哪些因素?

   A. 产品因素、地理因素、价格因素、客户因素

   B. 产品因素、组织因素、品牌因素、客户因素

   C. 产品因素、地理因素、价格因素、供应商因素

   D. 产品因素、组织因素、价格因素、客户因素

38. 在新式走向市场战略中,以下哪个不属于产品促销的内容?

   A. 将促销计划与目标市场保持一致　　B. 聚焦于目标市场中的决策者

   C. 了解决策者从哪里获取信息　　D. 开发新技术

39. 以正确的方式传达产品的正确信息至关重要。这些信息不仅能呈现产品的优势和特性,还能够使目标细分市场的客户产生强烈共鸣。这是走向市场战略中的哪个步骤?

   A. 促销计划　　B. 渠道　　C. 价值主张　　D. 传播信息

40. 在走向市场战略的八个步骤中，哪个不是"谁"这一象限的内容？

    A. 市场细分　　　　B. 价值主张　　　　C. 目标细分市场　　　D. 抢滩战略

41. 产品路线图有何作用？

    A. 对产品战略进行图解，呈现产品随时间的发展过程

    B. 包含即将推出的功能和产品的重要创新细节

    C. 强大的沟通工具，产品经理可以通过产品路线图让不同的部门保持一致

    D. 以上皆对

42. 关于技术路线图，以下哪个说法不正确？

    A. 技术路线图是将产品创新的具体解决方案与短期、长期经营目标相匹配以实现这些目标的计划

    B. 技术路线图是对产品路线图的重要补充

    C. 技术路线图确保新产品或新产品线所需技术的规划和开发工作，能够与产品整体上市计划协同一致

    D. 对战略上极为重视创新及产品创新所需技术的公司而言，技术路线图尤为重要

43. 在什么情境下，平台路线图非常重要？

    A. 在开发者要推出世界级新产品时

    B. 在开发者要进行突破式创新时

    C. 在开发者需要利用平台开发软件或硬件解决方案时

    D. 以上皆错

44. 在实际应用路线图时，不应该怎么做？

    A. 与非员工分享概略的路线图，与直接相关人员分享详细的路线图

    B. 对任何人公开路线图

    C. 使用不同详细程度的路线图版本

    D. 确保协同制定路线图，尽早并经常获得反馈

45. 可行性分析要素不包括以下哪个？

    A. 市场潜力、财务潜力、技术能力　　　　B. 营销能力、制造能力、知识产权

    C. 文化与氛围　　　　　　　　　　　　　D. 法规影响与投资需求

46. 巴斯模型、ATAR 模型和购买意向法都属于什么方法？

   A. 成本估算方法　　　　　　　　　B. 需求预测方法
   C. 投资回报方法　　　　　　　　　D. 绩效评估方法

47. 巴斯模型分为哪两种？

   A. 概率型和非概率型　　　　　　　B. 定性和定量
   C. 基本型和广义型　　　　　　　　D. 一级和二级

48. ATAR 模型中的字母分别指代什么？

   A. 知晓（Awareness）—测试（Test）—接受（Accept）—复购（Repeat）
   B. 知晓（Awareness）—试用（Trial）—购买（Availability）—复购（Repeat）
   C. 购买（Availability）—试用（Trial）—接受（Accept）—复购（Repeat）
   B. 知晓（Awareness）—试用（Trial）—接受（Accept）—复购（Repeat）

49. 对一款产品进行概念测试的结果如下：50%的人肯定会购买该产品，36%的人可能购买该产品。根据以往经验值进行估计，回答肯定购买的人中只有80%的人会真正购买，回答可能购买的人中只有33%的人会真正购买，根据购买意向法测算市场份额预测值为多少？

   A. 15.88%　　　　B. 5%　　　　C. 36%　　　　D. 33%

50. 以下哪个是应用财务分析方法对新产品进行评估的最佳说法？

   A. 新产品财务分析非常简单直接，只需生成预测数据再计算投资回报率即可
   B. 预测和财务分析是动态的，应随着对新产品或概念了解增多而进行演变和修订
   C. 所有类型的预测和财务分析应该用于所有项目类型：世界级新产品、公司级新产品、产品改进、平台产品等
   D. 可以为新产品预测和财务分析生成销售历史记录

51. 以下哪个是固定成本？

   A. 制造材料成本　　　　　　　　　B. 管理费用
   C. 生产用电费　　　　　　　　　　D. 生产人员工资

52. 以下关于可变成本的描述正确的是哪个？

   A. 在相关时间段或生产规模内，总额与业务活动不成比例变化的费用

B. 购买土地、建筑物和设备等的支出

C. 总额与业务活动成比例变化的费用

D. 在准备销售时，用于产品或服务相关的直接和可变成本中的资金

53. 以下关于营运资金的描述正确的是哪个？

   A. 反映了企业偿还短期负债的能力

   B. 在准备销售时，用于产品或服务相关的直接和可变成本中的资金

   C. 包括制造和销售的所有成本

   D. 以上皆对

54. 产品的零售价和以下什么因素有关？

   A. 出厂价　　　B. 批发成本　　　C. 零售成本　　　D. 以上皆对

55. 最低收益率取决于什么因素？

   A. 其他投资渠道的回报率　　　B. 风险水平

   C. A 和 B 选项　　　D. 净现值

56. 某项目投资为 100 万元，预计该项目年利润如下：

   第 1 年 15 万元；

   第 2 年 25 万元；

   第 3 年 40 万元；

   第 4 年 40 万元；

   第 5 年 60 万元；

   该项目的投资回收期是多久（不考虑折现率和资金时间价值的影响）？

   A. 2 年　　　B. 3 年　　　C. 3.5 年　　　D. 4 年

57. 某新产品 5 年期的收入与成本如下，折现率为 10%。该产品 5 年的累积净现值为多少万元？

   5 年间收入分别为：5000 万元；10000 万元；15000 万元；20000 万元；25000 万元

   5 年间成本分别为：3000 万元；5000 万元；5000 万元；8000 万元；10000 万元

   A. 44000　　　B. 30974　　　C. 75000　　　D. 31000

58. 某公司项目总投入 200 万元，产品上市后 3 年每年利润 100 万元。该项目的内部收益率 IRR 为多少？

  A. 15% B. 23% C. 33% D. 50%

59. 项目管理五个过程组分别是什么？

  A. 启动、规划、处理、指导、收尾 B. 启动、规划、执行、监控、收尾

  C. 启动、规划、执行、控制、指导 D. 启动、规划、执行、指导、收尾

60. 项目中的三重约束是什么？

  A. 范围、进度、成本 B. 任务、关键路径、可交付成果

  C. 进度、成本、质量 D. 范围、进度、质量

61. 项目范围是什么？

  A. 与项目与产品相关的里程碑

  B. 工作分解结构和关键路径

  C. 为交付具有特定特性和功能的产品、服务或成果所需完成的工作

  D. 某项产品、服务或成果所具有的特性和功能

62. 关键路径是什么？

  A. 一系列与项目排序、开始和结束以及完成日期相关的可交付成果和里程碑

  B. 工作分解结构中每个任务所需工期

  C. 从开始到完成的最长路径或总时差为零的路径

  D. 由关键技术任务组成的路径

63. 进度压缩包括以下哪些措施？

  A. 赶工 B. 快速跟进 C. 增加资源 D. 以上皆对

64. 先估算底层活动的成本，然后从下到上逐级汇总，最终得出整个项目总成本，这是什么成本估算方法？

  A. 历史数据法 B. 参数法

  C. 自下而上法 D. 自上而下法

65. 成本估算中的参数法是以下哪个？

    A. 先估算底层活动的成本，然后从下到上逐级汇总，最终得出整个项目总成本的方法

    B. 基于历史数据和项目参数，使用某种算法来计算当前项目成本的方法

    C. 基于过往项目数据来制定项目预算的方法

    D. 采用公司专有的模型和方法来制定预算

66. 根据过往项目数据来制定项目预算，这是什么项目预算方法？

    A. 历史数据法   B. 参数法

    C. 自下而上法   D. 自上而下法

67. 以下关于风险管理的正确描述是哪个？

    A. 对风险进行识别、评估和优先级排序，然后整合并有效地利用资源，通过监测和控制手段，将威胁的概率和/或影响最小化，或者最大限度地利用机会

    B. 项目经理如何应对风险

    C. 接受风险并尽一切努力来应对它

    D. 为减轻风险而采取的行动

68. 消极风险应对措施有哪些？

    A. 规避、转移、减轻、接受   B. 合作、包容、回避、折中

    C. 开拓、分享、提高、接受   D. 规避、转移、减轻、上报

69. 应对高概率、高影响风险，应该采取什么措施？

    A. 规避   B. 转移   C. 减轻   D. 接受

70. 应对低概率、高影响风险，应该采取什么措施？

    A. 规避   B. 转移   C. 减轻   D. 接受

71. 风险减轻策略用于应对什么风险？

    A. 高概率、高影响风险   B. 低概率、高影响风险

    C. 高概率、低影响风险   D. 低概率、低影响风险

72. 风险接受策略用于应对什么风险？

    A. 高概率、高影响风险   B. 低概率、高影响风险

C. 高概率、低影响风险 D. 低概率、低影响风险

73. 风险管理过程中的第一步是什么？
    A. 规划风险管理 B. 识别风险
    C. 分析风险 D. 监督风险

74. 风险管理过程中的最后一步是什么？
    A. 规划风险管理 B. 识别风险
    C. 分析风险 D. 监督风险

75. 项目风险和产品风险有所不同，以下哪个是产品风险？
    A. 资源可用性 B. 资金可得性
    C. 信息可靠性 D. 产品可能对客户造成伤害

76. 决策树是什么？
    A. 一种决策辅助工具，利用树形图或者决策模型得出可能的结果，包括项目成果、资源和成本
    B. 一种确定产品中所有功能的方法
    C. 一种用于确定哪些阶段可以跳过的决策技术
    D. 一种将制造方法进行图解的设计方法

77. 项目 A 和项目 B 都通过了商业论证。从预期货币值的角度，优选哪个项目？

项　目	投资(万元)	收益(万元)
项目 A	30	有 60%的概率市场需求强劲，可获得收益额为 60 有 40%的概率市场需求较弱，可获得收益额为 30
项目 B	20	有 60%的概率市场需求强劲，可获得收益额为 45 有 40%的概率市场需求较弱，可获得收益额为 20

A. 项目 A B. 项目 B C. 信息不足 D. 都不可

78. 以下哪个指标属于平衡计分卡中的学习与成长维度？
    A. 客户留存率 B. 市场份额
    C. 客户投诉 D. 员工核心能力

79. 以下哪些是常用于汇报和持续改进的度量指标?

　　A. 活力指数　　　　　　　　　　　　B. 研发费用占比

　　C. 专利数量和上市的新产品数量　　　D. 以上皆对

80. 在制定产品创新平衡计分卡时,建议选择几个度量指标?

　　A. 1~3个　　　B. 4~6个　　　C. 7~10个　　　D. 10个以上

试题答案与解析

序号	答案	知识点	教材页码
1	A	产品创新中的可控因素	P300 第7行
2	C	产品创新关键成功因素	P300 第4行
3	D	最佳公司的独特因素	P302 倒数第7行
4	C	最佳公司的模糊前端的实践	P303 第7行
5	C	产品管理的范围	P304 图7.1
6	B	产品经理的职责	P305 倒数第13行
7	D	产品经理的技能	P306 第3行
8	B	项目经理和产品经理	P306 倒数第11行
9	C	项目和产品	P307 第11行
10	D	项目管理和产品管理	P307 图7.2
11	D	产品经理专注点	P308 第1行
12	A	产品战略三角	P309 图7.3
13	A	产品生命周期阶段	P310 倒数第4行
14	B	产品生命周期缩短原因	P310 倒数第1行
15	A	产品生命周期成熟阶段	P311 倒数第6行
16	B	产品生命周期现金流	P312 图7.5
17	A	引入阶段特点	P312 图7.6
18	D	衰退阶段特点	P312 图7.6
19	B	引入阶段价格策略	P313 第1行
20	B	成长阶段分销策略	P313 第8行
21	C	成熟阶段促销策略	P313 倒数第8行

序号	答案	知识点	教材页码
22	A	衰退阶段产品策略	P313 倒数第 6 行
23	D	产品生命周期的产品组合	P314 倒数第 4 行
24	C	产品经理在产品生命周期中的 4 种角色	P315 图 7.8
25	D	产品经理在引入阶段的角色	P316 倒数第 8 行
26	B	产品经理在成长阶段的角色	P316 倒数第 5 行
27	C	产品经理在成熟阶段的角色	P317 第 8 行
28	A	产品经理在衰退阶段的角色	P315 图 7.8
29	A	跨越鸿沟	P318 图 7.9
30	D	跨越鸿沟的措施	P319 第 1 行
31	B	走向市场战略	P320 第 2 行
32	A	价值主张	P321 倒数第 4 行
33	C	整体解决方案	P322 第 4 行
34	A	出售给谁的关注点	P322 倒数第 2 行
35	C	准确定位目标市场	P323 倒数第 6 行
36	C	抢滩战略	P324 倒数第 2 行
37	D	选择渠道	P326 第 1 行
38	D	促销	P327 第 10 行
39	D	传播信息	P327 倒数第 4 行
40	B	走向市场战略的八个步骤	P328 图 7.24
41	D	产品路线图作用	P329 倒数第 10 行
42	A	技术路线图特点	P329 倒数第 4 行
43	C	平台路线图应用情境	P330 倒数第 2 行
44	B	路线图实践应用	P331 第 2 行
45	C	可行性分析要素	P332 第 9 行
46	B	需求与销售预测模型	P334 第 2 行
47	C	巴斯模型种类	P334 第 8 行
48	B	ATAR 模型内容	P334 倒数第 5 行
49	A	购买意向法计算	P335 倒数第 5 行
		80%×50%+33%×36%=15.88%	
50	B	财务分析特点	P335 倒数第 2 行
51	B	固定成本例子	P336 倒数第 7 行

序号	答案	知识点	教材页码
52	C	可变成本定义	P336 倒数第 6 行
53	D	营运资金定义	P336 倒数第 2 行
54	D	零售价	P337 图 7.30
55	C	最低收益率决定因素	P337 倒数第 3 行
56	C	投资回收期计算	P338 第 9 行
		3+[（15+25+40+40）−100]÷40=3.5（年）	
57	B	净现值计算	P339 倒数第 4 行
		NPV=（5000–3000）÷（1+10%）+（10000–5000）÷（1+10%）^{2}+（15000–5000）÷（1+10%）^{3}+（20000–8000）÷（1+10%）^{4}+（25000–10000）÷（1+10%）^{5} = 30974（万元）	
58	B	内部收益率计算	P341 第 2 行
		100÷（1+IRR）+100÷（1+IRR）^{2}+100÷（1+IRR）^{3}=200 IRR=23%	
59	B	项目管理过程组	P343 倒数第 9 行
60	A	项目中的三重约束	P344 图 7.36
61	C	项目范围定义	P344 倒数第 5 行
62	C	关键路径定义	P345 倒数第 5 行
63	D	进度压缩方法	P346 第 1 行
64	C	制定预算自下而上法	P346 第 5 行
65	B	制定预算参数法	P346 第 7 行
66	A	制定预算历史数据法	P346 第 9 行
67	A	风险管理定义	P346 倒数第 5 行
68	A	四种风险应对策略	P347 第 7 行
69	A	风险规避策略	P347 第 9 行
70	B	风险转移策略	P347 第 10 行
71	C	风险减轻策略	P347 第 11 行
72	D	风险接受策略	P347 第 12 行
73	A	风险管理流程中的第一步	P347 倒数第 7 行
74	D	风险管理流程中最后一步	P348 第 7 行
75	D	项目风险和产品风险差异	P348 倒数第 2 行
76	A	决策树定义	P349 第 7 行

序号	答案	知识点	教材页码
77	A	决策树计算	P349 图 7.38
		项目 A 的 EMV=[(60×60%)+30×40%]-30=18(万元)；项目 B 的 EMV=[45×60%+20×40%]-20=15(万元)。项目 A 的 EMV 比项目 B 的 EMV 更大，因此优选项目 A	
78	D	平衡计分卡	P351 图 7.40
79	D	产品创新度量指标	P352 第 7 行
80	B	产品创新平衡计分卡	P357 第 11 行

NPDP 期中测试

NPDP 期中综合试题

说明：考试时间为 3.5 小时（9:00—12:30），共 200 道题，均为单选题。答对 150 道（含）以上通过考试。

1. 通过增加产品特性和发布产品新型号来延长产品生命周期成了很多公司的产品策略。以下哪个例子没有采用该策略？
   A. 小米手机
   B. 苹果 iPhone 手机
   C. 华为智能手表
   D. 优步颠覆传统出租车服务

2. 默克公司为自己开发的产品申请了多项专利，以下哪个是专利的定义？
   A. 在一定时间阶段内生效并由政府授权或许可的权利，尤其指禁止他人制造、使用或销售一个发明的独有权利
   B. 在一个组织内保持秘密状态的与知识产权相关的信息
   C. 用于代表公司或产品并经由法定注册或许可的符号、单词或词组
   D. 在一定年限内，给予原创者独家的、指定的法律权利，包括印刷、出版、表演、放映、录制的文学艺术或音乐成果

3. 道格·兰尼提出了大数据的主流定义，即"3V"。"3V"指什么？
   A. 大量（Volume）、高速（Velocity）、差异（Variance）
   B. 大量（Volume）、高速（Velocity）、易变（Volatility）
   C. 大量（Volume）、高速（Velocity）、多样（Variety）
   D. 大量（Volume）、高速（Velocity）、有效（Valid）

4. 在产品生命周期的引入阶段，产品经理要成为洞察专家。在此阶段，产品经理的主要任务是什么？
   A. 产品详细设计与优化
   B. 与模糊前端相关的工作
   C. 关注并听取客户反馈，顺应市场需求，合理定价
   D. 与竞争对手开展竞争

5. 在产品生命周期中的哪个阶段，可以采取低价位的渗透定价法以获取市场份额，或者采取高价位的撇脂定价法以尽快收回投资？

   A. 引入阶段　　　B. 成长阶段　　　C. 成熟阶段　　　D. 衰退阶段

6. 创意人员将摩拜单车的车胎改为蜂窝结构，无须充气，减少了维护成本。这采用了 SCAMPER 法中的哪个方法？

   A. 调整（M）　　B. 逆向操作（R）　C. 去除（E）　　D. 改变用途（P）

7. 以下哪个是组合分析中的定性评估方法？

   A. 净现值　　　　B. 内部收益率　　C. 投资回收期　　D. 评分法

8. 肖恩对用户群体进行了广泛研究，并采用人口统计、行为、态度、生活方式和偏好等信息勾勒出典型用户。肖恩采用了什么方法？

   A. 用户体验地图　　　　　　　　　B. 用户故事
   C. 生命中的一天　　　　　　　　　D. 用户画像

9. 作为集团总裁，凯西带领高级管理团队制定多元化组织的整体战略，对不同的业务进行协同，从而提升整个集团的竞争力，请问她在制定什么？

   A. 公司战略　　　　　　　　　　　B. 经营战略
   C. 创新战略　　　　　　　　　　　D. 组合战略

10. 在开放式创新类型中，哪种类型创新渠道开放度高，合作方多样性也高？

    A. 开放型创新者　　　　　　　　　B. 整合型创新者
    C. 特殊型创新者　　　　　　　　　D. 封闭型创新者

11. 一位产品经理设计了一个直接触达潜在客户的研究项目。在此之前，他调查了技术出版物、电子数据库和网站。这种查阅出版物等资料的方法是以下哪个？

    A. 市场测试　　　　　　　　　　　B. 客户之声
    C. 组合管理　　　　　　　　　　　D. 二级市场调研

12. 将收集到的 24 个客户需求中的 8 个列为下一阶段的关键需求。最后，围绕相关"主题"对所有需求进行归集，用于指导创造性的探究。这是概念工程中哪个阶段的内容？

    A. 了解客户环境　　　　　　　　　B. 用专业方法进行落实

C. 将对客户的了解转化为需求　　D. 生成概念

13. 项目组合中除了支持型项目，还有哪种项目的风险较低？
   A. 突破型项目　　B. 世界级项目
   C. 平台型项目　　D. 衍生型项目

14. G 公司在开发一款新鞋时，采用了可降解材料以平衡可再生资源的流动。G 公司遵循了何种理念？
   A. 平台战略　　B. 技术 S 曲线
   C. 颠覆式创新　　D. 循环经济

15. 戴尼斯在制定不同的服务套餐。套餐中包括影响客户选择或决策的属性组合，如价格、功能和服务，他将这些属性量化为等级并组合起来，以满足不同消费者不同的选择。他使用了什么工具？
   A. 营销战略　　B. 联合分析
   C. 因子分析　　D. 功能分析

16. 皮特选出一些商店，在商店真实环境中摆放新产品，控制产品陈列架的位置，并记录产品在该商店内的销售额，随后，采访客户以获得他们对产品的反馈。这属于市场测试中的什么方法？
   A. 销售波调研　　B. 模拟试销
   C. 受控试销　　D. 试销

17. 玛丽是某家公司的高级管理者。该公司有一系列产品。玛丽和各部门负责人每季度都对产品组合评估一次，并为每个产品类别分配预算。例如，高端材料类 1000 万元，自动化装备类 900 万元，锂电类 800 万元。这是什么组合管理方法？
   A. 预算法　　B. 自上而下法
   C. 自下而上法　　D. 二者结合法

18. 你正在领导公司战略的制定，以下哪个工具你通常不会使用？
   A. SWOT 分析　　B. 商业模式画布
   C. PESTLE 分析　　D. 质量功能展开

19. 决策树通常和以下什么工具联合使用？

    A. 六项思考帽　　　B. SWOT 分析　　　C. 故事板　　　D. 预期货币价值

20. 不同类型开放式创新者的关键成功因素和管理风格有所不同，特殊型创新者的关键成功因素和管理风格分别是什么？

    A. 技术导向以及高度参与式

    B. 技术、服务、时间以及参与式

    C. 质量、服务、时间、品牌以及自上而下式

    D. 质量、服务、时间、品牌、技术以及自上而下式

21. 在跨越鸿沟模型中，哪类消费者会拒绝或非常被动地采用新技术？

    A. 早期采用者　　　B. 落后者　　　C. 晚期大众　　　D. 早期大众

22. 组合管理中资源配置有基于项目资源需求和基于新经营目标两种方法，其主要区别是什么？

    A. 基于项目资源需求是从企业现有资源角度配置资源，基于新经营目标是从业务所需资源角度配置资源

    B. 基于项目资源需求是从期望产出角度配置资源，基于新经营目标是从资源需求投入角度配置资源

    C. 基于项目资源需求是从资源需求投入角度配置资源，基于新经营目标是从期望产出角度配置资源

    D. 基于项目资源需求是从所需资源角度配置资源，基于新经营目标是从企业现有资源角度配置资源

23. 关于波士顿矩阵对产品的分类，以下哪个说法是错误的？

    A. 明星产品所占的市场份额较高，且该市场在不断增长

    B. 问题产品处于高增长的市场之中，但尚未获得显著的市场份额

    C. 现金牛产品所占的市场份额较高，且该市场在不断增长

    D. 瘦狗产品所占的市场份额较低，所处的市场增长较慢

24. 一个公司或组织花费更多的时间和资金通过广告与营销宣称公司采取的是"绿色"经营方式，而不是在其实际业务中努力减少对环境的影响，这是什么行为？

    A. 面向环境的设计（D4E）　　　　　　B. 可持续开发

C. 环保宣言　　　　　　　　　　　D. 漂绿

25. 一份定义明确的产品创新战略是新产品取得成功的关键基石，根据 PDMA 的 CPAS（2013 年）调查，拥有新产品战略的公司在最佳公司中的占比是多少？

   A. 52%　　　　B. 68%　　　　C. 78%　　　　D. 86%

26. 某汽车公司开发了一款车身又短又窄但易于停放的车。在交通拥挤时该车也可以在道路中穿行。消费者担心它的安全性，第三方进行的碰撞测试表明该车的性能优良。这款产品既要小，又要结实，这涉及了 TRIZ 中的哪方面？

   A. 矛盾　　　　B. 功能　　　　C. 资源　　　　D. 趋势

27. 在质量屋方法中，识别设计属性之后应该开展的下一步是什么？

   A. 连接客户需求与设计属性　　　　B. 对竞争产品进行评估
   C. 评估设计属性和开发目标　　　　D. 确定要在剩余部分中开发的设计属性

28. 科瑞斯公司在研发新产品时追求新技术，并期望率先上市，以下哪种战略最符合该公司的做法？

   A. 探索者　　　　B. 分析者　　　　C. 防御者　　　　D. 回应者

29. 在所有功能尚未完成的早期阶段，团队开发了原型，并邀请用户使用。针对使用结果，收集用户的建议和意见，然后对产品进行改进。这是一种什么原型法？

   A. 纸质原型法　　　　B. 功能原型法　　　　C. 阿尔法原型法　　　　D. 贝塔原型法

30. 在组合管理中，以下哪个组合管理评估标准的复杂度最高？

   A. 定性财务评分　　　　B. 项目成功概率
   C. 量化财务指标　　　　D. 定位

31. 迈克尔·波特认为可以通过以下哪个通用战略来确定组织的优势？

   A. 成本领先战略　　　　B. 可持续性战略
   C. 率先上市战略　　　　D. 知识产权战略

32. 针对现在的软件，客户需要增量功能，并希望能够快速交付，同时要求较低的风险，应该推荐哪种产品创新方法？

   A. 门径流程方法　　　　B. 敏捷产品创新方法

C. 精益产品创新方法　　　　　　　D. 集成产品开发方法

33. 谁负责制定创新战略？

    A. 营销部门　　　　　　　　　　B. 对创新感兴趣的员工
    C. 跨职能高级管理者组成的团队　　D. 董事会

34. 以下不适用于机会识别与评估阶段的市场调研方法是哪个？

    A. 二级市场调研　　　　　　　　B. 社交媒体
    C. 焦点小组　　　　　　　　　　D. 阿尔法测试

35. 以下哪个是项目经理在流程管理中的职责？

    A. 接受产品流程实施方面的培训，运用专业技能完成项目工作
    B. 对产品创新流程的战略性结果负责，包括流程的产出量、输出质量和组织内各级人员的参与度等
    C. 确保流程中的创意和项目按时、有序实施
    D. 采用公认的项目管理方法，确保准时实现项目里程碑，并在预算内交付成果

36. 公司打算开发一款产品，产生了很多创意，最后决定选出一个创意进行开发。在此过程中，先后使用了什么思维方式？

    A. 先用收敛思维，再用发散思维　　B. 先用发散思维，再用收敛思维
    C. 先用思维导图，再用亲和图　　　D. 先用亲和图，再用思维导图

37. 约翰新加入了一家高科技公司，公司要求和他签保密协议，协议中要求不得泄露对公司而言处于秘密状态的信息，这里涉及了什么类型的知识产权？

    A. 专利　　　　B. 商业秘密　　　C. 商标　　　　D. 版权

38. 在评估项目组合时，净现值方法的一个缺点是什么？

    A. 不能对项目进行排序
    B. 净现值不够量化
    C. 计算净现值的工具并非随时可用
    D. 很难确定项目准确的现金流数据，尤其在开发流程的早期

39. 产品创新团队中的成员更愿意分享信息，某个成员和另一个成员也消除了之前在产品创新上的分歧，大家开始进行合作，该团队处于哪个阶段？

    A. 形成阶段　　　　B. 震荡阶段　　　　C. 规范阶段　　　　D. 成熟阶段

40. 确保在产品组合中选定的项目能够实现产品创新战略中设定的财务目标。这属于组合管理目标中的哪一个？

    A. 价值最大　　　　B. 盈利充分　　　　C. 战略一致　　　　D. 管道平衡

41. 公司战略通常会有不同的层级，对战略层级的理解有助于董事会和管理者厘清公司的责任和使命。在年度会议上，B 资源管理公司的领导者对多种战略进行了讨论，其中的一个战略就是提升信息系统基础设施的安全性，这属于哪个层级的战略？

    A. 职能战略　　　　B. 经营战略　　　　C. 创新战略　　　　D. 使命

42. 不属于可行性分析内容的是以下哪个？

    A. 产品质量　　　　B. 知识产权　　　　C. 市场潜力　　　　D. 投资需求

43. 杰克识别出了一个风险，该风险发生概率很低，可一旦发生会对项目产生很大的影响，应该采取什么应对措施来应对该风险？

    A. 规避　　　　　　B. 转移　　　　　　C. 减轻　　　　　　D. 接受

44. 在 FF 公司，查尔斯一直在为一款新型无人机开发项目做商业论证。公司总经理正在推动该项目，但财务可行性表明该项目不会产生任何回报。FF 公司采用了严格的门径流程。查尔斯深知关口在流程中的重要性，因为关口可以确保什么？

    A. 只有可能成功的项目才会被继续开发

    B. 总经理支持的项目会被优先考虑

    C. 除了仍在持续开发的项目，所有的项目都要被评估

    D. 所有的项目都要被记录在案

45. 六西格玛设计的定义是什么？

    A. 通过产品和工艺设计来满足需求的方法

    B. 市场调研定义产品需求的方法

    C. 根据既定程序开发新产品方法

    D. 将客户需求与技术规格相结合的方法

46. 集成产品开发成熟度最高级别是以下哪个?

   A. 注重客户需求
   B. 注重知识积累、能力开发和创新文化形成
   C. 注重工具使用
   D. 注重战略和组合

47. 某产品运输成本4元,固定成本可以忽略不计,可变成本2元,实现利润3元,定价应该为多少?

   A. 3元   B. 6元   C. 9元   D. 10元

48. 某公司将手机知识产权战略与公司战略保持一致,持续分析竞争对手的产品,并对知识产权进行保护,请问该公司的知识产权管理方法属于以下哪个类型?

   A. 战略型   B. 主动型   C. 被动型   D. 优化型

49. A公司推出一款新的应用程序,聚焦在比较狭小的市场上,用户非常小众。这是什么战略?

   A. 细分市场战略
   B. 蓝海战略
   C. 抢滩战略
   D. 成本领先战略

50. 以下哪个不是系统工程设计框架中的步骤?

   A. 研讨和采用工作原则
   B. 挖掘客户需求
   C. 选择合理的解决方案组合
   D. 确定原理解

51. 产品给客户带来的利益描述了产品的哪种属性?

   A. 价值主张   B. 竞争优势   C. 特性   D. 功能

52. 人种学方法的优点是什么?

   A. 花费的时间比较长,特别是当研究者想要调查目标市场中众多的受访者时
   B. 依赖研究者对观察到的内容的解读
   C. 可以识别出未阐明的需求,这些隐形需求是产品创新的基础
   D. 缺乏统计信度的依据

53. 在什么会议上,团队给产品负责人演示并接受其评价。产品负责人将依照冲刺会议上设定的标准,决定接受或拒收这些工作?

   A. 冲刺规划会
   B. 冲刺评审会

C. 每日站会 D. 冲刺回顾会

54. 请根据以下表述选择正确答案。
    表述 1：回收期提供了关于项目财务风险持续时间的信息。
    表述 2：项目盈利所需时间会受到回收期的影响。
    A. 表述 1 正确，表述 2 错误 B. 表述 1 错误，表述 2 正确
    C. 二者皆对 D. 二者皆错

55. 快速原型法也被称作什么？
    A. 实体自由成形技术 B. 增材制造
    C. 3D 打印 D. 以上皆对

56. 杰克是一名精益产品创新顾问。他正在审核一家新汽车公司的产品创新流程。审核结果显示，该公司在产品创新流程的多个阶段都存在大量返工，他应向首席执行官提出什么建议？
    A. 减少正在进行的设计数量 B. 制定产品创新章程
    C. 对任务标准化以改进产品创新流程 D. 雇用额外的工作人员来处理变异性

57. 公司需要制定一组度量指标以监控公司产品创新项目绩效，你的上司就此征询你的意见。在选择成功指标时，不应该推荐以下哪个？
    A. 用度量指标进行监控，制定措施，立即行动
    B. 选择数量恰当的度量指标
    C. 了解度量指标能做什么和不能做什么
    D. 选择独立于公司目标之外的度量指标

58. 对技术模式和商业模式进行综合分析，帮助制定组织创新战略的是以下哪个战略框架？
    A. 安索夫矩阵 B. 波特竞争战略
    C. 皮萨诺创新景观图 D. 迈尔斯和斯诺战略框架

59. 马克在组合管理时按照项目需求进行资源配置，以下是最终结果。他应该充分利用哪些资源，以解决资源未能有效利用这一问题？

专业领域	A 项目	B 项目	C 项目	总需求	总供给	利用率
ID 设计师	1	1	1	3	2	150%
结构工程师	3	5	7	15	16	94%
电子工程师	1	2	3	6	8	75%
软件工程师	2	4	5	11	10	110%

A. ID 设计师和软件工程师
B. 软件工程师和电子工程师
C. ID 设计师和电子工程师
D. 结构工程师和电子工程师

60. 在精益创业中，实施开发—测量—学习循环时不会用到以下哪种技术？

　　A. 案头研究、访谈、观察和线上调查　　B. 共创、模仿、实物模型和社交网络
　　C. 测试最小可行产品　　D. 六西格玛

61. 产品生命周期中的产品管理措施首先由以下哪个因素决定？

　　A. 生命周期评估　　B. 可持续性计划
　　C. 产品、价格、促销和地点　　D. 产品生命周期的阶段

62. 对传统出租车行业而言，优步（Uber）意味着什么？

　　A. 延续式创新　　B. 颠覆式创新
　　C. 没有什么创新价值可言　　D. 不好判断

63. 刚刚完成了满足各方需求的程序编写之后，团队将一个新的应用程序推向市场并选择部分真实用户进行测试，以下何种测试最好地描述了这种情形？

　　A. 阿尔法测试　　B. 贝塔测试
　　C. 伽马测试　　D. 阿尔法、贝塔和伽马测试的结合

64. 唐纳德先生受聘于泰勒国际集团。在入职培训的当天，他需要了解公司的愿景、使命与核心价值观。例如，他了解到公司中的每个人都要全力以赴追求以下目标：以身作则、成本意识、简洁、接纳多样性，这代表了公司的哪个方面？

　　A. 公司使命　　B. 公司愿景
　　C. 公司价值观　　D. 以上皆错

65. 以下关于组合管理的描述，正确的是哪个？

　　A. 组合管理是对"正确"产品的选择和维护，与组织的经营战略和创新战略协调一致

B. 在产品的引入阶段、成长阶段，需要以产品为核心

C. 在产品创新阶段，重点放在产品上

D. 在产品的成长阶段、成熟阶段，重点放在产品上

66. 上市时间常常是创新成功的关键因素。一家制造企业正全力推动产品创新流程的实施，但还是发现上市时间被延迟了，管理层认为问题主要在于某些关键阶段缺乏资源和能力，该公司应该聚焦于何种具体战略？

   A. 财务战略   B. 技术战略   C. 能力战略   D. 运营战略

67. 在产品生命周期的哪个阶段，公司重点放在开始建立品牌并进行市场开发上？

   A. 引入阶段   B. 成长阶段   C. 成熟阶段   D. 衰退阶段

68. 某一流程旨在通过一系列固定时长的迭代进行产品创新，该流程能够以有规律的节奏交付软件，该流程被称作什么？

   A. 冲刺   B. 精益产品创新方法
   C. Scrum   D. 精益创业

69. DAMIC 是六西格玛的重要组成部分，其目的是什么？

   A. 把定性化需求转换成定量参数
   B. 使用结构化的问题解决技术来满足政府法规要求
   C. 改进现有流程，使其满足客户需求
   D. 考虑了通货膨胀因素的销售预测

70. 在前期测试时，创业团队发现他们开发的宠物产品并没有解决客户真正的痛点。团队转而改进产品功能，最终满足了客户需求。这属于什么转型？

   A. 客户细分市场转型   B. 客户需求转型
   C. 平台转型   D. 商业架构转型

71. 在迈尔斯和斯诺模型中，那些迅速跟随探索者的公司扮演了什么角色？

   A. 探索者   B. 防御者   C. 分析者   D. 回应者

72. 以下哪个是定量市场调研方法？

   A. 深度访谈   B. 焦点小组   C. 问卷调查   D. 人种学方法

73. 哪对变量在平衡组合的气泡图中不常被用到？
   A. 净现值与投资回报率　　　　　　B. 风险与回报
   C. 市场风险与用户风险　　　　　　D. 技术新颖度与产品新颖度

74. 企业的愿景是什么？
   A. 产品创新项目的目标　　　　　　B. 表述公司观念的哲学
   C. 价值取向　　　　　　　　　　　D. 企业最期望的未来状态

75. 在产品生命周期中的哪个阶段，产品销量下降，公司要做出艰难的决策？
   A. 引入阶段　　B. 成长阶段　　C. 成熟阶段　　D. 衰退阶段

76. 在组建产品创新项目团队时，最常见的一个成功因素是什么？
   A. 跨职能代表　　　　　　　　　　B. 许多有创意的团队成员
   C. 强大的项目领导者　　　　　　　D. 团队成员互相喜欢对方

77. 为公司选择度量指标时，以下哪个是需要考虑的因素？
   A. 度量的范围（如项目范围、事业部范围）
   B. 度量的时间跨度（如过去的结果、当前的绩效）
   C. 度量的对象（如高级管理者、中层管理人员）
   D. 以上皆对

78. 谁应该对新产品创意进行评分？
   A. 跨职能团队　　　　　　　　　　B. 仅限营销经理
   C. 仅限产品经理　　　　　　　　　D. 仅限首席执行官

79. 一家公司决定为其新产品命名。该公司已经进行了广泛的搜索，并确定没有其他公司或产品使用该名称。该公司申请注册该名称，这属于什么知识产权类型？
   A. 专利　　　B. 商标　　　C. 版权　　　D. 商业秘密

80. 谁对组织中产品创新流程的战略结果负责？
   A. 项目经理　　B. 首席执行官　　C. 流程负责人　　D. 敏捷教练

81. 以下哪个说法是正确的？
   A. 组织身份是组织在情感上坚守的原则

B. 愿景表明了"我是谁"

C. 使命表述了组织商业准则，以确保资源得以聚焦

D. 价值观是提供独一无二价值的一系列行动

82. 在可持续开发中，DFE 代表什么？
   A. 面向退市的设计　　　　　　　　B. 开发的环境
   C. 面向环境的设计　　　　　　　　D. 面向经济性的设计

83. SWOT 分析可用于制定战略。SWOT 分析包括什么？
   A. 优势、劣势、机会和威胁　　　　B. 战略、意愿、组织和团队合作
   C. 战略、缺点、组织和威胁　　　　D. 优势、意愿、机会和团队合作

84. 一个公司收购了某创新型产品公司，将要召开技术研讨会制定战略。该会议应聚焦以下哪个战略？
   A. 人力资源战略　　　　　　　　　B. 销售战略
   C. 技术战略　　　　　　　　　　　D. 营销战略

85. 什么时候制定新产品的市场营销组合？
   A. 在产品开发前制定　　　　　　　B. 与产品生命周期并行
   C. 在产品开发后制定　　　　　　　D. 在营销部门做决定时制定

86. 某新产品的开发成本是 1000000 元，预计该产品的年利润如下：第 1 年为 60000 元；第 2 年为 150000 元；第 3 年为 350000 元；第 4 年为 440000 元；第 5 年为 600000 元。那么该产品的投资回收期是多久（不考虑折现率和资金时间价值的影响）？
   A. 3 年　　　　B. 5 年　　　　C. 4 年　　　　D. 以上皆错

87. 团队在一次冲刺迭代周期中完成足够小的工作单元被称作什么？
   A. 产品待办项　　　　　　　　　　B. Scrum
   C. 概念评估　　　　　　　　　　　D. TPS 丰田生产系统

88. 以下哪个不是产品创新治理的内容？
   A. 产品创新流程是否适合组织或产品的特定需求
   B. 是否为产品创新流程的每个阶段设定了度量指标
   C. 是否采用了合适的市场调研方法

D. 是否按照度量指标定期评审产品创新流程

89. 以下哪个不是成本的基本构成要素？
    A. 固定成本　　　B. 可变成本　　　C. 资本支出　　　D. 机会成本

90. 价值主张应该聚焦于_____，而不是_____。
    A. 特性、收益　　B. 收益、成本　　C. 收入、成本　　D. 收益、特性

91. 估算中的参数法是什么？
    A. 将每个项目分解到任务级别并估算每个任务的成本的方法
    B. 使用当前市场数据来预测成本的方法
    C. 基于历史数据和项目参数，使用某种算法来计算当前项目成本的方法
    D. 采用公司专有的模型和方法来制定预算

92. 山姆公司高级管理层决定在今年通过新产品来树立自身在市场上的品牌形象，至少启动20个公司级产品创新项目。高级管理层对于这些项目都很重视，并亲自参加每个项目的启动会，强调每个项目都很重要。遗憾的是，这些项目启动后并没有达到预期效果，项目间也因为争抢资源而导致部门关系紧张。你认为其中最大的问题是什么？
    A. 组合管理不完善　　　　　　　B. 高级管理层支持力度不够
    C. 产品经理不胜任工作　　　　　D. 资源配置不合理

93. 产品创新章程包括以下哪个：Ⅰ.聚焦领域；Ⅱ.总体目标和具体目标；Ⅲ.详细的财务分析和项目计划？
    A. Ⅰ和Ⅱ　　　B. Ⅰ和Ⅲ　　　C. Ⅱ和Ⅲ　　　D. Ⅰ、Ⅱ和Ⅲ

94. 以下哪个最能描述产品组合管理系统？
    A. 每年生成一次产品创新项目投资清单的决策流程
    B. 一个动态的决策过程，不断更新企业活跃产品创新项目清单
    C. 一个多项目管理流程，资源在各个项目之间平衡，生成一个持续的投资项目清单
    D. 以上皆错

95. A公司是一家世界500强公司。该公司拥有多条产品线，某些产品在市场上非常成功。但是，公司高级管理层认为产品间缺乏衔接，而且产品研发时间过长，导致产

品的整体更新换代速度非常缓慢。如果请你来提出建议，你会提什么建议？

    A. 更换产品经理   B. 检查该公司的项目组合管理体系

    C. 制定公司的产品平台战略   D. 审查产品创新流程是否合理

96. 关于组合管理，以下哪个表述最适合？

    A. 最好的新产品组合是选择净现值最高的项目

    B. 最好的新产品组合是选择蒙特卡罗模拟最好结果的项目

    C. 最好的新产品组合是根据管理输入得分最高的项目

    D. 最好的新产品组合是通过上述方法和其他方法结合选择出来的项目

97. 关于高级管理层参与产品创新，以下哪个说法最合适？

    A. 高级管理层应该较晚参与，这样就不会浪费时间

    B. 高级管理层应该尽早参与产品创新，以便最有效地影响结果

    C. 高级管理层应该从头到尾大量参与产品创新，因其不能完全指望项目领导者

    D. 高级管理层不应参与产品创新，因为这么做不能很好地利用他们自己的时间

98. 产品创新章程因为以下哪个原因而极具价值？

    A. 为新产品概念提供聚焦点和方向

    B. 澄清产品创新项目目的和团队成员的角色与责任

    C. 定义产品创新项目里程碑和详细的团队可交付成果

    D. 确定产品创新项目风险、应急计划和财务状况

99. 以下哪个可用来区分产品创新中的赢家与输家？

    A. 高级管理层在其中承担微观管理的角色

    B. 强烈的市场导向：以市场为导向，以客户为重点

    C. 节约资源投资，不惜牺牲速度和质量

    D. 无须在开发之前的任务上浪费时间，直接进入开发和实施

100. 以下哪些是新产品概念的较好来源？

    A. 来自研发、营销和/或运营等内部资源

    B. 来自教育机构、发明家和纯研究机构等外部资源

    C. 客户等外部资源，包括领先用户

    D. 以上皆对

101. 应对新概念进行概念测试，主要基于以下哪个原因？
   A. 测试整体产品及其营销计划，便于预测成功概率
   B. 筛选和淘汰不良概念，帮助开发良好概念
   C. 确定产品是否按预期实现功能
   D. 确定新产品是否满足客户需求以及新产品是否具备成本效益性

102. 对标是什么？
   A. 收集一些优秀组织的绩效数据，组织将自身绩效与其他优秀组织的绩效进行比较
   B. 产品设计和制造的迭代流程
   C. 一种自下而上的技术，用于发现数据之间的联系
   D. 平衡四个绩效维度的综合绩效衡量指标

103. 以下哪个是使用财务分析评估新产品的最佳说法？
   A. 新产品的财务分析非常简单直接，只需生成预测并计算投资回报率即可
   B. 预测和财务分析应被视为一个动态的过程，即随着对新产品或概念的更多了解而进行演变和修订
   C. 所有类型的预测和财务分析应该用于所有项目类型：世界级新产品、公司级新产品、改进型新产品、平台型新产品等，因为这种一致性可以带来更准确的分析
   D. 可以并应该为新产品预测和财务分析生成销售历史记录

104. W公司要进行生命周期评估，产品经理应遵循的评估流程应该为以下哪个？
   A. 资源开采、材料生产、制造和使用
   B. 发现、筛选、商业论证、开发、测试与确认、上市
   C. 明确生命周期评估的目标与范围；对产品生命周期所有阶段的能源和材料投入进行检查；对生命周期中与输入和输出相关的环境影响进行评估；对结果进行说明并采取纠正措施
   D. 启动、规划、执行、监控和收尾

105. 某组织掌握的原有技术已无法实现进一步发展，要寻求新技术转型，说明该技术处于技术S曲线的什么阶段？
   A. 引入阶段　　　B. 成长阶段　　　C. 成熟阶段　　　D. 衰退阶段

106. 在衡量员工满意度时，以下哪种度量指标最有用？
   A. 员工流失率　　　　　　　　　B. 生产线周期时间

C. 平台产生的收入　　　　　　　　D. 员工休息次数

107. 德尔菲技术是在一组专家中进行反复协商最终达成共识，据此得出对未来情况的最可靠预测的一种技术，其较为常用的情境不包括哪个？
    A. 制定战略前的准备　　　　　　B. 技术预测
    C. 创意生成　　　　　　　　　　D. 用财务函数计算财务指标

108. 通过产品使用测试，要回答以下哪些问题？
    A. 产品是否工作　　　　　　　　B. 在开发时产品出现的问题是否得到解决
    C. 产品是否解决了客户的所有问题　　D. 以上皆对

109. 以下哪个是定性市场调研方法？
    A. 概念测试与概念分类　　　　　B. 焦点小组
    C. 眼动追踪　　　　　　　　　　D. 生物特征反馈

110. 投资中最常用的3个度量指标是什么？
    A. 投资回收期、净现值、现金流
    B. 投资回收期、净现值、内部收益率
    C. 净现值、内部收益率、总成本
    D. 净现值、内部收益率、盈亏平衡点

111. 以下哪个对高绩效团队而言非常重要？
    A. 共同目标、领导力和开放式沟通　　B. 授权、互信和冲突管理
    C. 自尊、高效流程和多元化　　　　　D. 以上皆对

112. 在塔克曼团队发展模型中，在形成阶段之后的阶段是什么？
    A. 解散阶段　　B. 规范阶段　　C. 震荡阶段　　D. 成熟阶段

113. Cox公司采取创新方法是：很少与合作方进行合作，同时创新渠道的开放度较低。Cox公司属于哪种开放式创新类型？
    A. 封闭型创新者　　　　　　　　B. 整合型创新者
    C. 特殊型创新者　　　　　　　　D. 开放型创新者

114. 在可持续创新中，经常会提到外部性这个概念。外部性指的是什么？

    A. 企业在可持续创新时，考虑外部竞争者的影响，从而制定相应的可持续发展战略

    B. 与三重底线概念相同

    C. 企业考虑外部环境，比如行业结构、行业规模、行业增速等，制定可持续创新战略

    D. 产品对人或环境的影响，而该影响并未反映在产品的市场定价中

115. 作为一种工作风格评估方法，DISC 有何价值？

    A. 为团队成员提供了工具和共同语言，可用于改进沟通和协作

    B. 可成为团队原则和指南，帮助团队成员就问题、激励因素和压力因素等进行探讨

    C. 可指导团队成员进行建设性对话

    D. 以上皆对

116. 与职能型团队、轻量型团队和自治型团队相比，以下哪个是重量型团队的缺点？

    A. 刚性和官僚　　　　　　　　　　B. 项目不够聚焦

    C. 对团队成员而言有难度　　　　　D. 不能和组织保持一致

117. 一家饮料公司打算开发新型饮料产品线，现有 10 种不同口味的配方。该公司进行了累计不重复触达率与频度分析。得出的结果表明，喜欢前 5 种口味的目标消费者数量占 83%。作为产品经理，你决定开发几种口味？

    A. 10 种口味　　　　　　　　　　B. 5 种口味

    C. 上报首席执行官，让其决策　　　D. 以上皆错

118. 在产品创新项目中，产品经理的责任是发现和定义范围，项目经理的责任是什么？

    A. 发现和定义范围　　　　　　　　B. 执行和交付

    C. 管理生命周期　　　　　　　　　D. 门径流程中的阶段 1 和 2

119. 直接或间接地对员工行为有重大影响的工作环境特征集合，被称作什么？

    A. 文化　　　　B. 环境　　　　C. 氛围　　　　D. 组织结构

120. 关于 A/B 测试，以下哪个说法是错误的？

    A. 适用于对世界级新产品的概念进行深入洞察

    B. 多变量研究方法中的一种，可以测试和比较两个版本或变量

    C. 在 A/B 测试中，会平均分配每个变量的测试样本

D. 在多变量测试中使用 A/B 测试的考虑因素是所需时间和流量、洞察深度及产品或概念的成熟度

121. 创意评估与早期商业分析阶段中使用的市场调研方法包括以下哪些？
    A. 客户现场访问和问卷调查　　　　B. 焦点小组和概念测试
    C. 产品使用测试和焦点小组　　　　D. 市场测试和试销

122. 塔克曼提出了团队发展的五个阶段：形成阶段、震荡阶段、规范阶段、成熟阶段和解散阶段。形成阶段会发生什么？
    A. 遣散团队成员　　　　　　　　　B. 组织团队并使成员开始相互了解
    C. 授权给团队　　　　　　　　　　D. 解决团队成员之间的分歧

123. 塔克曼提出了团队发展的五个阶段，分别是形成阶段、震荡阶段、规范阶段、成熟阶段和解散阶段。震荡阶段会出现什么后果？
    A. 团队领导掌权　　　　　　　　　B. 有些团队成员离开了团队
    C. 解决了团队成员之间的冲突　　　D. 制订了项目计划

124. 某公司决定启动一个高风险项目，要开发的产品不属于公司传统品类。哪种团队结构最适合这种类型的项目？
    A. 自治型团队　　　　　　　　　　B. 轻量型团队
    C. 职能型团队　　　　　　　　　　D. 重量型团队

125. 根据预设的标准来选择不同类型的项目，并实现项目平衡。标准包括长期与短期、高风险与低风险、产品或市场类型等。这属于组合管理五个目标中的哪一个？
    A. 价值最大　　　B. 管道平衡　　　C. 战略一致　　　D. 项目平衡

126. 泰德根据高级管理层的要求制定组合绩效度量指标。高级管理层希望通过组合绩效度量指标用于实现什么目标？
    A. 工具的合理性和适用性
    B. 流程的有序和标准化，提高产品开发效率
    C. 选择项目，与战略保持一致，组合的平衡和有效性
    D. 战略的合理性和灵活性

127. 基于政治、经济、社会、技术、法律和环境的结构化分析工具是什么？

A. SWOT 分析 B. 可行性分析
C. 德尔菲技术 D. PESTLE 分析

128. 生命周期成本分析有何特点？

A. 分析产品生命周期中所有相关方（供应商、制造商和消费者）
B. 考虑在产品生命周期内产生的与产品、流程和活动相关的所有成本
C. A 和 B 选项
D. 不考虑外部成本和生命周期结束成本

129. 喜欢快节奏的工作，做决策很快，要求也很高，以行动为导向。这在 DISC 工作评估工具中属于哪一类型的人？

A. 支配型 B. 影响型 C. 稳健型 D. 谨慎型

130. 产品经理在产品生命周期的衰退阶段扮演的是什么角色？

A. 洞察专家 B. 增长黑客 C. 留存大师 D. 方案达人

131. 在产品生命周期中呈现以下特点：销量增加、单位客户成本下降、利润上升、客户数量增加、竞争对手增多，这说明处于产品生命周期的哪个阶段？

A. 引入阶段 B. 成长阶段 C. 成熟阶段 D. 衰退阶段

132. 杰夫在思考几个问题：产品的用户画像是怎样的？产品能够解决哪些问题？如何对产品成功进行度量？杰夫在做什么工作？

A. 树立产品愿景 B. 制定产品战略 C. 项目实施 D. 产品上市

133. "现金牛"产品的定义是什么？

A. 具有显著未来市场潜力的产品
B. 奶制品
C. 销售下滑的产品
D. 在整体增长缓慢的市场上具有较高市场份额的产品

134. 针对波士顿矩阵中的"瘦狗"产品，应采用什么策略？

A. 加强产品推广 B. 投资研发改进产品

C. 放弃或改变价值主张 D. 降低价格

135. 在产品生命周期中呈现以下特点：销量下降，单位客户成本低，利润下降，签订合同的客户减少、竞争对手减少，这说明处于产品生命周期的哪个阶段？

    A. 引入阶段   B. 成长阶段   C. 成熟阶段   D. 衰退阶段

136. 在大多数产品创新流程最初阶段，你的期望是什么？

    A. 进行深入的技术、营销和业务分析
    B. 测试新的产品及其商业化计划的各个方面
    C. 快速了解市场机会、技术需求和能力的可获得性
    D. 完善产品的设计、原型、制造设计、制造准备和上市计划

137. QR 公司正在开发一款新产品。团队对产品中的一项功能进行分析时发现，用户认为必须有该功能，如果没有该功能，用户就不会使用该产品。在卡诺模型中，这属于什么属性？

    A. 魅力属性   B. 期望属性   C. 必备属性   D. 无差异属性

138. 关于巴斯模型，以下哪个说法是不正确的？

    A. 巴斯模型有两种形式，即基本型和广义型
    B. 基本型需要评估三个参数，分别是 p、q 和 N
    C. 需要考虑重复购买或替换性购买
    D. N 表示目标中最终购买产品的消费者总数

139. 在精益创业的学习计划中，人员配置、预算编制和组织结构等信息归属于以下哪方面？

    A. 市场   B. 组织   C. 商业   D. 技术

140. 循环经济强调什么因素？

    A. 减少、再生产和再循环
    B. 减少、再利用和再循环
    C. 反向、再利用和再循环
    D. 减少、再利用和资源

141. 以下哪个是产品增强特性的例子？

    A. 食物在冰箱里可以存放更久
    B. 增强引擎性能的化学添加物
    C. 有多个清洗附件的吸尘器
    D. 免费的售后服务

142. 病毒式传播、客户黏性和付费增长模式都属于什么转型方式？

   A. 价值获取转型　　　　　　　　　B. 增长引擎转型
   C. 渠道转型　　　　　　　　　　　D. 技术转型

143. 功能性设计包括什么？

   A. 安全性设计　　　　　　　　　　B. 简单化设计
   C. 重新设计　　　　　　　　　　　D. 以上皆对

144. 制定可持续经营战略的步骤不包括哪个？

   A. 将客户需求和设计属性进行关联　　B. 评估问题并明确目标
   C. 在组织使命中纳入可持续性　　　　D. 制定可持续战略

145. 在托马斯冲突管理模型中，包容策略有何特点？

   A. 合作水平和自信水平都低　　　　　B. 合作水平高和自信水平低
   C. 合作水平和自信水平都居中　　　　D. 合作水平低和自信水平高

146. 上市前产品与市场测试阶段所需的关键市场信息有哪些？

   A. 市场规模、销售潜力、竞争对手、竞争产品、目标市场特征和客户愿意支付的价格
   B. 将最初创意转化为详细的概念说明。将用户需求与产品属性、功能进行关联，从而制定产品设计规格
   C. 在开发最终形式和功能的产品时，需要提供有关目标市场偏好和产品改进的信息
   D. 目标市场对产品的接受度（可能和竞争对手有关）、销售潜力、定价及有利于商业化的所有信息

147. 以下哪个不是 TRIZ 工具？

   A. 40 个发明原理　　　　　　　　　B. 分离原理
   C. 76 个标准解　　　　　　　　　　D. IDOV 法

148. 在平衡计分卡中，员工流失率、员工核心能力、员工满意度等指标属于哪个维度？

   A. 财务　　　　　　　　　　　　　B. 客户
   C. 内部流程　　　　　　　　　　　D. 学习与成长

149. 可服务性设计主要集中在哪些方面?

　　A. 产品再利用和再加工

　　B. 用户如何与产品（或用户界面）进行交互，如何使用产品，都有哪些行为，在哪里使用产品

　　C. 提升在维修和排除故障时诊断、拆卸或更换产品的零件、部件、子组件或组件的能力

　　D. 在确保质量标准的同时，尽量减少产品成本和生产时间

150. 在虚拟团队模式中,任务导向、现场访问和80/20倾听等实践活动归属于什么要素?

　　A. 启动与组建团队　　　　　　　　B. 沟通
　　C. 知识管理　　　　　　　　　　　D. 领导力

151. 田口方法主要应用在产品概念选择和设计参数优化上，其目的是什么?

　　A. 将变异的影响降至最低　　　　　B. 提高零部件的精度
　　C. 应用更好的设计软件　　　　　　D. 提高设计者的技能水平

152. 一个项目的五个阶段是什么?

　　A. 启动、规划、执行、监控、收尾　　B. 规划、识别、实施、测试、收尾
　　C. 启动、筛选、实施、监控、收尾　　D. 筛选、规划、执行、监控、收尾

153. 产品创新章程包括什么内容?

　　A. 详细的发布计划　　　　　　　　B. 总体目标和具体目标
　　C. 新产品的具体规格　　　　　　　D. 成功所需的市场调研计划

154. 项目三重约束是什么?

　　A. 范围、进度和成本　　　　　　　B. 流程、时间和预算
　　C. 产品、流程和客户　　　　　　　D. 计划、性能和成本

155. 产品经理在成熟阶段的角色是什么?

　　A. 洞察专家　　B. 增长黑客　　C. 留存大师　　D. 方案达人

156. 哪种压缩项目时间的方法通常会增加成本，但可以使项目按时完成?

　　A. 快速跟进　　　　　　　　　　　B. 减少工作范围
　　C. 增加资源　　　　　　　　　　　D. 增加时差

157. 一个项目的进度表如下，该项目的关键路径是哪条？

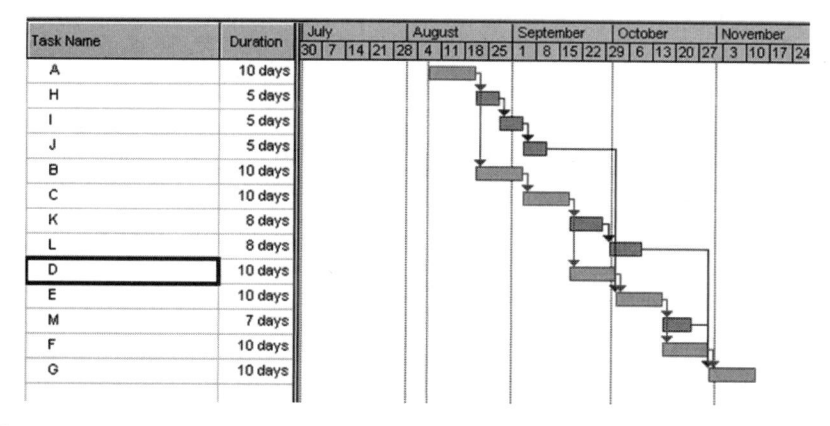

A. A-B-C-D-E-F-G-H-I-J-K-L-M
B. H-I-J-K-L-M
C. A-B-C-D-E-F-G
D. 不确定

158. 在平衡计分卡中，六西格玛水平、单位成本、机器停机时间、能源消耗、新产品上市时间等指标属于哪个维度？

A. 财务
B. 客户
C. 内部流程
D. 学习与成长

159. 万艾可药物本来是为心血管疾病患者开发的，后来转而用于治疗男性疾病，这属于什么转型？

A. 客户细分市场转型
B. 客户需求转型
C. 平台转型
D. 商业架构转型

160. 参与者从118张写有产品词汇的卡片中选出与该产品或设计相关的卡片，并解释为什么所选卡片中的词汇要体现在该产品或设计上，最后得出结论。这是什么方法？

A. 感性工学
B. 情感分析
C. 神经网络法
D. 微软反应卡

161. 资源争夺归属组合管理的范畴。可是，受到资源数据难以获得和数据提供迟缓等制约，要对资源进行精准管理难度较大。那么，组合经理的对策是什么？

A. 进一步细化和量化资源
B. 限制并定义组合所覆盖的范围
C. 增加组合管理人员数量
D. 将资源冲突问题交给他人管理

162. 在以下哪种类型的团队中，项目经理的权力最大？

A. 重量型团队
B. 自治型团队
C. 轻量型团队
D. 职能型团队

163. 抽样方法是指什么？

    A. 邀请 8~12 人的焦点小组　　　　B. 使用少量参与者来代表更大群体的方法

    C. 产品使用测试技术　　　　　　　D. 根据设计输出进行估算的方法

164. 库珀提出组合管理需要和战略协同，并且要实现哪三个目标？

    A. 战略匹配、战略贡献、战略相关性　　B. 战略匹配、战略吻合、战略一致

    C. 战略匹配、战略贡献、战略优先级　　D. 战略匹配、战略聚焦、战略相关性

165. 在敏捷产品创新方法中，促进和协助开发团队的人被称作什么？

    A. 产品负责人　　　　　　　　　　B. 团队领导者

    C. 冲刺领导者　　　　　　　　　　D. 敏捷教练

166. 在敏捷方法中，代表客户利益和需求的人是谁？

    A. 产品负责人　　　　　　　　　　B. 项目经理

    C. 客户关系经理　　　　　　　　　D. 敏捷教练

167. 以下哪个说法最能反映特定产品创新流程模型的价值？

    A. 敏捷适合所有产品

    B. 敏捷和精益的结合通常是最好的选择

    C. 门径流程是唯一适用于所有类型产品的流程

    D. 高绩效公司将根据一系列不同产品创新流程模型的要素开发自己的模型，以适应其特定的公司环境和要求

168. 以下价值观是哪种产品创新流程宣言中的核心组成——"个体和互动高于流程和工具，响应变化高于遵循计划"？

    A. 精益产品创新方法　　　　　　　B. 敏捷

    C. 门径流程　　　　　　　　　　　D. 集成产品开发

169. 在敏捷方法中，产品待办列表是指什么？

    A. 一个足够小的工作单元，可以由团队在一个冲刺迭代中完成

    B. 工作落后于计划

    C. 客户提出的需求清单

    D. A 和 C 选项

170. 以下哪个工具在技术预测中不常用？
    A. 专家小组法或德尔菲技术　　　　B. SWOT 分析
    C. 专利分析法和趋势分析法　　　　D. 人种学方法

171. 环境质量功能展开遵循公理化设计逻辑，要求每项设计都应考虑哪四个方面？
    A. 客户、功能、实物和流程　　　　B. 环境、质量、功能和特性
    C. 客户、市场、产品和技术　　　　D. 战略、组合、流程和工具

172. 以下哪个是集成产品开发成熟度模型的最低级别？
    A. 知识、技能与创新　　　　　　　B. 基本工具
    C. 项目与团队　　　　　　　　　　D. 聚焦客户

173. 与职能型团队相比，轻量型团队的优点是什么？
    A. 项目工作优先于职能工作　　　　B. 改善了沟通，更快地完成项目工作
    C. 提供职业发展道路的一致性　　　D. 聚焦在项目上，对项目的承诺更强

174. 关于团队领导者，以下哪个说法是对的？
    A. 给团队提出目标　　　　　　　　B. 依靠人力资源部门进行激励
    C. 不能容忍失败　　　　　　　　　D. 发出指令，要求团队成员无条件执行

175. 初创团队希望商业模式画布给他们带来什么？
    A. 产品创意　　　　　　　　　　　B. 整体经营策划
    C. 技术发展路线　　　　　　　　　D. 促销计划

176. 杰克在公司领导数字化战略制定工作。在制定数字化战略前，他首先要明确什么？
    A. 公司具备的数字化技术　　　　　B. 愿景、使命、价值观及支持战略
    C. 董事会对数字化转型的要求　　　D. 消费者对数字化产品的需求

177. 制定组合绩效度量指标通常会用以下哪个？
    A. 评分法　　　B. 通过/失败法　　　C. 组合评估标准　　　D. 气泡图

178. 系统工程是什么？
    A. 综合了许多以技术和人为中心的学科。在系统生命周期中，将工业、机械、制造、控制、软件、电气、土木工程及控制论、组织研究和项目管理整合起来。通过技术和管理流程，

确保实现系统用户的需求

B. 在产品设计和制造流程中，采用跨职能团队同时协同展开而不是按单个职能顺序展开的方式进行开发。旨在使开发团队从项目一开始就考虑从概念到退市整个产品生命周期的所有要素，包括质量、成本和维护

C. 系统地运用由多功能学科集成而得的团队成果，有效果、有效率地开发新产品，以满足客户需求的一种理念

D. 按时间维度将工作划分为不同的阶段，阶段之间有管理决策关口。多职能团队在获得管理层批准进入下一个产品开发阶段之前，必须在前一个阶段成功完成所有要求的任务

179. LP 公司采用了一种新型产品创新方法。该方法特点为快速开发原型，将其推向市场，在不消耗不必要资源的情况下衡量产品是否成功，并使用早期营销测试手段获得的数据来进行下一轮开发。这是什么产品创新方法？

　　A. 快速原型法　　　B. 精益创业　　　C. 敏捷方法　　　D. 系统工程

180. 所有流程模型都遵循以下什么原则？

　　A. 注重战略一致性，整个组织采用结构化流程框架并达成共识
　　B. 基于知识制定决策，以降低产品失败风险，在做设计决策时考虑相关方反馈
　　C. 采用跨职能团队
　　D. 以上皆对

181. 概念工程的核心特点是什么？

　　A. 以客户为中心，目的是开发产品概念
　　B. 以产品为中心，目的是开发产品概念
　　C. 以技术为中心，目的是开发技术概念
　　D. 以市场为中心，目的是开发市场概念

182. JD 产品团队正在开发一款新产品。在用卡诺模型对其中一个产品属性进行分析时，发现增加它后消费者就会非常满意，而不增加它时，消费者也不会不满意。这属于什么属性？

　　A. 魅力属性　　　B. 期望属性　　　C. 必备属性　　　D. 无差异属性

183. 科恩在带领团队开发一款新产品。他首先选出几个重要的产品要素，然后在每个产品要素下纵向开发出不同的创意，最后将每个要素下的创意横向组合起来，形成多

个解决方案。这是什么方法？

A. 组合分析　　B. 联合分析　　C. 形态分析　　D. TURF 分析

184. 在应对组合管理复杂性时，可以遵循组合管理准则。以下哪个不是组合管理准则？

A. 估算资源
B. 资源调整
C. 变更管理
D. 正确的流程应该聚焦在高效和有效地交付正确结果上

185. 研究功能载体和功能对象之间作用关系的是什么方法？

A. 价值流分析　　B. 根因分析　　C. 功能分析　　D. 趋势分析

186. FAST 技术图建立在什么分析的基础上？

A. 功能分析　　B. 联合分析　　C. 模拟分析　　D. 形态分析

187. 逆向工程的价值是什么？

A. 将产品功能之间的因果关系可视化，从而加深对产品工作原理的理解
B. 识别被研究对象的功能，从而与竞争对手的产品和生产工艺进行比较，有针对性地开发产品
C. 用相对抽象的语言代替具体的产品运行和应用描述，更利于提升创造力和设计水平
D. 创造性开发可供选择的多元化解决方案

188. DFX 的价值是什么？

A. 为产品设计者节约了设计时间
B. 为产品设计者提出了更多的、更高的、不切实际的要求
C. 为产品设计者提供了成本最小化、产品稳健性、可靠性和达到质量目标的关键方法
D. 为产品设计者提供了更为便捷、高效的设计工具

189. 以下哪个不属于情感化设计？

A. 感性工学　　B. 情感分析　　C. 神经网络法　　D. 稳健设计

190. 产品团队运用原型的目的是什么？

A. 设计产品

B. 验证产品的运行、部件、布局、功能、外观和体验

C. 生成创意

D. 试销

191. 深度访谈是什么调研方法？

    A. 定性调研方法　　　　　　　　B. 间接调研方法

    C. 定量调研方法　　　　　　　　D. 次级调研方法

192. 研究者用专门的装置跟踪参与者目光所及之处，并生成参与者目光停留在被测对象上的痕迹图。将该图提供给设计者作为信息布局和摆放位置的参考。这是什么方法？

    A. 微软反应卡　　　　　　　　　B. 生物特征反馈

    C. 眼动追踪　　　　　　　　　　D. 感官检验

193. 在进行产品创新时，团队采用某种方法可以识别哪些变量会对研究主题产生影响，并用多个变量的已知值来预测变量的结果值。该方法是以下哪种？

    A. 多元回归分析　　　　　　　　B. TURF 分析

    C. 联合分析　　　　　　　　　　D. 多维尺度分析

194. 沃尔玛在购物车把手上安装了传感装置。该装置用来收集使用购物车购物的消费者的脉搏、体温和血压等体征参数，通过这些指标来判断消费者对哪些商品感兴趣。这是什么技术的例子？

    A. 生物特征反馈　　　　　　　　B. 感性工学

    C. 神经网络法　　　　　　　　　D. 微软反应卡

195. 多变量研究方法的优点是什么？

    A. 有助于理解产品属性和当前产品之间的关系

    B. 可以识别市场空白

    C. 提供了能够识别隐性或模糊需求的机会，并了解客户的潜在需求

    D. 以上皆对

196. 在虚拟团队的沟通中容易产生什么问题？

    A. 没有协作工具　　　　　　　　B. 无法安排任务

C. 无法配置资源　　　　　　　　　　D. 文化、种族或语言障碍

197. 基于三个参数，即创新系数、模仿系数和目标中最终购买产品的消费者总数量，对销售进行预测的方法是什么？

    A. 巴斯模型　　　B. ATAR 模型　　　C. 购买意向法　　　D. 跨越鸿沟

198. 在制定平衡计分卡时，会选择收入、净利润、毛利率、销量、息税前利润、投资回报率等指标，这属于哪个维度？

    A. 财务　　　　　B. 客户　　　　　C. 内部流程　　　　D. 学习与成长

199. 以下哪个是产品平台的示例？

    A. 微软公司的 Windows 框架　　　　B. 苹果公司的 MacOS
    C. 谷歌公司的 Android　　　　　　　D. 以上皆对

200. 大卫是一位产品经理。他在团队管理中善于了解他人的情绪，控制自己的情绪，并能将不良情绪转化为正能量。因此，大卫受到了团队成员的欢迎。这体现了大卫具备了什么情商要素？

    A. 自我认知　　　B. 自我调节　　　C. 激励　　　　　　D. 移情和社交技能

试题答案与解析

序号	答案	知识点	教材页码
1	D	创新管理/产品生命周期/产品生命周期对产品组合的影响	P314 倒数第 10 行
2	A	战略/创新支持战略/知识产权战略/知识产权类型/专利/定义	P33 倒数第 8 行
3	C	市场调研/定量市场调研方法/大数据/定义	P232 倒数第 6 行
4	C	创新管理/产品生命周期/产品经理在产品生命周期中的角色/引入阶段/重点工作	P315 图 7.8 和 P316 第 4 行
5	A	创新管理/产品生命周期/管理产品生命周期/引入阶段/价格	P313 第 1 行
6	A	工具/创意生成阶段/创意生成工具/SCAMPER 法/调整	P157 倒数第 6 行
7	D	组合/新产品机会评估与选择/定性评估方法/评分法	P75 倒数第 9 行

序号	答案	知识点	教材页码
8	D	工具/创意生成阶段/创意生成工具/用户画像	P159 倒数第 2 行
9	A	战略/经营战略与公司战略/公司战略	P9 倒数第 2 行
10	A	战略/开放式创新/开放式创新类型/开放型创新者	P48 图 1.26
11	D	市场调研/一级与二级市场调研/二级市场调研方法	P214 第 1 行
12	C	工具/概念设计阶段/概念工程/第二阶段/内容	P161 倒数第 9 行
13	B	组合/什么是产品组合/什么是组合管理/组合中的项目类型/衍生型项目	P69 倒数第 5 行
14	D	战略/可持续创新/可持续产品创新/循环经济与创新/原则	P56 第 7 行
15	B	工具/实体化设计阶段/联合分析/步骤	P173 倒数第 1 行
16	C	市场调研/试销与市场测试/受控试销	P243 第 1 行
17	B	组合/组合与战略的连接方法/自上而下法	P71 第 10 行
18	D	战略/制定战略前的准备/战略制定工具	P11 倒数第 9 行
19	D	创新管理/风险管理/决策树	P349 图 7.38
20	B	战略/开放式创新/开放式创新类型/特殊型创新者的关键成功因素与管理风格	P48 图 1.27
21	B	创新管理/产品生命周期中的鸿沟/跨越鸿沟	P318 图 7.9
22	C	组合/资源配置/资源配置方法	P82 第 2 行
23	C	战略/创新支持战略/营销战略/分析现有产品组合/波士顿矩阵	P39 图 1.21
24	D	战略/可持续创新/可持续产品创新/可持续性与战略/漂绿	P440 倒数第 8 行
25	C	战略/什么是战略/战略在产品创新中的重要作用	P4 倒数第 1 行
26	A	工具/概念设计阶段/TRIZ/矛盾	P166 第 6 行
27	A	工具/详细设计与规格阶段/质量功能展开/构建质量屋的步骤	P181 倒数第 1 行
28	A	战略/创新战略与战略框架/迈尔斯和斯诺战略框架/探索者	P23 图 1.10 和倒数第 1 行
29	B	工具/制造与装配阶段/原型法/功能原型法	P190 第 7 行
30	B	组合/组合管理系统应用/组合管理复杂度变化	P86 图 2.14
31	A	战略/创新战略与战略框架/波特竞争战略/成本领先战略	P20 图 1.9 和 P21 第 1 行
32	B	流程/产品创新流程模型/敏捷产品创新方法	P120 倒数第 5 行

序号	答案	知识点	教材页码
33	C	文化/管理职责/产品创造流程中的角色/创新战略制定者	P260 倒数第 5 行
34	D	市场调研/产品创新各阶段的市场调研/机会识别与评估/市场调研方法	P246 图 5.3
35	D	文化/管理职责/产品创新流程中的角色/项目经理	P262 第 8 行
36	B	工具/创意生成阶段/什么是创意生成/发散思维和收敛思维	P157 第 3 行
37	B	战略/创新支持战略/知识产权战略/知识产权类型/商业秘密	P33 倒数第 1 行
38	D	组合/新产品机会评估与选择/定量评估方法/净现值/缺点	P77 倒数第 2 行
39	C	文化/团队发展/塔克曼团队发展模型/规范阶段	P270 倒数第 3 行
40	B	组合/什么是组合管理/组合管理 5 个目标/盈利充分	P68 第 1 行
41	A	战略/什么是战略/战略层级	P5 图 1.1
42	A	创新管理/可行性分析/可行性分析要素	P332 第 8 行
43	B	创新管理/风险管理/什么是风险管理/转移	P347 第 10 行
44	A	流程/产品创新流程模型/门径流程/什么是关口	P110 倒数第 8 行
45	A	工具/制造与装配阶段/六西格玛设计/应用	P192 倒数第 2 行
46	B	流程/产品创新流程模型/集成产品开发/集成产品开发体系的组织实践等级	P116 图 3.8
47	C	创新管理/财务分析/售价/计算 售价=成本+利润=4+2+3=9（元）	P337 图 7.30
48.	A	战略/创新支持战略/知识产权战略/知识产权管理方法/战略型	P34 图 1.16
49	A	战略/创新战略与战略框架/波特竞争战略/细分市场战略	P22 倒数第 6 行
50	B	流程/产品创新流程模型/系统工程/系统工程设计框架中的步骤	P128 第 6 行
51	A	创新管理/产品生命周期中的鸿沟/走向市场流程/价值主张	P321 第 4 行
52	C	市场调研/定性市场调研方法/人种学方法/优点和缺点	P222 第 8 行
53	B	流程/产品创新流程模型/敏捷方法/关键要素/评审	P122 倒数第 6 行
54	B	创新管理/财务分析/投资回收期	P338 第 9 行
55	D	工具/制造与装配阶段/原型法/快速原型法	P192 第 1 行

序号	答案	知识点	教材页码
56	C	流程/产品创新流程模型/精益产品创新方法/13 项精益原则/第 4 项	P119 倒数第 8 行
57	D	创新管理/度量指标与关键绩效指标	P350 第 1 行
58	C	战略/创新战略与战略框架/皮萨诺创新景观图	P27 图 1.12 和 P27 第 1 行
59	D	组合/资源配置/资源配置工具	P85 图 2.13
60	D	流程/产品创新流程模型/精益创业/开发—测量—学习循环/技术	P133 倒数第 8 行
61	D	创新管理/产品生命周期/管理产品生命周期	P312 第 4 行
62	B	战略/创新战略与战略框架/克里斯坦森颠覆式创新/示例	P26 倒数第 10 行
63	B	市场调研/产品使用测试/阿尔法测试、贝塔测试与伽马测试/贝塔测试	P241 第 3 行
64	C	战略/明确组织方向/价值观	P7 倒数第 7 行
65	A	组合/什么是产品组合/什么是组合管理	P67 第 9 行
66	C	战略/创新支持战略/能力战略	P39 倒数第 5 行和 P41 图 1.22
67	A	创新管理/产品生命周期/产品生命周期阶段介绍/引入阶段	P311 第 8 行
68	C	流程/产品创新流程模型/敏捷方法/Scrum	P122 倒数第 10 行
69	C	工具/制造与装配阶段/六西格玛设计/六西格玛/DMAIC	P193 倒数第 12 行
70	B	流程/产品创新流程模型/精益创业/转型/客户需求转型	P137 第 10 行
71	C	战略/创新战略与战略框架/迈尔斯和斯诺战略框架/分析者	P24 倒数第 10 行
72	C	市场调研/定量市场调研方法/问卷调查	P227 倒数第 10 行
73	B	组合/平衡组合/气泡图/维度	P80 图 2.7
74	D	战略/明确组织方向/愿景/定义	P7 第 5 行
75	D	创新管理/产品生命周期/衰退阶段/特点	P312 图 7.6
76	A	流程/本章小结/流程模型/共同原则	P143 第 5 行和 P357 第 9 行
77	D	创新管理/度量指标与关键绩效指标/选择度量指标考虑因素	P350 第 1 行及常识

序号	答案	知识点	教材页码
78	A	组合/新产品机会评估与选择/定性评估方法/通过失败法	P75 第 6 行
79	B	战略/创新支持战略/知识产权战略/知识产品类型/商标	P33 倒数第 4 行
80	C	文化/管理职责/流程中的角色/流程负责人	P262 第 2 行
81	C	战略/明确组织方向/使命/定义	P7 第 10 行
82	C	工具/制造与装配阶段/可持续性设计/面向环境的设计	P384 第 11 行
83	A	战略/制定战略前的准备/战略制定工具/SWOT 分析/内容	P11 倒数第 6 行
84	C	战略/创新支持战略/技术战略	P30 第 4 行
85	B	创新管理/产品生命周期/管理产品生命周期	P312 第 5 行
86	C	创新管理/财务分析/投资回收期/计算	P338 第 8 行
		前 4 年累计利润=60000+150000+350000+440000=1000000（元），正好收回投资。因此投资回收期为 4 年。	
87	A	流程/产品创新流程模型/敏捷方法/Scrum/产品待办列表/产品待办项	P122 第 8 行
88	C	流程/产品创新流程控制/产品创新治理/内容	P141 倒数第 7 行
89	D	创新管理/财务分析/成本/构成要素	P336 第 2 行
90	D	战略/创新支持战略/营销战略/价值主张	P38 第 8 行和 P321 第 8 行
91	C	创新管理/项目管理/预算/参数法	P346 第 7 行
92	A	组合管理/作用	P66 倒数第 2 行
93	A	流程/产品创新章程/内容	P104 第 7 行
94	B	组合/产品组合管理系统/定义	P68 第 5 行和图 2.1
95	C	战略/创新支持战略/产品平台战略/优势	P28 倒数第 2 行
96	D	组合/新产品机会评估与选择	P72 倒数第 2 行
97	B	流程/产品创新引论/在产品创新流程中"前端"的重要性	P103 第 10 行
98	A	流程/产品创新章程/价值	P103 倒数第 4 行
99	B	创新管理/产品创新关键成功因素/项目方面	P300 倒数第 1 行
100	D	战略/开放式创新	P47 第 5 行
101	B	市场调研/定量市场调研方法/概念测试与概念分类	P230 第 4 行
102	A	创新管理/度量指标/对标与持续改进	P358 第 2 行和 P425 第 12 行
103	B	创新管理/财务分析	P335 倒数第 2 行

序号	答案	知识点	教材页码
104	C	工具/制造与装配阶段/可持续性分析工具/生命周期评估/步骤	P198 第 2 行
105	C	战略/创新支持战略/技术战略/技术 S 曲线/成熟阶段	P32 图 1.14 和倒数第 2 行
106	A	创新管理/度量指标与关键绩效指标/平衡计分卡	P351 图 7.40
107	D	战略/制定战略前的准备/战略制定工具/德尔菲技术/应用情境	P13 第 1 行、P30 倒数第 3 行和 P159 第 4 行
108	D	市场调研/产品使用测试/目的	P240 第 9 行
109	B	市场调研/定性市场调研方法/焦点小组	P218 第 7 行
110	B	创新管理/财务分析/投资回报率/常用指标	P338 第 4 行
111	D	文化/团队发展/什么是高绩效团队/高绩效团队/成功因素	P269 图 6.7
112	C	文化/团队发展/塔克曼团队发展模型	P270 第 8 行
113	A	战略/开放式创新/开放式创新类型/封闭型创新者	P48 图 1.26
114	D	战略/可持续创新/可持续产品创新/外部性	P54 倒数第 3 行
115	D	文化/团队发展/工作风格/DISC/作用	P271 倒数第 6 行
116	C	文化/产品创新团队结构/重量型团队/缺点	P268 图 6.6
117	B	市场调研/多变量研究方法/TURF 分析	P239 第 10 行
118	B	创新管理/管理产品创新/项目经理	P306 倒数第 11 行
119	C	文化/创新文化与氛围/氛围/定义	P258 第 9 行
120	A	市场调研/多变量研究方法/A/B 测试/特点	P238 第 8 行
121	A	市场调研/产品创新各阶段的市场调研/创意评估与早期商业分析阶段/市场调研方法	P247 图 5.3
122	B	文化/团队发展/塔克曼团队发展模型/形成阶段/内容	P270 倒数第 10 行
123	B	文化/团队发展/塔克曼团队发展模型/震荡阶段/内容	P270 倒数第 4 行
124	A	文化/产品创新团队结构/自治型团队/应用情境	P266 倒数第 4 行
125	D	组合/什么是组合管理/组合管理五个目标/项目平衡	P67 倒数第 7 行
126	C	组合/组合绩效度量指标/目标	P89 倒数第 4 行
127	D	战略/制定战略前的准备/战略制定工具/PESTLE 分析	P12 倒数第 5 行
128	C	工具/制造与装配阶段/可持续性分析工具/生命周期成本/特点	P199 倒数第 3 行

序号	答案	知识点	教材页码
129	A	文化/团队发展/工作风格/DISC/支配型	P272 第1行
130	D	创新管理/产品生命周期/产品经理角色/方案达人	P315 图 7.8
131	B	创新管理/产品生命周期/管理产品生命周期/成长阶段	P312 图 7.6
132	A	创新管理/管理产品创新/产品管理战略/树立愿景	P308 倒数第13行
133	D	战略/营销战略/分析现有产品组合/波士顿矩阵/现金牛/特点	P39 图 1.21
134	C	战略/营销战略/分析现有产品组合/波士顿矩阵/瘦狗/策略	P39 图 1.21
135	D	创新管理/产品生命周期/管理产品生命周期/衰退阶段	P312 图 7.6
136	C	流程/产品创新流程模型/门径流程/筛选阶段/内容	P108 倒数第3行
137	C	工具/概念设计阶段/卡诺模型/必备属性/特点	P163 第7行
138	C	创新管理/需求与销售预测/巴斯模型/内容	P334 倒数第10行
139	B	流程/产品创新流程模型/精益创业/学习计划/组织/内容	P135 第2行
140	B	流程/产品创新章程/可持续性/循环经济/内容	P106 第9行
141	D	战略/营销战略/产品的三个层次/增强特性	P37 图 1.20
142	B	流程/产品创新流程模型/精益创业/转型/增长引擎转型	P137 倒数第1行
143	D	工具/初始设计与规格阶段/功能性设计/内容	P176 第10行
144	A	战略/可持续创新/制定可持续经营战略的方法	P51 倒数第3行
145	B	文化/团队发展/冲突管理/托马斯模型/包容/特点	P275 图 6.9
146	D	市场调研/产品创新各阶段的市场调研/上市前产品与市场测试/所需市场信息	P247 图 5.3
147	D	工具/概念设计阶段/TRIZ/主要方法	P167 第5行
148	D	创新管理/度量指标与关键绩效指标/平衡计分卡/学习与成长	P351 图 7.40
149	C	工具/初始设计与规格阶段/可服务性设计/内容	P179 倒数第7行
150	D	文化/虚拟团队/领导力	P279 图 6.12 和 P283 倒数第12行
151	A	工具/详细设计与规格阶段/稳健设计/田口方法/特点	P186 倒数第8行
152	A	创新管理/项目管理/产品创新中的项目管理/5个过程组	P343 倒数第9行
153	B	流程/产品创新章程/总体目标和具体目标	P104 第10行
154	A	创新管理/项目管理/三重约束	P344 第2行和图 7.36
155	C	创新管理/产品生命周期/产品经理角色/留存大师	P315 图 7.8

序号	答案	知识点	教材页码
156	C	创新管理/项目管理/进度压缩/赶工	P346 第1行
157	C	创新管理/项目管理/关键路径	P345 倒数第5行
158	C	创新管理/度量指标与关键绩效指标/平衡计分卡/内部流程	P351 图7.40
159	A	流程/产品创新流程模型/精益创业/转型/客户细分市场转型	P137 倒数第12行
160	D	工具/详细设计与规格阶段/情感化设计/微软反应卡	P188 第1行
161	B	组合/组合管理系统应用/组合管理准则/组合的范围	P87 倒数第12行
162	C	文化/产品创新团队结构/自治型团队/特点	P267 第4行
163	B	市场调研/市场调研方法/抽样方法/抽样/定义	P216 倒数第8行
164	C	组合/组合与战略关系/组合与战略的连接方法/三个目标	P70 第5行
165	D	流程/产品创新流程模型/敏捷方法/敏捷教练/作用	P124 第2行
166	A	流程/产品创新流程模型/敏捷方法/产品负责人/作用	P123 倒数第4行
167	D	流程/产品创新流程模型比较/最佳实践	P141 第3行
168	B	流程/产品创新流程模型/敏捷方法/敏捷软件开发宣言/内容	P121 第6行
169	C	流程/产品创新流程模型/敏捷方法/产品待办列表/内容	P122 第5行
170	D	战略/创新支持战略/技术战略/技术预测/工具	P30 倒数第3行
171	A	工具/制造与装配阶段/可持续性分析工具/环境质量功能展开/考虑方面	P199 第4行
172	B	流程/产品创新流程模型/集成产品开发/成熟度模型/最高级	P116 图3.8
173	B	文化/产品创新团队结构/轻量型团队/优点	P265 第1行
174	A	文化/领导力/角色与责任/团队领导者的角色	P276 倒数第10行
175	B	战略/战略制定工具/商业模式画布/作用	P15 第5行
176	B	战略/数字化战略/制定流程	P45 倒数第4行
177	C	组合/本章小节/组合绩效度量指标和组合评估标准	P92 第4行
178	A	流程/产品创新流程模型/系统工程/定义	P128 第3行
179	B	流程/产品创新流程模型/精益创业/定义	P133 第2行
180	D	流程/本章小结/流程模型/共同原则	P143 第2行
181	A	工具/概念设计阶段/概念工程/特点	P161 第5行
182	A	工具/概念设计阶段/卡诺模型/魅力属性	P163 第3行

序号	答案	知识点	教材页码
183	C	工具/概念设计阶段/形态分析/内容	P164 第 5 行
184	D	组合/组合管理系统应用/组合管理准则	P87 第 1 行和 P141 第 9 行
185	C	工具/实体化设计阶段/功能分析/内容	P174 第 7 行
186	A	工具/实体化设计阶段/FAST 技术图/特点	P175 第 2 行
187	B	工具/实体化设计阶段/逆向工程/价值	P175 倒数第 7 行
188	C	工具/本章小节/初始设计与规格阶段/DFX 的价值	P200 倒数第 1 行
189	D	工具/详细设计与规格阶段/情感化设计	P187 第 8 行
190	B	工具/制造与装配阶段/原型法	P188 倒数第 8 行
191	A	市场调研/定性市场调研方法/深度访谈	P220 第 2 行
192	C	市场调研/定量市场调研方法/眼动追踪/特点	P231 第 3 行
193	A	市场调研/多变量研究方法/ 多元回归分析	P238 倒数第 4 行
194	A	市场调研/定量市场调研方法/生物特征反馈	P231 倒数第 7 行
195	D	市场调研/多变量研究方法/优点	P239 倒数第 8 行
196	D	文化/虚拟团队/沟通	P279 倒数第 4 行
197	A	创新管理/需求与销售预测/巴斯模型/内容	P334 第 8 行
198	A	创新管理/度量指标/平衡计分卡	P351 图 7.40
199	D	创新管理/产品路线图与技术路线图/平台路线图	P330 倒数第 1 行
200	B	文化/领导力/情商/自我调节	P278 第 7 行

NPDP 考前冲刺

考前冲刺试题一

说明：考试时间为 3.5 小时（9:00—12:30），共 200 题，均为单选题。答对 150 道（含）以上通过考试。

1. What is the product scope?

    A. The work that needs to deliver a product, service, or result with specific features and functions

    B. The features and functions that characterize a product, service, or result

    C. The person assigned responsibility for overseeing all of the various activities that concern a particular product

    D. All goods, services, or knowledge sold

1. 产品范围是什么？

    A. 为交付具有特定特性和功能的产品、服务或成果所需完成的工作

    B. 某个产品、服务或成果所具有的特性和功能

    C. 负责监督与产品有关所有活动的个人

    D. 用来销售的所有商品、服务或知识

2. What are the first three stages of Tuckman team development model?

    A. Storming, norming, performing
    B. Storming, norming, forming
    C. Forming, storming, norming
    D. Forming, norming, performing

2. 塔克曼团队发展模型的前三个阶段分别是什么？

    A. 震荡阶段、规范阶段、成熟阶段
    B. 震荡阶段、规范阶段、形成阶段
    C. 形成阶段、震荡阶段、规范阶段
    D. 形成阶段、震荡阶段、成熟阶段

3. Which of the following descriptions of the project is correct?

    A. A constant endeavor to deliver new products to marketplace

    B. A temporary endeavor undertake to create a unique product, service or result

    C. An attempt to change the way work is done

    D. No clear deadline

3. 以下关于项目的描述正确的是哪个？

   A. 源源不断向市场提供新产品的工作

   B. 为创造独特的产品、服务或成果而进行的临时性工作

   C. 试图改变工作方式的努力

   D. 没有明确的截止时间

4. Jack is using a popular Agile framework that emphasizes the use of information radiators such as task boards and burndown charts and includes three major phases; pre-game, game and post-game. Which framework is Jack most likely using?

   A. Lean   B. Crystal   C. Scrum   D. XP

4. 杰克正在使用一种较为流行的敏捷框架，该方法强调信息发布工具的运用，如任务板和燃尽图，其中包括三个主要阶段：冲刺前、冲刺和冲刺后。杰克用的是哪种敏捷方法？

   A. 精益   B. 水晶
   C. Scrum   D. 极限编程

5. In the BCG's Matrix, we have Dogs, Cash cows, Question mark, and Stars quadrants. Which represents "low arena attractiveness and low business strength/relative market share"?

   A. Dogs   B. Cash cows
   C. Question mark   D. Stars

5. 在波士顿矩阵中，有瘦狗、现金牛、问题和明星四类产品。以下哪类产品的特点是低市场增长率和低市场份额？

   A. 瘦狗   B. 现金牛   C. 问题   D. 明星

6. What is the product platform?

   A. A grouping of similar customers that are targets of new product ideas

   B. An element of PIC that need definition before developing effort begin

   C. Basic architectures or underlying structures common across a group of products or that will be the basis of a series of products commercialize over a number of years

   D. The project plan of a new product that has been placed in the portfolio

6. 产品平台是什么？

   A. 一群相似的客户群，他们是新产品创意的目标人群

   B. 在开发活动前，需要进行定义的产品创新章程要素

   C. 一组产品所共有的底层结构或基础架构，成为未来一系列产品的基础

   D. 已经列入项目组合的产品创新项目计划

7. Which customers are noted as early adopters?

   A. Customers who rely on their own intuition and buy into new product early on

   B. Customers that seek out enhanced product

   C. Customers used for Alpha and Beta test to help determine which features will be best appreciated

   D. Customers that stake out particular product and continue to support it throughout its life cycle

7. 哪些客户被称作早期采用者？

   A. 那些根据自己的判断在初期就购买新产品的客户

   B. 寻找增强版产品的客户

   C. 参与阿尔法测试和贝塔测试，帮助确定哪些产品特性会受欢迎的客户

   D. 关注某个产品，并在其整个生命周期中持续支持该产品的客户

8. Which type of chart is most commonly used to indicate that the portfolio is balanced?

   A. X-Y chart   B. Histogram

   C. Bubble chart   D. Quality function expansion matrix

8. 最常用来呈现项目组合平衡的是以下哪种图？

   A. X-Y 图   B. 直方图   C. 气泡图   D. 质量功能展开

9. What does customer on-site visits mean in product innovation?

   A. A very specific event where the customer and the developer interact

   B. Conducting a focus group event

   C. Visiting a current customer to make a sale and get product innovation ideas

   D. Improving customer relations in order to later sell product

9. 在产品创新中，客户现场访问是一种什么方法？

   A. 客户和开发者进行互动的特定活动

B. 进行焦点小组活动

C. 访问现有客户，开展销售并获取新产品创意

D. 改善客户关系以确保后续产品的销售

10. When using a bubble chart to represent the new product portfolio balance, what variables can be used in the X-Y chart?

    A. Risk and return

    B. Market and technology novelty

    C. Market and technology risks

    D. All of the above are right

10. 当使用气泡图将新产品组合可视化时，可以将什么变量用于 X-Y 图？

    A. 风险和回报   B. 市场新颖度和技术新颖度

    C. 市场风险和技术风险   D. 以上皆对

11. Tom is giving a report to the senior management. He is illustrating the product strategy and demonstrating how products will evolve over time. What kind of roadmap does Tom use?

    A. Technology roadmaps   B. Product roadmaps

    C. Platform roadmaps   D. Business model roadmap

11. 汤姆正在向高级管理层汇报。他将产品战略进行了图解，并呈现了一些产品随时间的发展过程。汤姆采用了什么路线图？

    A. 技术路线图   B. 产品路线图

    C. 平台路线图   D. 商业模式路线图

12. What are the two major causes of new product failure?

    A. Too long to market and failure to identify customer needs

    B. Poor execution of process and market research

    C. Poor market research and lack of thoroughness in identifying real needs in the marketplace

    D. Poor market research and lack of project planning

12. 新产品失败的两个主要原因是什么？

    A. 上市周期长和未能识别客户需求

    B. 糟糕的执行力和市场调研

    C. 糟糕的市场调研和未能识别真正的市场需求

    D. 糟糕的市场调研和缺乏项目计划

13. A value proposition should focus on _____ , not _____ .

    A. features, benefits
    B. benefits, costs
    C. revenue, features
    D. benefits, features

13. 价值主张应聚焦于_____，而不是_____。

    A. 特性，收益
    B. 收益，成本
    C. 收入，特性
    D. 收益，特性

14. What does test marketing refer to?

    A. A type of market testing usually conducted with a chosen portion of the market

    B. Controlled sales event

    C. A research method used during concept generation

    D. A type of full sale

14. 试销指的是什么？

    A. 在选定的某一市场中开展的市场测试

    B. 控制销售活动

    C. 在概念生成阶段所采用的一种调研方法

    D. 一种全面销售方法

15. What is product pipeline?

    A. Units of new product in inventory with suppliers

    B. The existence of a new product within the distribution chain but not yet solid to end customer

    C. The scheduled stream of products in development for release to the market

    D. Has nothing to do with new product develop activities

15. 什么是产品管道?

    A. 供应商的新产品库存数量

    B. 已进入分销渠道中,但还未销售给客户的产品

    C. 准备投放市场的一系列开发中的产品

    D. 与产品创新活动无关

16. What is the critical path?

    A. A set of activities that must be completed for the project to be finished successfully. The path is a set of task linkages through the project that determine how long a project should take

    B. The time it takes to complete every task listed in the WBS

    C. A set of deliverables and milestones associated with project sequencing, start and finish, and completion date

    D. Can not prove how long the project will take

16. 关键路径是什么?

    A. 由确保项目顺利完成的一系列相关活动组成的路径,贯穿整个项目,决定了完成项目所需时间

    B. 在工作分解结构中列出每项任务的完成时间

    C. 与项目排序、开始和结束日期、完成日期等相关的一系列可交付成果和里程碑

    D. 并不能证明完成项目需要多长时间

17. Which schedule compression method usually adds cost but attempts to allow the project to be completed on time?

    A. Following critical path   B. Reducing the scope of work
    C. Adding resources   D. Adding slack

17. 哪种进度压缩方法通常会增加成本,但可以使项目能够按时完成?

    A. 遵循关键路径   B. 缩减工作范围
    C. 增加资源   D. 增加时差

18. What is the main purpose of portfolio management to achieve?

    A. Strategic fit   B. Strategic contribution
    C. Strategic priorities   D. All of the above are right

18. 项目组合管理的主要目的是要实现什么?

   A. 战略匹配   B. 战略贡献   C. 战略优先级   D. 以上皆对

19. Jimmy and the team use the purchase intention methods to measure the market share of new products. It is known that 30% of potential consumers will definitely buy this product, and 70% may buy this product. In addition, the company estimated that only 80% of the people who answered yes would really buy, and only 20% of the people who answered yes would really buy. What is the predicted market share of the new product?

   A. 24%   B. 14%   C. 38%   D. 37%

19. 吉米和团队用购买意向法来测算新产品的市场份额。已知30%的潜在消费者肯定会购买该产品，70%的人可能购买该产品。此外，该公司估计，回答肯定购买的人中只有80%的人会真正购买，回答可能购买的人中只有20%的人会真正购买，最终得出该新产品的市场份额预测值为多少?

   A. 24%   B. 14%   C. 38%   D. 37%

20. What is one of the major weakness of using focus groups in selecting new product options ?

   A. Can provide fresh insights and in-depth understanding

   B. Not a quantitative technique — statistical conclusions cannot be made

   C. Behavior of participants can be observed

   D. Questions can be changed quickly in response to participants' comments

20. 用焦点小组来选择新产品方案的主要缺点之一是什么?

   A. 能提供新的洞察并促进深度了解   B. 非定量方法，无法得出统计结论

   C. 可观察参与者的行为   D. 可根据参与者的意见快速更新问题

21. Which of the following team trait is most important for performance?

   A. Mutual trust   B. Experience

   C. Expertise   D. Role of the project manager

21. 以下哪个团队特征对绩效而言是最重要的?

   A. 互信   B. 经验   C. 专业技能   D. 项目经理的角色

22. Which of the following ideation tool is used by participants to write ideas to solve specific problems in a written rather than oral way?

　　A. Brainstorming　　　　　　　　B. Six thinking hats

　　C. Ethnographic approaches　　　　D. Brainwriting

22. 参与者用书面而非口头的方式写出解决具体问题的创意，这是以下哪个创意生成工具？

　　A. 头脑风暴　　　　　　B. 六项思考帽

　　C. 人种学方法　　　　　D. 头脑书写法

23. Companies often conduct what type of market research to measure customer perception of a product and its ability to perform as promised?

　　A. Concept testing　　　　　　　　B. Product use testing

　　C. Market opportunity analysis　　　D. Secondary market research

23. 公司一般采用哪种市场调研方法来衡量客户对产品的看法和产品能否达到其所承诺的水平？

　　A. 概念测试　　　　　　B. 产品使用测试

　　C. 市场机会分析　　　　D. 二级市场调研

24. Better practice of product innovation ideas include_____.

　　A. more ideas are better than less　　　B. ideas come from all aspects

　　C. have a formal program for getting ideas　　D. all of the above are right

24. 关于产品创新的创意，较好的做法包括_____。

　　A. 创意多好过创意少　　　　　B. 创意应来自各个方面

　　C. 采取获得创意的正式活动　　D. 以上皆对

25. Resource adjustment is a part of portfolio management. Apart from which of the following, are all good practices for portfolio managers to adjust resources?

　　A. Further refine and quantify the supply and demand of resources

　　B. Leave resource conflicts to others for management

　　C. Monitor the project resource increases or decreases resulting from reprioritization

　　D. The resource change decisions need to be closely coordinated with the leaders of project teams

25. 资源调整是组合管理中的内容。除了以下哪个，其他都是组合管理人员对资源进行调整的良好实践？

   A. 不断细化和量化资源供给和需求

   B. 将资源冲突问题交给他人处理

   C. 跟踪优先级变化导致的项目资源变化

   D. 项目团队领导者通过协同制定资源变更决策

26. What the definition of Intellectual Property (IP)?

   A. Required information that is critical to the success of the project

   B. A term used to describe the information

   C. Information including properly knowledge, technical competencies, and design information, which provides commercially exploitable competitive benefit to an organization

   D. Cannot be sold

26. 什么是知识产权？

   A. 对项目的成功至关重要的必备信息

   B. 一个描述特定技术信息的术语

   C. 能为组织在商业活动中所用且富有竞争力的知识、技术能力和设计信息

   D. 不能出售

27. What does VOC refer to?

   A. A process for eliciting needs form customers that uses structured and sin-depth means

   B. A potential customer's opinion of new product concept

   C. A logical set of features and attributes noted by market research

   D. A document used by engineers to develop specifications

27. 客户之声是什么？

   A. 运用结构化和深入的方式启发客户需求的过程

   B. 潜在客户对新产品概念的看法

   C. 市场调研中提到的一系列有逻辑性的特性和属性

   D. 工程师用以开发产品规格的文档

28. Limitations of secondary market research include_____.

    A. low cost and short time required to collect information.

    B. wide range of data sources available

    C. a lack of specific and focus

    D. provides a sound basis for further and focused primary research

28. 二级市场调研的局限性包括_____。

    A. 收集信息所需的时间短、成本低

    B. 数据来源广泛

    C. 不够具体和聚焦

    D. 可为深入和聚焦的一级市场调研打下良好的基础

29. What is risk management?

    A. The process of identifying, measuring and mitigating project risks

    B. How project managers avoid potential problems

    C. About accepting risk and doing everything to prevent it

    D. Action taken to reduce risk

29. 风险管理是什么？

    A. 识别、测量和减少项目风险的过程

    B. 项目经理如何避免潜在的问题

    C. 接纳所有的风险并尽可能避免它们

    D. 为减少风险而采取的行动

30. What determines the success rate of product innovation for a company?

    A. Research and development

    B. The quality of the organization's product innovation practices

    C. Contact with stakeholders

    D. Shorten time to market for new products

30. 企业的产品创新成功率是由什么决定的？

    A. 研究和开发

    B. 该组织产品创新实践的质量

C. 与相关方的联系

D. 缩短的新产品投放到市场的时间

31. For product developers, what does a quality product innovation process mean?

    A. Reduce cost and increase uncertainty

    B. Increase cost

    C. Helps ensure that uncertainty is reduced as project cost increase

    D. Make product development more interesting

31. 对产品开发者而言，高质量的产品创新流程意味着什么？

    A. 降低成本和增加不确定性

    B. 增加成本

    C. 有助于确保在项目成本增加时能够降低不确定性

    D. 使产品创新更为有趣

32. SWOT analysis covers strengths, weaknesses, opportunities, and threats. Many companies use this method to develop strategies. Generally speaking, when a company adopts this method, what are the advantages and disadvantages based on?

    A. External of the industry   B. Internal of the company

    C. External of the company   D. Internal of the industry

32. SWOT 分析包含优势、劣势、机会和威胁。很多公司用该方法来制定战略。通常而言，当某一公司采用该方法时，其中的优势和劣势是基于什么而言的？

    A. 行业外部   B. 公司内部   C. 公司外部   D. 行业内部

33. What kind of project is a lightweight team suitable for?

    A. Minor product improvements in which the development work requires coordination among functions

    B. New to the company project

    C. Disruptive project

    D. New to the world project

33. 轻量型团队适用于什么样的项目？

    A. 小型产品改进项目，且项目需要职能部门之间的协作

    B. 公司级新产品项目

    C. 颠覆型新产品项目

    D. 世界级新产品项目

34. What is the most commonly used TRIZ tool?

    A. Brainwriting　　　　　　　　　　B. Altshuller's 40 principles

    C. Crosby's 7 thinking hats　　　　D. Scientific method

34. 什么是最常用的 TRIZ 工具？

    A. 头脑书写法　　　　　　　　　　B. 阿奇舒勒的 40 个发明原理

    C. 克罗斯比的 7 项思考帽　　　　D. 科学方法

35. Which of the following stages does the technical S-curve not include?

    A. Introduction phase　　　　　　B. Growth stage

    C. Decline stage　　　　　　　　D. Maturity stage

35. 技术 S 曲线不包含以下哪个阶段？

    A. 引入阶段　　B. 成长阶段　　C. 衰退阶段　　D. 成熟阶段

36. Which of the following statement is true about conflict?

    A. Conflict is always bad for the team　　　B. Conflict can be positive

    C. Conflict is best solved by the project leader　　D. Conflict should be avoided

36. 关于冲突，以下哪个说法是正确的？

    A. 对团队而言，冲突有百害而无一利　　B. 冲突可以是积极的

    C. 冲突最好由项目领导者来解决　　　　D. 必须避免冲突

37. Which of the following descriptions about the top-down approach is correct?

    A. Also called the strategic bucket approach

    B. Strategic selection criteria applicable to each project

    C. Determined by high-quality resources

D. The project are not prioritized within buckets

37. 以下关于自上而下法的描述正确的是哪个？
    A. 又被称为战略桶
    B. 适用于每个项目的战略选择标准
    C. 取决于有多少优质资源
    D. 项目无法用战略桶进行排序

38. Prototyping is typical in what stage of new product innovation process?
    A. Commercialization
    B. Launch
    C. Development
    D. Opportunity identification

38. 原型在产品创新流程中的哪个阶段最为常见？
    A. 商业化
    B. 上市
    C. 开发
    D. 机会识别

39. Product decline stage, the last stage of product life circle develops primarily due to_____.
    A. technology advancements, customer/user preference changes, global competition, and environmental changes
    B. lack of innovation in the product line
    C. too many competitors resulting in terrible price wars
    D. the stage where the market leaders are clearly defined for the rest of the product life

39. 产品衰退阶段是产品生命周期的最后阶段，出现它的主要原因是_____。
    A. 技术进步、用户需求改变、国际竞争和环境变化
    B. 产品线缺乏创新方法
    C. 竞争对手众多导致了惨烈的价格战
    D. 该阶段是市场领导者为产品生命周期最后阶段所下的定义

40. Diana is ready to develop a balanced scorecard for product innovation. As a product innovation consultant, what would you advise her to do?
    A. Develop a balanced scorecard based on consultant recommendations and best company practices
    B. Establish a cross functional team for product innovation and improvement, and develop a balanced scorecard framework
    C. Develop a balanced scorecard based on her own experience

D. Seek guidance and suggestions from senior management and develop a balanced scorecard framework

40. 黛安娜准备制定产品创新平衡计分卡。作为产品创新顾问，你会建议她怎么做？
    A. 根据顾问建议和最佳公司实践制定平衡计分卡
    B. 组建产品创新改进跨职能团队，制定平衡计分卡框架
    C. 按照自己的从业经验制定平衡计分卡
    D. 征求高管层的指导和建议，制定平衡计分卡框架

41. In the BCG's Matrix, which represents "high arena attractiveness and low business strength/ relative market share"?
    A. Dogs
    B. Cash Cows
    C. Stars
    D. Question mark

41. 在波士顿矩阵中，位于高市场增长率和低市场份额象限的是什么产品类型？
    A. 瘦狗
    B. 现金牛
    C. 明星
    D. 问题

42. Christensen's efforts in sustaining and disruptive technologies suggest that_____.
    A. boot technologies have similar customer benefits
    B. sustaining technologies are seldom profitable
    C. disruptive technologies introduce a different value proposition
    D. disruptive technologies work in high growth markets

42. 关于延续式和颠覆式技术，克里斯坦森提出了_____的建议。
    A. 引导技术满足类似的客户利益
    B. 延续式技术很少能够获利
    C. 颠覆性技术要带来不同的价值主张
    D. 颠覆性技术在高增长市场中很奏效

43. Qualitative market research usually_____.
    A. represent the view of the generally population
    B. is associated with the voice of customer research
    C. in quantitative form, with data value
    D. is conducted using a small number of participants

43. 定性市场调研通常____。

   A. 代表大部分人的观点   B. 与客户之声研究有关

   C. 以量化形式出现，有数据价值   D. 在少数参与者中开展

44. What is market segmentation?

   A. Often used to determine what prices is appropriate for new product in the marketplace

   B. To dividing up of a market into group of customer with similar needs

   C. A market research technology that assist organization in determining what product to develop for the masses

   D. Thought to be important: to understanding what product will serve the needs of the most people

44. 市场细分是什么？

   A. 一般用于新产品的市场定价

   B. 将市场划分为具有相似需求的客户群体

   C. 一种帮助公司决定开发哪种产品的市场调研技术

   D. 在了解哪款产品能满足绝大部分客户需求时非常重要

45. Booz, Allen, and Hamilton propose an early new product innovation process including ____.

   A. 6 basic stages   B. multiple sets of work packages

   C. a series of decisions   D. impact and probability effort

45. 博思·艾伦和汉森密尔顿在早期提出的产品创新流程包含____。

   A. 六个基本阶段   B. 多个工作包

   C. 一系列决策   D. 影响和概率

46. What are the metrics can be defined as?

   A. A set of measurements to track product development and allow a firm to measure the impact of process improvements over time

   B. A set of measures used to anticipate customer needs and utilize the information to match internal resources with external opportunities

   C. A measures for measuring the effect and frequency of performance indicators

   D. A matrix that break down a product by needs met and technological components allowing for targeted analysis

46. 度量指标是什么？

    A. 一组用于跟踪产品开发的指标，公司用其评估流程改进的影响

    B. 预测客户需求和利用信息将内部资源和外部机遇进行匹配的一系列措施

    C. 衡量性能指标作用和频率的方法

    D. 一种矩阵工具，根据所需满足的需求对产品进行分析，以及用于针对性目标分析的技术组件

47. Which of the following is risk transfer measure?

    A. Cancel the project
    B. Purchase insurance

    C. Choose reliable suppliers
    D. Adopt more testing

47. 以下哪个是风险转移措施？

    A. 取消项目
    B. 购买保险

    C. 选择可靠的供应商
    D. 采用更多的测试

48. What is the core of differentiation strategy?

    A. Increase the company's market share by focusing on cost sensitive consumers

    B. Reduce the production cost of products

    C. Develop products with high quality, unique and outstanding characteristics

    D. Gain market share by expanding new product lines

48. 差异化战略的核心是什么？

    A. 通过专注于对成本敏感的消费者来增加公司的市场份额

    B. 降低产品的生产成本

    C. 开发优质、独特及卓越的产品

    D. 通过拓展新的产品线来获取市场份额

49. Which should be considered when designing a new product?

    A. All answers listed

    B. Speed market

    C. Customer needs

    D. Base of manufacture

49. 在设计新产品时,应该考虑哪些方面?

    A. 全部选项   B. 上市速度   C. 客户需求   D. 可制造性

50. Which type of project in a portfolio fills a gap in an existing product line?

    A. Breakthrough   B. Platform   C. Derivative   D. Support

50. 在项目组合中,哪种类型的项目可以弥补现有产品线的空白?

    A. 突破型项目   B. 平台型项目

    C. 衍生型项目   D. 支持型项目

51. A group method of creative problem solving frequently used in concept generation, which of the methods is this?

    A. Convergent thinking   B. Brainstorming

    C. Affinity charting   D. Bottom up approach

51. 在概念生成阶段,经常使用的一种创造性问题解决的小组方法是以下哪种方法?

    A. 收敛思维   B. 头脑风暴

    C. 亲和图   D. 自上而下法

52. In the open innovation, what kind of participants using user innovation, outsourcing or alliances?

    A. Innovation seeker   B. Innovation provider

    C. Intermediary   D. Open innovator

52. 在开放式创新的参与机制中,利用用户创新、外包或联盟等方法的属于哪类参与者?

    A. 寻求者   B. 提供者   C. 中介者   D. 开放者

53. How to define financial success?

    A. The ability of the organization to meet its goals

    B. Return on investment

    C. The extend to which a new product meets its profit, margin and return on investment goals

    D. Can be defined in terms of customer satisfaction

53. 如何定义财务成功?

    A. 用组织达成目标的能力来定义

    B. 用投资回报率来定义

    C. 用新产品达到其利润、毛利率和投资回报率目标的程度来定义

    D. 用客户满意度来定义

54. Managers may adopt different methods when resolving conflicts. Which of the following is often viewed as a lose-lose conflict management solution?

    A. Compromising B. Avoiding C. Accommodating D. Competing

54. 管理者在解决冲突时会采用不同的方法。以下哪个往往会被视为双输的冲突解决方法?

    A. 折中 B. 回避 C. 包容 D. 竞争

55. What should be considered in systems engineering?

    A. Technical system and product system

    B. System design and project management

    C. Schedule management and cost management

    D. Product system and profit system

55. 系统工程要考虑什么?

    A. 技术系统和产品系统 B. 系统设计和项目管理
    C. 进度管理和成本管理 D. 产品系统和盈利系统

56. Gates are defined as decision points based on delivery, criteria, and output. What does the output include?

    A. Financial Statements B. Peaks and valleys of probability and impact
    C. Go,kill,hold,rework decision D. Pass, eliminate, manage, recycle and reuse decision

56. 关口被定义为基于交付成果、标准和输出的决策点,关口输出包括什么?

    A. 财务报表

    B. 概率和影响的峰值和谷值

    C. 通过、否决、搁置、重做的决策

D. 过关、淘汰、管理、回收、再使用的决策

57. A phase is usually defined by three factors—activity, comprehensive analysis, and _____.

    A. opportunity identification   B. deliverables

    C. influence and probability   D. product development

57. 一个阶段通常是由三个因素来定义，包括活动、综合分析和_____。

    A. 机会识别   B. 可交付成果

    C. 影响和概率   D. 产品开发

58. The responsibility for the portfolio management usually falls to whom?

    A. Senior management   B. Project managers

    C. Functional managers   D. Program managers

58. 项目组合管理的责任通常落在谁的身上？

    A. 高级管理者   B. 项目经理

    C. 职能经理   D. 项目集经理

59. The main success factors and appropriate managerial styles differ for these different types of open innovators. What are the main success factors and the managerial style of open innovator?

    A. Quality, service, time, brand and top-down

    B. Technological, service, time and participative

    C. Technological leadership and highly participative

    D. Quality, service, time, brand, technology and top-down

59. 不同类型开放式创新者的关键成功因素和管理风格有所不同，开放型创新者的关键成功因素和管理风格分别是什么？

    A. 质量、服务、时间、品牌和自上而下式

    B. 技术、服务、时间和参与式

    C. 技术导向和高度参与式

    D. 质量、服务、时间、品牌、技术和自上而下式

60. Which of the following statements is wrong about concept engineering?

   A. Customer-centered processes

   B. Clarified the "fuzzy front end" of product innovation process

   C. The purpose is to develop the product concept

   D. The purpose is to generate ideas

60. 关于概念工程，以下哪个说法是错误的？

   A. 以客户为中心的流程

   B. 对产品创新流程的"模糊前端"进行了明确

   C. 目的是开发产品概念

   D. 目的是生成创意

61. What can an attractive markets offer?

   A. High ROI potential

   B. Lots of customers

   C. Opportunities for incremental projects

   D. High potential for product innovation customers who need the product and feel it is important and low competition level

61. 一个有吸引力的市场可以提供什么？

   A. 高投资回报率的潜质

   B. 庞大的客户群

   C. 增量型项目机会

   D. 潜在意向高的客户，这些客户需要产品创新，也认为产品很重要，且竞争较少

62. What does the house of quality relate primary customer requirements to?

   A. Major design attribute about which the team will make design choice

   B. Features chosen to be included in the final product

   C. The design and tooling for the final product

   D. Time to launch

62. 质量屋将客户需求和什么联系在一起？

   A. 开发团队进行设计选择的主要设计属性

B. 包含在最终产品中的产品特性

C. 最终产品的设计和模具

D. 产品上市时间

63. A few years ago, there was a new product named Transit Elevated Bus to solve traffic. This vehicle can seat people on it, and there is a cavity in the middle where cars can pass through. What principle of invention in TRIZ is used in this product?

   A. Universality B. Nested doll
   C. The other way round D. Segmentation

63. 前些年，出现了一款解决交通拥堵的新公交车——巴铁。该公交车上面可以坐人，中间有个空腔，空腔大到可以让轿车从中穿过。该产品运用了 TRIZ 中的什么发明原理？

   A. 多用性 B. 嵌套 C. 反向作用 D. 分割

64. What does a product innovation charter remind us?

   A. Product innovation process is required
   B. Failure is not an option
   C. The specifications for the product
   D. Goals and objectives

64. 产品创新章程提醒我们应该关注什么？

   A. 产品创新流程是必要的
   B. 失败不是一种选择
   C. 产品规格
   D. 总体目标和具体目标

65. What is a business case?

   A. The financial analysis of the proposed new product
   B. Transactions with non-consumers such as manufactures, resellers, distributors, wholesalers and retailers
   C. An analysis of the business situation surrounding a proposed project
   D. The case that defines the product, business plan, end projects as well as includes the results of the market, technical and financial analysis

65. 商业论证是什么？

    A. 新产品的财务分析

    B. 与非消费者的交易，如生产者、经销商、分销商、批发商和零售商

    C. 围绕项目的商业环境分析

    D. 对产品、商业计划、项目、市场结果、技术和财务等方面的分析和论证

66. What is one type of project budget used to estimate the cost of a product innovation effort that utilizes data from past projects that are similar in nature?

    A. Historical data   B. Parametric

    C. Bottom-up   D. Top-down

66. 以下哪个是根据过往类似项目数据来估计产品创新成本的项目预算方法？

    A. 历史数据法   B. 参数法

    C. 自下而上法   D. 自上而下法

67. What are the cash flow characteristics of cash cow products?

    A. Negative   B. High and stable

    C. Flat   D. Negative or flat

67. 现金牛产品的现金流特点是什么？

    A. 负的   B. 高且稳定的

    C. 持平的   D. 负的或持平的

68. What are the two situations where scoring methods are commonly used in product innovation?

    A. Product use testing and marker testing

    B. Concept generation and concept evaluation

    C. Market testing and test marketing efforts

    D. Concept evaluation and portfolio management

68. 在产品创新中，通常会使用评分法的两个场合是什么？

    A. 产品使用测试和市场测试   B. 概念生成和概念评估阶段

    C. 市场测试和营销测试工作   D. 概念评估和组合管理

69. When implementing a digital strategy, a large amount of data will be generated. Without effective use of these data, digital strategy can become inefficient. After generating and identifying these data, what should we do next?

    A. Identify   B. Prioritize   C. Design   D. Implement

69. 在实施数字化战略时,会有大量的数据生成。如果无法有效利用这些数据,数字化战略就可能会变得很低效。生成和识别了这些数据后,接下来应该如何处理这些数据?

    A. 识别   B. 排序   C. 设计   D. 实施

70. What type of team is typically used for disruptive and/or game changer type project?

    A. Heavyweight team   B. Lightweight team
    C. Autonomous team   D. Functional team

70. 哪种类型的团队最常用于颠覆式创新和/或改变游戏规则的项目?

    A. 重量型团队   B. 轻量型团队
    C. 自治型团队   D. 职能型团队

71. Which of the following is important for a high-performing team?

    A. Common goal, leadership, and open communication
    B. Empowerment, mutual trust, and conflict management
    C. Maintenance of self-esteem, effective team processes, and diversity
    D. All of the above are right

71. 以下哪个对高绩效团队而言非常重要?

    A. 共同目标、领导力和开放式沟通   B. 授权、互信和冲突管理
    C. 自尊、高效流程和多元化   D. 以上皆对

72. What is project portfolio ?

    A. A list of product features related to customer importance for a new product concept
    B. An analysis of resources to project cost
    C. The set of projects in development at any point in time, These will vary in the extent of newness or innovativeness

D. An element of the SBU's new product strategy

72. 项目组合是什么？

    A. 针对新产品概念，与客户重要程度相关联的一系列产品特性
    B. 项目成本的资源分析
    C. 一组新颖和创新程度各异的开发项目
    D. 事业部新产品战略的基本元素

73. Miles and Snow suggest that which of the follow strategies can lead to success in product innovation?

    A. Prospectors   B. Defenders   C. Reactors   D. All of the above are right

73. 迈尔斯和斯诺认为，以下哪个战略对产品创新而言最有效？

    A. 探索者   B. 防御者   C. 回应者   D. 以上皆对

74. For Miles and Snow, what are the characteristics of analyzer strategy?

    A. Often seen as using new to the world technologies
    B. Seldom first-to-market
    C. Always protect business opportunities
    D. Same as first-to-market

74. 迈尔斯和斯诺认为，分析者战略有何特点？

    A. 通常表现为使用全新技术   B. 很少率先进入市场
    C. 总是保护商业机会   D. 率先进入市场

75. How to deal with resource changes caused by changes in project priorities in teams using Lean and Agile?

    A. Reject changes
    B. Strictly prevent and control changes
    C. Report to sponsor
    D. Be closely coordinated with the leaders of project teams to make resource change decisions

75. 在运用精益方法和敏捷方法的团队中，如何应对项目优先级变化导致的资源变化？

    A. 拒绝变更

B. 严格防止和控制变更

C. 上报发起人

D. 与项目团队领导者密切协作，制定资源变更决策

76. What type of team has proved most successful in product innovation?

A. Functional
B. Work groups
C. Autonomous
D. Cross-functional

76. 哪种类型的团队已被证明在产品创新中是最成功的？

A. 职能型　　B. 工作组型　　C. 自治型　　D. 跨职能型

77. The Kano model focuses on the competitive demand of similar products and makes corresponding analysis. Which of the following does the Kano model not include?

A. Kano questionnaire design
B. Kano evaluation table
C. Noise analysis
D. Frequency analysis

77. 卡诺模型将产品聚焦在同类产品中具有竞争力的需求上，并进行相应分析。卡诺模型不包括以下哪个？

A. 卡诺问卷设计　　B. 卡诺评估表　　C. 噪声分析　　D. 频度分析

78. Which of the following main components are delivery, criteria and output in the Stage-Gate process?

A. Opportunity identification
B. Project briefing
C. Project completion
D. Gate

78. 在门径流程中，可交付成果、标准和输出是以下哪个的主要构成部分？

A. 机会识别　　B. 项目汇报会　　C. 项目竣工　　D. 关口

79. Who is going to do the comprehensive analysis at a certain stage in the Stage-Gate process?

A. Chief executive officer
B. Cross-functional team
C. Process owner
D. Team leader

79. 在门径流程中，应由谁来开展阶段中的综合分析？

   A. 首席执行官   B. 跨职能团队   C. 流程负责人   D. 团队领导者

80. Which of the following does not represent the characteristics of the bottom-up approach of portfolio management?

   A. Develop project selection criteria

   B. Starting from a list of individual projects

   C. Starting from developing business strategy and innovation strategy

   D. Items that meet the standard can be selected

80. 以下哪个不是项目组合管理中自下而上法的特点？

   A. 制定项目选择标准   B. 从具体项目清单开始

   C. 从制定经营战略和创新战略开始   D. 满足选择标准的项目就可以入选

81. What is decision tree?

   A. A decision-making technique used to determine which stage can be skipped

   B. A way to determine all the features that can be build into a product

   C. A diagram used for making decisions in business or computer programming. The "branches" of the tree diagram represent choices with associated risks, costs, results, and outcome probabilities. By calculating outcomes (profits) for each of the branches, the best decision for the firm can be determined

   D. A design for manufacturing method for diagramming specifications

81. 决策树是什么？

   A. 决定可以跳过哪个阶段的决策技术

   B. 决定产品要包括哪些特性的方法

   C. 在商业或计算机程序设计中用来做决策的图形。树形图中的"分支"表示具有相关风险、成本、成果和结果概率的选择。通过计算每个分支的结果（利润），可以确定企业的最佳决策

   D. 用于绘制规格的制造工艺设计方法

82. Which of the following scenarious might be more appropriate for a work group or functional team?

   A. A slight product change

B. A new product line development

C. A new to the company project development

D. A new platform product development

82. 工作组或职能型团队更适合以下哪种情境?

A. 产品微改进   B. 新的产品线开发

C. 公司级新产品开发   D. 新的平台产品开发

83. Which of the following participants participate in open innovation through outsource, form alliances, mergers and acquisitions, venture capital licensing?

A. Seeker   B. Provider   C. Intermediary   D. Open innovator

83. 以下哪类参与者采用外包、联盟、并购、风险投资或授权许可等方式参与开放式创新?

A. 寻求者   B. 提供者   C. 中介者   D. 开放者

84. What is the method of Quality Function Deployment?

A. A way to sure quality manufacture of products

B. A plan to produce high quality products that customers will buy

C. A mean of translating market needs to technical requirements

D. A way to transform creativity into new products

84. 质量功能展开是什么方法?

A. 确保产品生产质量的方法

B. 生产客户愿意购买的高质量产品的计划

C. 将市场需求转化为技术需求的方法

D. 将创意转化为新产品的方法

85. PepsiCo is preparing to optimize its subsidiaries and brands and develop a new strategy. What is this strategy?

A. Business strategy   B. Corporate strategy

C. Marketing strategy   D. Overall strategy

85. 百事公司准备将其各子公司和子品牌进行统筹优化，以便制定一个新的战略。这是什么战略？

　　A. 经营战略　　　　B. 公司战略　　　　C. 营销战略　　　　D. 总体战略

86. What are the Diffusion and ATAR models often used to forecast?

　　A. Sales of products with trial and repeat characteristics

　　B. Sales of new products to a particular niche

　　C. Sales of a line of platform products over time

　　D. Sales by region

86. 扩散模型和 ATAR 模型经常用于预测什么？

　　A. 具有试用和复购特性的产品销售情况

　　B. 将新产品销售给利基市场的情况

　　C. 随着时间推移，平台产品的销售情况

　　D. 产品按地区销售的情况

87. Adam is a product designer. He hopes to use the information collected in the early exploration stage to generate more concepts. As a product manager, what method would you recommend?

　　A. Robust design　　　　　　　　　　B. Morphological analysis

　　C. House of Quality　　　　　　　　D. Prototype

87. 亚当是一个产品设计者。他希望应用前期探索阶段收集到的信息来形成更多的概念。作为产品经理，你会推荐他采用什么方法？

　　A. 稳健设计　　　B. 形态分析　　　C. 质量屋　　　D. 原型

88. Avon hopes to become a company that knows women around the world best and meets their needs in products, services and self realization. What is this description?

　　A. Strategy　　　B. Mission　　　C. Vision　　　D. Values

88. 雅芳公司希望成为最了解全球女性的公司，满足她们在产品、服务和自我实现方面的需求。这是什么描述？

　　A. 战略　　　B. 使命　　　C. 愿景　　　D. 价值观

89. In which situation would the company choose a heavyweight team?

   A. Product improvement project
   B. New category entry project
   C. Product repositioning project
   D. Product line extension project

89. 公司会在哪种情况下选择重量型团队？

   A. 产品改进项目
   B. 新品类开发项目
   C. 产品重新定位项目
   D. 产品线延伸项目

90. Which of the following statements about the level of uncertainty is correct during a new product innovation project?

   A. Highest at the start (fuzzy front end) and drops off as the projects moves forward
   B. Gets progressively higher
   C. Low at the start and peaks during intermediate stage/phases of the project.
   D. Is the same throughout the project

90. 产品创新项目中，以下哪个关于不确定性水平的描述是正确的？

   A. 在启动阶段（模糊前端）最高并随着项目开展逐渐降低
   B. 逐渐提高
   C. 在项目开始阶段低，在中间阶段达到峰值
   D. 在整个项目都相同

91. Kickstarter proposed "to help you bring creative projects into life". What is this description?

   A. Strategy
   B. Vision
   C. Mission
   D. Values

91. Kickstarter 公司提出"帮助你将创意项目带入生活"。这是关于什么的描述？

   A. 战略
   B. 愿景
   C. 使命
   D. 价值观

92. What is product innovation charter?

   A. A short document that is used as a sale piece for internal support gathering
   B. The summary strategy statement that guide a department or project team in their efforts to generate a new product
   C. The business case that answers all the questions regarding a specific new product concept

D. A critical strategic tool, is the heart of any organized effort to commercialize a new product

92. 产品创新章程是什么？

　　A. 用作内部支持收集销售单的简短文档

　　B. 指导一个部门或项目团队完成产品创新工作的概括性战略文件

　　C. 可以回答任一具体新产品概念的商业论证

　　D. 一种关键战略工具，是组织对新产品价值进行商业化的核心

93. What is risk management about?

　　A. Understanding project cost　　　　B. Understanding scope management

　　C. Project uncertainty　　　　　　　　D. Time on task

93. 风险管理是有关什么的？

　　A. 理解项目成本　　　　　　　　　　B. 理解范围管理

　　C. 项目的不确定性　　　　　　　　　D. 完成任务所需时间

94. Which of the following statements is incorrect about product innovation metrics?

　　A. The company uses the balanced scorecard to consider the performance of resources, progress, cost and quality

　　B. Product innovation metrics are clearly linked to the performance and development framework within the company

　　C. Product innovation metrics are changed from time to time according to specific areas identified for improvement

　　D. Vitality index is the metrics used by senior management for reporting

94. 关于产品创新度量指标，以下哪个表述不正确？

　　A. 公司应用平衡计分卡考核资源、进度、成本和质量等方面的绩效

　　B. 产品创新度量指标应与公司的绩效和发展框架有明确联系

　　C. 产品创新度量指标应根据识别出的具体改进领域进行调整

　　D. 活力指数是用于向高级管理层汇报的度量指标

95. What are lean product innovation processes mainly concentrated?

　　A. Set more discipline in the process　　　　B. Make the process more agile

C. Eliminate waste   D. Encourage cross-functional integration

95. 精益产品创新流程聚焦于什么？

   A. 在流程中制定更多的规则   B. 使流程更敏捷
   C. 消除浪费   D. 鼓励跨职能整合

96. In Pisano's innovation landscape map, radical innovation focus on _____.

   A. extensive research and development
   B. creating a new market with a new technology
   C. a new family of products
   D. high budget, high risk projects

96. 在皮萨诺创新景观图中，激进型创新聚焦于_____。

   A. 广泛地研究和开发   B. 采用新技术来开发新市场
   C. 新产品族   D. 高预算、高风险的项目

97. Agile is a method that can be used to accelerate _____.

   A. risk management   B. lean project management
   C. product innovation   D. scrum

97. 敏捷是用于加速_____流程的方法。

   A. 风险管理   B. 精益项目管理
   C. 产品创新   D. Scrum

98. What is derivative product?

   A. A new product that is slight change or improvement
   B. A new product based on changes to an existing product that modifies and/or improves same product features
   C. A new product change based on market research and customer service records
   D. Not a new product

98. 衍生产品是什么？

   A. 有细微改变或改进的新产品
   B. 基于现有产品做出改变的新产品，调整和/或改进了某些产品特性

C. 以市场调研和客户服务为基础，发生了改变的新产品

D. 不属于新产品

99. What does the number of stages of the Stage-Gate process and levels depend on?

  A. The idea we want to achieve   B. Specific situation and level of risk

  C. Feasible solution   D. Distribution channel to be utilized

99. 门径流程中的阶段和关口的数量取决于什么？

  A. 想要实现的创意   B. 具体情况和风险水平

  C. 可行的方案   D. 要利用的分销渠道

100. When will the value of portfolio management be diminished?

  A. Senior management control the process

  B. Scoring models are used

  C. Subordinate employees and stakeholders do not understand the decision process

  D. Financial and nor-financial ensures are used to determine balance of the portfolio

100. 项目组合管理的价值会在什么时候变弱？

  A. 高级管理层控制了流程

  B. 运用了评分法

  C. 下属员工和相关方不理解决策过程

  D. 运用资金或非资金措施决定项目组合平衡

101. How to apply Delphi technique?

  A. Service records to build a better product

  B. Interactive rounds of consensus development across a group of experts to predict

  C. New product developers from across technical fields to develop a new to the world type product

  D. Alpha and beta testing technique to develop a new product, service requirements, and customer service procedures

101. 如何应用德尔菲技术？

  A. 记录服务，以便创造更好的产品

  B. 组织专家就预测主题进行多轮讨论，并达成共识

C. 组织跨技术领域的产品创新人员，以开发一个全新的产品类型

D. 使用阿尔法测试和贝塔测试技术来开发新产品、服务需求和客户服务流程

102. What are the characteristics of secondary market research?

A. More accurate than primary research

B. Confirmatory in nature

C. Less expensive

D. All the research needed in a new product development effort

102. 二级市场调研方法有何特点？

A. 比一级市场调研更准确

B. 更具确定性

C. 成本低

D. 所有研究都要在所开发的新产品基础上展开

103. The results of the survey conducted by the Product Development Management Association show that the difference between the best company and other companies in product innovation lies in the best company has＿＿＿.

A. a good CEO

B. stage-Gate process

C. high quality product development practices and processes

D. rich product development funds

103. 产品开发与管理协会的调查结果表明，最佳公司和其他公司在产品创新上的区别在于前者具有＿＿＿。

A. 一个好的首席执行官　　　　　　B. 门径流程

C. 高质量的产品创新实践和流程　　D. 充裕的产品开发资金

104. Portfolio management includes two important aspects, what are these?

A. Portfolio selection and portfolio review

B. Portfolio initiation and completion

C. Resource assignment and portfolio support

D. Meeting marketing and technical requirements

104. 项目组合管理包括两个重要方面，分别是什么？

　　A. 组合选择和组合评审　　　　B. 组合启动和完成

　　C. 资源分配和组合支持　　　　D. 满足营销和技术要求

105. There are a lot of uncertainties in the early stages of the product innovation process, which are often referred to as?

　　A. Concept generation　　　　B. Fuzzy front end

　　C. Product framework development　　D. Concept assessment

105. 在产品创新流程的早期阶段有很多不确定性，该阶段通常被称作什么？

　　A. 概念生成　　　　　　　　　B. 模糊前端

　　C. 产品框架开发　　　　　　　D. 概念评估

106. What is one of the shortcomings of the classic waterfall process?

　　A. Not suitable for projects that require easy changes

　　B. Simple and easy to understand and use

　　C. Complete one stage at a time

　　D. Can be used very well for small projects with clear requirements

106. 经典瀑布模型的缺点之一是什么？

　　A. 不适合需求容易变化的项目　　B. 简单、易于理解和使用

　　C. 一次完成一个阶段　　　　　　D. 可以很好地用于需求明确的小型项目

107. What are the responsibilities of product process manger in produce innovation?

　　A. Success of new product launches

　　B. Allocation resources

　　C. Ensuring the product portfolio decisions are implemented in an orderly manner

　　D. That all project managers meets process time lines

107. 在产品创新中，流程经理承担什么职责？

　　A. 新产品成功上市

　　B. 资源配置

　　C. 确保产品组合决策得到有序实施

D. 所有项目经理都应满足流程中的时间要求

108. In lean startup, a good learning plan has the following characteristics, except for_____.

    A. fail quickly and learn quickly, as the stage progresses, the probability of success usually increases

    B. early verification and early understanding of low probability events

    C. provide evidence or pivot points for problem solving in stages

    D. must cover all aspects of the market, organization, business and technology

108. 在精益创业中，良好的学习计划具有以下特点，除了_____。

    A. 快速失败，快速学习；随着阶段的进展，成功概率通常会上升

    B. 可以提前验证，并能尽早了解低概率事件

    C. 分阶段为问题解决提供证据或转型点

    D. 必须覆盖市场、组织、商业和技术等所有方面

109. Customers can be segmented by_____.

    A. age   B. race and gender
    C. income   D. all of the above are right

109. 客户可以按_____维度进行细分。

    A. 年龄   B. 种族和性别   C. 收入   D. 以上皆对

110. Consumers used a 10-point scale to rate the brand and features of digital cameras. As a rule will not consider any brand that scores below a 6 on any attribute. If the brand Sony scores a 9 or 10 on the first four attributes and a 5 on Zoom, the consumer will rule out Sony. What is this method?

    A. Compensatory model   B. Non-compensatory model
    C. Financial analysis   D. Surveys

110. 消费者采用了 10 分制给数码相机品牌和特性打分。只要有一项得分低于 6 分，那么该品牌就会被淘汰。如果索尼在前四个特性上得分为 9~10 分，而在变焦倍数上得分为 5 分，那么消费者就会剔除索尼。这是什么方法？

    A. 补偿模型   B. 非补偿模型   C. 财务分析   D. 问卷调查

111. What is the ideal focus group size?

  A. Less than five people   B. Eight to twelve people

  C. Approximately fifteen people   D. More than twenty people

111. 理想的焦点小组人数是多少？

  A. 少于 5 人   B. 8 到 12 人   C. 约 15 人   D. 超过 20 人

112. In project management, what does total float or slack mean?

  A. The number of days over schedule the project is projected to come in

  B. Allows for work order and scope changes

  C. The amount of time an activities may be delay from its early start without delaying the project finish date

  D. Should not be zero

112. 在项目中，总时差指什么？

  A. 超出项目计划的天数

  B. 允许工作顺序和范围变化

  C. 在一项活动中，在不影响项目完成时间情况下，该活动可以宽延的时间

  D. 不能为 0

113. Which of the following is a project risk rather than a product risk?

  A. Fails to meet the project funding needs

  B. Fails to deliver promised benefits

  C. Fails to meet regulatory requirements

  D. Does not meet customer expectations, such as aesthetics, features, functionality, or price

113. 以下哪个是项目风险而不是产品风险？

  A. 未能满足项目资金需求

  B. 未能实现承诺的利益

  C. 未能满足监管要求

  D. 未满足客户期望，如外观、特性、功能或价格

114. What is problem-based ideation?

    A. Is an excellent method for discovering new technologies

    B. Is a method that doesn't fit in well with other ideation methods

    C. Is a productive approach of finding and solving customer problems

    D. Is a simple process for finding and evaluating ideas

114. 基于问题的创意生成是什么？

    A. 发现新技术的绝佳方法

    B. 一种与其他概念生成方法不匹配的方法

    C. 一种发现和解决客户问题的有效方法

    D. 寻找并评估创意的简单过程

115. When the user is using the TV, ① he presses the TV channel switch button; ② the TV changes channels. From the perspective of functional analysis, which of the following is correct?

    A. ① is an extrinsic function; ② is an intrinsic function

    B. ① is an intrinsic function; ② is an extrinsic function

    C. Both ① and ② are intrinsic functions

    D. Both ① and ② are extrinsic functions

115. 用户在使用电视机：①他按下电视频道切换按钮；②电视机切换频道。从功能分析的角度而言，以下哪个是正确的？

    A. ①是外部功能；②是内部功能

    B. ①是内部功能；②是外部功能

    C. ①和②都是内部功能

    D. ①和②都是外部功能

116. A project costs $100000 and takes four months to deliver. It is estimated that the project will make a profit of $10000 in the first month after launching and $20000 every month thereafter. What is the payback period of this project?

    A. 6 months   B. 4 months   C. 9.5 months   D. 8.5 months

116. 一个项目耗资100000美元，用4个月交付。预计项目上市后首月盈利10000美元，之后每个月盈利20000美元，该项目的回收期是多长？

    A. 6个月   B. 4个月   C. 9.5个月   D. 8.5个月

117. Which of the following scenarios can decision trees be used for?

    A. Ideation   B. Support decision-making

    C. Improve emotional intelligence   D. People-oriented

117. 决策树可以用于以下什么情境？

    A. 创意生成   B. 辅助决策   C. 提高情商   D. 以人为本

118. What questions should answer when analyzing from right to left when using FAST technical diagram?

    A. Is this a basic function   B. How is this function carried out

    C. Is this function a secondary function   D. Why do we need this function

118. 使用FAST技术图，当从右到左进行分析时，要回答什么问题？

    A. 该功能是基本功能吗   B. 该功能是如何实现的

    C. 该功能是次要功能吗   D. 为什么需要该功能

119. What is risk mitigation?

    A. Actions taken to reduce the probability and impact of the risk to below some threshold of acceptability

    B. The process of identifying and quantifying risks

    C. The acceptance of risk as part of any product innovation project

    D. Changing the plan to eliminate possibility of risk occurring

119. 什么是风险减轻？

    A. 采取行动，把风险发生概率和影响降低到可接受的临界值内

    B. 识别并量化分析风险的过程

    C. 把风险当作产品创新项目的一部分并接受

    D. 改变计划，以消除风险发生的可能性

120. What is risk tolerance?

   A. The term used to describe a company's product innovation efforts that have every low risk. Example is defensive type projects

   B. A concept that describes the complete belief that only new product will create shareholder value and a company must learn to tolerate the risk associated with product innovation

   C. A best practice is to establish a single metric for risks assessment that is common for all new product projects

   D. The level of risk project stakeholders are willing to accept

120. 什么是风险容限？

   A. 用于描述公司的产品创新工作具有很低的风险，如防御型项目

   B. 一个深信只有新产品才能创造股东价值的概念，认为公司必须学会承受产品创新带来的风险

   C. 最好的做法是建立一个对任何产品创新项目都适用的风险评估体系

   D. 项目相关方可以接受的风险水平

121. What should the developers and explorers of world-class new products do when formulating strategies?

   A. To launch platform projects as quickly as possible

   B. To be the first to deliver a new technology to the marketplace

   C. To launch as many platform projects as possible to meet the demands of the marketplace

   D. To provide the masses with a new product

121. 世界级新产品的开发者和探索者在制定战略时应该怎么做？

   A. 尽快启动平台项目

   B. 成为将新技术推向市场的首家提供商

   C. 推出尽可能多的平台项目，尽最大可能满足市场需求

   D. 为大众提供新产品

122. What is a key management function in the capability strategy?

   A. Identify what resource and capability gaps need to be filled in order to maintain a competitive advantage

   B. Ability to quickly find target markets

   C. Ability to bring products to market quickly

D. Ability to develop new business models

122. 在能力战略中，一个关键的管理能力是什么？

　　A. 识别需要填补哪些资源和能力空白，以保持竞争优势的能力
　　B. 迅速找到目标市场的能力
　　C. 将产品快速上市的能力
　　D. 开发新商业模式的能力

123. Mark is reviewing the feasibility analysis report. In the feasibility analysis report, it includes arguments on market potential, financial potential, technical capability, marketing capability, manufacturing capability, regulatory implications, and investment requirements, but what is missing?

　　A. Source of manufacturing equipment　　B. Intellectual Property
　　C. Distribution channels　　D. Source of raw materials

123. 马克正在审阅可行性分析报告。该可行性分析报告涵盖了市场潜力、财务潜力、技术能力、营销能力、制造能力、法规影响和投资需求等方面的论证，但是缺少了什么内容？

　　A. 制造设备来源　　B. 知识产权
　　C. 分销渠道　　D. 原材料来源

124. What is one of the core concept of the lean product innovation process?

　　A. Process integration　　B. Continuous creativity
　　C. Knowledge growth　　D. Embrace changes

124. 精益产品创新流程的核心概念之一是什么？

　　A. 流程整合　　B. 持续的创造力
　　C. 知识增长　　D. 拥抱变化

125. Who is an analyzer?

　　A. An organization that focus on market research to lead the development of the new products
　　B. A strategy that follows an ease of use focus with in a known product family
　　C. A strategy that follows an imitative strategy where the goal is set to the market with an equivalent

or betted product

D. Develop new technology and innovative strategies to create a new market and new value proposition

125. 分析者是什么角色？

    A. 专注于市场调研的组织，从而引领新产品开发

    B. 专注于已知产品族，遵循易用性原则

    C. 采用模仿策略，目标是推出相似或更好的产品

    D. 制定新技术或创新策略，开发新市场或价值主张

126. What is the technology foresighting?

    A. The company's technical expert team predicts the technology trend

    B. Forecast technology trends by an external team of technical experts

    C. The company and the external technical expert team predict the technology trend based on published information, business and social events and key technologies

    D. The company and the external technical expert team predict the technology trend based on the company's existing technology reserves and competitors' technology development

126. 什么是技术预测？

    A. 由公司的技术专家团队进行技术趋势预测

    B. 由公司外部的技术专家团队进行技术趋势预测

    C. 由公司或外部技术专家团队根据公开信息、商业与社会事件及关键技术进行技术趋势预测

    D. 由公司和外部技术专家团队根据公司现有的技术储备和竞争对手的技术开发情况进行技术趋势预测

127. In the traditional product life cycle, which phrase has the most sales?

    A. Introduction   B. Crossing the chasm

    C. Growth   D. Maturity

127. 在传统的产品生命周期中，哪个阶段的销量最高？

    A. 引入   B. 跨越鸿沟   C. 成长   D. 成熟

128. What are the good practice of the best company's measurement of product innovation?

　　A. Only measure innovation results

　　B. Only measure the innovation process

　　C. Measuring not only the results of innovation, but also the process of innovation

　　D. Neither the innovation result nor the innovation process is measured

128. 最佳公司衡量产品创新的良好实践是什么？

　　A. 只衡量创新结果

　　B. 只衡量创新过程

　　C. 不仅衡量创新结果，也衡量创新过程

　　D. 既不衡量创新结果，又不衡量创新过程

129. The company is screening product innovation projects. The senior management hopes that the product innovation project can not be lower than the minimum rate of return of 20%, and the NPV of the project should also be considered. Which of the following project should be selected?

　　A. ROI=15%　NPV=$100k　　　　B. ROI=22%　NPV=$50k

　　C. ROI=18%　NPV=$70k　　　　　D. ROI=22%　NPV=$80k

129. 公司正在筛选产品创新项目。高级管理层希望产品创新项目的收益率不能低于20%，同时也要考虑项目的净现值情况。应选择以下哪个项目？

　　A. ROI=15%　NPV=$100k　　　　B. ROI=22%　NPV=$50k

　　C. ROI=18%　NPV=$70k　　　　　D. ROI=22%　NPV=$80k

130. Jennifer leads the product development team to carry out reverse engineering. What is their purpose for doing so?

　　A. Understand the customer's emotional changes when experiencing the product

　　B. Compare with competitors' products and production processes

　　C. Collect market research data

　　D. Conduct team building activities and build a good team climate

130. 杰尼弗带领产品开发团队采用逆向工程，通过该方法，他们想达到什么目的？

　　A. 了解客户在体验产品时的情绪变化

B. 与竞争对手的产品和生产工艺进行比较

C. 收集市场调研的数据

D. 开展团队建设活动，构建良好的团队氛围

131. Which of the following is an example of core benefits?

   A. Communicate with other personnel providing emergency services over large distances with clarity, ease, and reliability

   B. The product includes high-performance main radio unit and the earpiece

   C. Ongoing support services including a 24/7 service desk and online service portal.

   D. Provides USB cable and docking station

131. 下列哪项是产品核心利益的例子？

   A. 与其他提供紧急服务人员能够在远距离情况下实现清晰、方便和可靠的通信

   B. 产品由高性能的无线接收器和耳机组成

   C. 提供不间断的支持服务，包括 7×24 小时服务的服务台和线上服务门户网站

   D. 提供 USB 线和扩展坞

132. In the design for serviceability, what does the total cost of serviceability include?

   A. Cost of diagnostics   B. Cost of logistics and transportation

   C. Actual service time   D. All of the above are right

132. 在可服务性设计中，可服务性总成本包括什么？

   A. 故障诊断成本   B. 物流和运输成本

   C. 实际服务时间   D. 以上皆对

133. Company A take the lead develop a new product. This product is a wireless door lock with Wi-Fi function. What type of the product is this?

   A. Platform   B. Breakthrough

   C. Improved   D. Derivative

133. A 公司率先开发了一款新产品。该产品是具备 Wi-Fi 功能的无线门锁。这是一款什么类型的产品？

   A. 平台型   B. 突破型   C. 改进型   D. 衍生型

134. Steve is a product manager of a company. He is responsible for generating revenue and providing value to his organization by selling products to customers. Which aspect of product management is he responsible for?

    A. Business   B. User experience

    C. Technology   D. Project management

134. 史蒂夫是一家公司的产品经理。他负责通过向客户销售产品，获得收入并向其组织提供价值。他这是承担了产品管理中哪方面的工作？

    A. 经营   B. 用户体验   C. 技术   D. 项目管理

135. Knowledge greatly influences decision making. In the new product innovation process, where should knowledge come from?

    A. Mainly from internal resources   B. Mainly from external resources

    C. From internal and external resources   D. Corporate shareholders

135. 知识会极大地影响决策。在产品创新流程中，知识来自哪里？

    A. 主要来自内部资源   B. 主要来自外部资源

    C. 来自内部和外部资源   D. 企业股东

136. Compared with project management, which is product management more inclined to?

    A. Development   B. Technical knowledge

    C. Complete the project   D. Business-oriented

136. 与项目管理相比，产品管理聚焦于哪里？

    A. 开发   B. 技术知识   C. 完成项目   D. 经营导向

137. What are the features of Kansei engineering?

    A. Consider user feelings and emotional needs

    B. Identify Kansei words

    C. Make product or process insensitive to variation

    D. A and B

137. 感性工学的特点是什么？

    A. 考虑用户感觉和情感需求   B. 识别感性词语

C. 使得产品或流程对变异不敏感   D. A 和 B 选项

138. In the service industry, service maps or blueprints are created to identify the "critical moments" or moments of truth that may create an imbalance or misspecification of the value delivery. What kind of this prototyping?

    A. Functional prototyping   B. Experience prototyping
    C. Paper prototyping   D. Rapid prototyping

138. 在服务行业中，通过创建服务地图或蓝图来识别"关键时刻"，以及可能造成价值交付不足或遗漏的时刻。这是什么原型法？

    A. 功能原型法   B. 可体验原型法   C. 纸质原型法   D. 快速原型法

139. The key performance indicators in market research do not include_____.

    A. core competence of employees   B. pride
    C. use and purchase intention   D. willingness to pay

139. 市场调研中的关键绩效指标不包括_____。

    A. 员工核心能力   B. 自豪感
    C. 使用和购买意向   D. 付费意愿

140. The marketing strategy for a company should_____.

    A. be developed independently by the marketing department
    B. be developed so as to be consistent with the overall business strategy
    C. be developed every five years
    D. be developed without consideration of the overall business strategy

140. 公司的营销战略应该_____。

    A. 由营销部门独立开发   B. 符合总体经营战略
    C. 每五年制定一次   D. 制定时无须考虑总体经营战略

141. What is the main purpose and value of market research in product innovation?

    A. Identify personal needs
    B. Provide marketing solutions
    C. Predict the future

D. Provide information to help the organization make decisions

141. 在产品创新中要进行市场调研，其主要目的和价值是什么？

  A. 识别个人需求 B. 提供营销解决方案

  C. 预测未来 D. 为组织决策提供信息

142. Which of the following is fixed cost?

  A. Plant rent cost B. Manufacturing material cost

  C. Production labor cost D. Production electricity cost

142. 以下哪个是固定成本？

  A. 厂房租金 B. 生产用材料成本

  C. 一线人员工资 D. 生产用电电费

143. Key principles of Agile product development include team empowerment, small incremental releases, completing one feature before the next, and_____.

  A. eliminate waste B. linear process

  C. active user involvement D. ignore risk

143. 敏捷产品创新方法的主要原则包括团队授权、小型增量发布、一次完成一个功能，以及_____。

  A. 杜绝浪费 B. 线性过程 C. 用户积极参与 D. 忽略风险

144. Which of the following is correct about divergent thinking?

  A. Performed early in the idea generation process

  B. Performed in the concept evaluation phase

  C. Often used to move from a largest number of ideas to a small number

  D. Used to evaluate product design and development activities

144. 关于发散思维，以下哪个是正确的？

  A. 应用在创意生成的早期阶段

  B. 应用在概念评估阶段

  C. 通常用于将非常多的创意归纳为几个之时

  D. 用于评估产品设计和开发活动

145. What does convergent thinking help?

   A. Move from a largest number of ideas to select few

   B. Generate a large number of ideas

   C. Generate lots of ideas early in the concept generation phase

   D. Move form a small number of ideas to large number of ideas

145. 收敛思维有助于什么？

   A. 从一大堆创意中选出几个　　　　B. 促进大量创意的产生

   C. 在概念生成阶段促进大量创意的产生　　D. 将少量创意变成大量创意

146. What is one of the potential sources of waste in product innovation?

   A. Stakeholders participate in the process as early as possible

   B. Too many invalid meetings

   C. Ordered workflow

   D. Clearly defined product requirements

146. 产品创新的潜在浪费来源之一是以下哪个？

   A. 相关方尽早参与流程　　　　B. 过多的无效会议

   C. 有序的工作流程　　　　　　D. 清楚定义的产品需求

147. Agile uses sprints, scrum master and product backlog. What does the waterfall model use?

   A. Linear process　　　　B. Lean principles

   C. Stages and gates　　　D. Scrum master

147. 敏捷方法使用冲刺、敏捷教练和产品待办列表。瀑布模型使用什么？

   A. 线性流程　　B. 精益原则　　C. 阶段和关口　　D. 敏捷教练

148. The Triple bottom line of sustainable product innovation requires reporting product innovation performance from three aspects. Which of the following statements is wrong?

   A. Scope, Schedule, and Cost　　　　B. Profit, People, and Planet

   C. Financial, Social, and Environmental　　D. 3P

148. 可持续产品创新中的三重底线要求从三个方面报告产品创新绩效,以下哪个说法是错误的?

　　A. 范围、进度和成本　　　　　　　B. 利润、人类和地球

　　C. 财务、社会和环境　　　　　　　D. 3P

149. Which organizational culture factor has a positive impact on the success of new products?

　　A. Managers set goals　　　　　　　B. Understanding failure

　　C. Respect for adventurous spirit　　D. All of the above are right

149. 以下哪个组织文化因素对新产品成功有积极影响?

　　A. 管理人员树立目标　　　　　　　B. 理解失败

　　C. 尊重冒险精神　　　　　　　　　D. 以上皆对

150. Key features of organizations with strong innovation capabilities include＿＿＿.

　　A. centralized innovation strategy　　B. close contact with the market

　　C. clear thinking and direction　　　D. all of the above are right

150. 具有较强创新能力的组织的主要特点包括＿＿＿。

　　A. 聚焦的创新战略　　　　　　　　B. 与市场联系紧密

　　C. 清晰的思路和方向　　　　　　　D. 以上皆对

151. Kris is going to draw the business model canvas. He begins to consider intellectual property, brands, capital, fixed assets and human resources. What is he thinking about?

　　A. Key partners　　　　　　　　　B. Value propositions

　　C. Key resources　　　　　　　　　D. Key activities

151. 克瑞斯在构思商业模式画布。他开始考虑知识产权、品牌、资金、固定资产和人力资源。他在思考什么方面的内容?

　　A. 重要合作　　B. 价值主张　　C. 核心资源　　D. 关键业务

152. Who is responsible for building a product strategy in an organization?

　　A. Executive vice president　　　　B. Senior product manager

C. Business manager D. Customer

152. 在一个组织中，通常由谁来负责制定产品战略？

   A. 执行副总裁 B. 高级产品管理者
   C. 业务经理 D. 客户

153. What is a Solid State Drive for a mechanical Hard Disk Drive?

   A. Disruptive technological innovation B. Disruptive business model innovation
   C. Slight innovation D. All of the above are wrong

153.对于机械硬盘而言，固态硬盘是什么创新？

   A. 颠覆式技术创新 B. 颠覆式商业模式创新
   C. 微创新 D. 以上皆错

154. The startup team developed a sports equipment, but the sales volume was low due to the COVID-19c. In turn, the team has created a platform to provide sports enthusiast community services, and also sell products, resulting in a sharp increase in sales. What pivot does this belong to?

   A. Customer segment pivot B. Customer need pivot
   C. Platform pivot D. Business architecture pivot

154. 创业团队开发了一款运动器械，因新冠疫情原因，销量惨淡。团队转而打造了一个平台，为运动爱好者提供社群服务，同时也售卖产品，最终销量暴增。这属于什么类型的转型？

   A. 客户细分市场转型 B. 客户需求转型
   C. 平台转型 D. 商业架构转型

155. Which is one of the benefits of systems engineering?

   A. Design-related decisions are fairly detailed and made upfront due to intense customer involvement
   B. Over-analyses of the problem and too much detail upfront may cause the risk of delay and a focus on the incorrect elements for solutioning
   C. As the project progresses over time, the initial requirements may become outdated because they

were based on knowledge that was generated at a historical point in time, and may no longer be appropriate or relevant

D. Exerting influence and the ability to effect change become increasingly difficult as the product innovation progresses toward the final phases due to "operational and resource commitments" to the project

155. 以下哪个是系统工程的优点？

A. 与设计相关的决策非常详细，并可在客户深度参与下提前做出决策

B. 对问题的过度分析和过多的预设细节会造成延迟风险，也会导致将重点放在不恰当的解决方案要素上

C. 随着项目进展，最初的需求可能会变得过时、不再合适或相关，因为它们是基于历史时间点产生的知识

D. 由于对项目的运营和资源做出承诺，所以当产品创新过程进入尾声时，有效应对变化的能力会越来越弱

156. Tangible characteristics of a product include_____.

A. features, styling, packaging
B. installation, credit and warranty
C. price and promotion
D. all of the above are right

156. 产品的有形特性包括_____。

A. 特性、风格和包装
B. 安装、信用和质保
C. 价格和促销
D. 以上皆对

157. What is ethnography?

A. A confirmatory research technical used for studying a customer group in relationship to his or her needs and wants

B. A market research method used to illicit new product ideas by noting the issues and problems faced by customers

C. An exploratory research tech used to determine what type of solution will work

D. A descriptive qualitative research method for studying customer in relation to his or her environment

157. 什么是人种学方法？

　　A. 一种确认性调研技术，用于研究某一消费群体与其消费需求和期望之间的关系

　　B. 一种市场调研方法，用于通过识别消费者面临的问题来非法获取某些新产品创意

　　C. 一种探索性调研技术，用于确定哪种能解决方案能奏效

　　D. 调研客户与其所处环境的一种描述性的定性调研方法

158. A "cash cow" product is defined as＿＿＿．

　　A. a product that has significant future market potential

　　B. a product produced from milk

　　C. a product with declining sales

　　D. a product that has a high market share in a market of slow overall growth

158. "现金牛"产品被定义为＿＿＿。

　　A. 具有显著未来市场潜力的产品

　　B. 奶制品

　　C. 销量下滑的产品

　　D. 总体市场增长率较低，但市场份额较高的产品

159. In order to solve the space problem of stool legs, developers changed the original four-leg design and adopted a new no-leg design. Which of the SCAMPER was used?

　　A. E（Eliminate）　　　　　　　　B. R（Reverse）

　　C. M（Modify）　　　　　　　　　D. P（Put to another use）

159. 开发人员为了解决凳子腿占用空间问题，一改原来四条腿设计，采用新型无腿设计，这是采用了 SCAMPER 法中的哪个方法？

　　A. E（去除）　　　　　　　　　　B. R（逆向操作）

　　C. M（调整）　　　　　　　　　　D. P（改变用途）

160. The marketing mix is defined as＿＿＿．

　　A. the set of products being marketed at the same time

　　B. the combination of product, price, place and promotion

　　C. the group of individuals involved in marketing a product

　　D. the combination of marketing strategies and plans

160. 营销组合被定义为_____。

    A. 在同一时间内销售一系列产品   B. 产品、价格、地点和促销的组合
    C. 参与产品营销的团队   D. 营销战略和计划的组合

161. Why is Intellectual Property important in product innovation?

    A. It is good for the product development manger's reputation
    B. It can establish a basis for on-going revenue generation
    C. It encourages creativity
    D. It is an indicator of a good product development process

161. 为什么知识产权对产品创新而言很重要？

    A. 它有利于产品开发经理的声誉   B. 它可以为产生收益奠定基础
    C. 它鼓励创造力   D. 它是良好的产品开发流程的一个指标

162. What does "D" stand for in the Six Sigma Process DMAIC and Design for Six Sigma IDOV respectively?

    A. Both are "Define"
    B. Both are "Design"
    C. "Define" in DMAIC and "Design" in IDOV
    D. "Design" in DMAIC and "Define" in IDOV

162. 在六西格玛流程 DMAIC 和六西格玛设计 IDOV 中，"D"分别代表什么？

    A. 两者都代表"定义"
    B. 两者都代表"设计"
    C. DMAIC 中的 D 代表"定义"，IDOV 中的 D 代表"设计"
    D. DMAIC 中的 D 代表"设计"，IDOV 中的 D 代表"定义"

163. Value from a new product with specific Intellectual Property can be generated through_____.

    A. marketing the product under your company's brand
    B. selling the intellectual property rights to another company
    C. licensing the intellectual property to another company
    D. all of the above are right

163. 具有知识产权的新产品可以通过_____实现价值。

A. 用公司品牌来销售产品 B. 把知识产权卖给另一家公司

C. 把知识产权授权给另一家公司 D. 以上皆对

164. In six thinking hats, which hat is used to express emotions, such as likes, dislikes, fears, etc.?

A. White B. Yellow C. Green D. Red

164. 在六顶思考帽中，哪顶帽子用来表达喜欢、不喜欢、害怕等情绪？

A. 白色 B. 黄色 C. 绿色 D. 红色

165. The GK team create and identify a scenario around each concept: actor, context, process to achieve goal. Evaluate and reformulate the concept as you go through the scenario. Illustrate the scenarios by reflecting on all activities, users, and other participants involved in real-life situations where the concept is being used. What method does GK team use?

A. Conceptual engineering B. Conceptual scenario

C. Concept generation D. All of the above are wrong

165. GK 团队围绕每个概念创建并确定一个场景，包括参与者、环境和实现目标的流程。在整个场景中，对概念进行评估并优化。将概念在现实生活中的应用，包括用户、其他参与者和所有活动，用场景的方式体现出来。该团队用了什么方法？

A. 概念工程 B. 概念场景 C. 概念生成 D. 以上皆错

166. The need to constantly refresh a company's products is the result of shortening the_____.

A. stage-Gate B. concept testing

C. ideation D. product life cycle

166. 公司对产品需求的不断变化会导致_____的缩短。

A. 阶段—关口 B. 概念测试

C. 思维能力 D. 产品生命周期

167. Multiple regression analysis is used to identify which variables will affect the research topic. How many variables will be studied at most?

   A. 1   B. 2   C. 3   D. Multiple

167. 多元回归分析用于识别哪些变量会对研究主题产生影响，其研究的变量最多可以有多少？

   A. 1个   B. 2个   C. 3个   D. 多个

168. A software company has multiple product lines and plans to develop a new powerful product. This product will enable anyone in the organization to build intelligent applications or workflows from scratch. This product integrates the development of non code or low code applications, automation of robot processes and self-service analysis into an integrated system, which has changed the current model of application development, Which of the following terms best describes the applications, workflows, and robotic processes built on this new product?

   A. Breakthrough project
   B. Platform project
   C. Derivative project
   D. Supporting project

168. 一家软件公司有多条产品线并计划开发一款强大的新产品，该产品将使组织内的任何人都能够从头开始构建智能应用程序或工作流。该产品将无代码或低代码应用程序开发、机器人流程自动化以及将自助分析集成于一个整合的系统之内。该项目改变了目前应用程序开发模式。以下哪个最好地描述了构建于这个新产品之上的应用程序、工作流和机器人流程？

   A. 突破型项目
   B. 平台型项目
   C. 衍生型项目
   D. 支持型项目

169. Which of the following is the typical hierarchy?

   A. Strategy, Portfolio, Program, Project, Subproject
   B. Platform, Portfolio, Program, Strategy, Project, Subproject
   C. Program, Portfolio, Platform, Project, Subproject, Strategy
   D. Strategy, Program, Portfolio, Project, Subproject

169. 以下哪个是典型的层级结构？

   A. 战略、组合、项目集、项目、子项目
   B. 平台、组合、项目集、战略、项目、子项目
   C. 项目集、组合、平台、项目、子项目、战略
   D. 战略、项目集、组合、项目、子项目

170. Portfolio performance metrics include _____.

   A. commercial risk
   B. time to market
   C. investment size
   D. all of the above are right

170. 组合绩效度量指标包括_____。

   A. 商业风险
   B. 产品上市时间
   C. 投资规模
   D. 以上皆对

171. Someone are highly energetic and talkative, build social relationships easily and will seek new people with whom to engage. What kind of person does this person belong to in the DISC work assessment tool?

   A. Dominance   B. Influence   C. Steady   D. Conscientious

171. 有些人精力充沛且非常健谈，很容易建立社会关系，并喜欢接触新人。在DISC工作评估工具中，这属于哪一类型的人？

   A. 支配型   B. 影响型   C. 稳健型   D. 谨慎型

172. Successful team have a_____.

   A. a common purpose and goal
   B. highly skilled team members
   C. history together
   D. strong leader

172. 成功的团队拥有_____。

   A. 共同的目的和目标
   B. 技能水平很高的团队成员
   C. 共同的经历
   D. 优秀的领导者

173. In the Thomas-Kilmann conflict model, what are the features of avoiding strategy?

   A. Low level of cooperativeness and low level of assertiveness

B. High level of cooperativeness and low level of assertiveness

C. Moderate level of cooperativeness and moderate level of assertiveness

D. Low level of cooperativeness and high level of assertiveness

173. 在托马斯冲突管理模型中，回避策略有何特点？

    A. 合作水平和自信水平都低
    B. 合作水平高和自信水平低
    C. 合作水平和自信水平都居中
    D. 合作水平低和自信水平高

174. In the virtual team model, what practical activities are included in the meeting elements?

    A. E-mail, language and customs and celebrate diversity
    B. Meeting format, rigorous planning and quality standards
    C. Task oriented, site visits and 80/20 listening
    D. Systems engineering, collaboration tools and lessons learned

174. 在虚拟团队模式中，会议要素包含了什么实践活动？

    A. 使用电子邮件、语言和习俗和鼓励多元化
    B. 会议形式、严格的计划和质量标准
    C. 任务导向、现场访问和 80/20 倾听
    D. 系统工程、协作工具和经验教训

175. When rewarding, one should use_____.

    A. reward individual
    B. reward team
    C. reward outstanding team members
    D. always reward the project leader

175. 在进行奖励时，应该_____。

    A. 奖励个人
    B. 奖励团队
    C. 奖励优秀团队成员
    D. 总是奖励项目领导者

176. What are the disadvantages of using NPV as a criteria?

    A. Ignores probabilities and risk
    B. Assume financial forecasts are accurate
    C. Only considers financial goals
    D. All of the above are right

176. 用净现值作为标准，会有什么缺点？

    A. 忽略了概率和风险
    B. 假设财务预测是正确的

C. 仅考虑了财务目标　　　　　　D. 以上皆对

177. A company widely uses product sustainability metrics as a source of competitive advantage. Lead the competition in design, supplier management, intellectual property and other aspects. At what level is the company in the Sustainability Maturity Model?

   A. Succeeding　　B. Improving　　C. Beginning　　D. Leading

177. 一家公司广泛使用产品可持续性度量指标，并将其作为竞争优势的来源，在设计、供应商管理、知识产权等各个方面全面领先对手。该公司处于可持续性成熟度模型中的什么级别？

   A. 成功级　　　　B. 改进级　　　　C. 初始级　　　　D. 领先级

178. An iterative approach that is performed in a collaborative environment by self-organizing teams is known as_____.

   A. integrated product development　　B. spiral waterfall model
   C. lean new product process　　　　　D. agile methodology

178. 在合作环境下，由自治式团队进行产品迭代开发，该方法被称作_____。

   A. 集成产品开发　　　　B. 螺旋瀑布模型
   C. 精益产品创新流程　　D. 敏捷方法

179. What is the role of the product manager in the growth stage?

   A. Solution seeker　　　B. Subject expert
   C. Growth hacker　　　　D. Retention strategist

179. 在成长阶段，产品经理应该承担什么角色？

   A. 洞察专家　　B. 方案达人　　C. 留存大师　　D. 增长黑客

180. The principles of sustainable product design do not include _____.

   A. use non-toxic, sustainably produced, or recycled materials with low environmental impact
   B. use manufacturing processes and produce products which are energy
   C. materials should come from sustainably managed renewable sources that can be composted when their usefulness is exhausted
   D. meet users' emotional requirements

180. 可持续性产品设计的原则不包括____。

    A. 使用无毒、可持续生产或对环境影响较低的可回收材料

    B. 使用节能的生产流程来生产产品

    C. 选用可再生材料，在其功用耗尽时，可将其制成肥料

    D. 满足用户的情感需求

181. Dennis is forecasting the sales volume of a product and obtains the following data:

    The number of buying units: 1,000,000

    Percent aware: 40%

    Percent trial: 20%

    Percent availability: 40%

    Percent repeat: 50%

    Annual units bought: 1.5

    What is the expected sales volume of this product?

    A. 32,000   B. 16,000   C. 1,000,000   D. 24,000

181. 丹尼斯正在对一个产品进行销量预测，得到以下数据：

    购买单位数量：1000000

    知晓率：40%

    试用率：20%

    购买率：40%

    复购率：50%

    年度购买次数：1.5

    那么，该产品的预计销量为多少？

    A. 32000   B. 16000   C. 1000000   D. 24000

182. What is the definition of product value?

    A. Revenue minus cost

    B. New product innovation income and new product innovation cost

    C. Revenue minus expenses

    D. Number of benefits

182. 产品价值的定义是什么？

　　A. 收入减去成本

　　B. 新产品创新收入和新产品创新成本

　　C. 收入减去费用

　　D. 带来的利益多少

183. What is the method of taking strategy as the starting point and emphasizing project selection according to the strategy?

　　A. Strategic bucket　　　　　　　　B. Bottom-up approach

　　C. Top -down approach　　　　　　D. A and C options

183. 以战略为出发点，强调按照战略进行项目选择，这是什么方法？

　　A. 战略桶　　　　　　　　　　　　B. 自下而上法

　　C. 自上而下法　　　　　　　　　　D. A 和 C 选项

184. What are the common indicators used to prove the value of product innovation and other functions of the company?

　　A. Time to market　　　　　　　　B. Number of projects released

　　C. Project budget　　　　　　　　D. Number of resources allocated

184. 用于证明产品创新价值以及与公司其他职能相关的常用指标是什么？

　　A. 上市时间　　　　　　　　　　　B. 项目发布数量

　　C. 项目预算　　　　　　　　　　　D. 所配置资源的数量

185. What is the definition of benchmarking?

　　A. A collection of date and information from a number of organizations that allows a organization to compare their performance to the performance of other companies

　　B. The iterative process from product design to product completion

　　C. A bottom-up technology for discovering connections between pieces of date

　　D. A comprehensive performance measure that balances four performance dimensions

185. 对标的定义是什么？

　　A. 收集其他组织的数据和资料，以便组织能够将其绩效与组织的绩效进行对比

B. 产品从设计到生产完成的迭代过程

C. 用于发现数据间联系的自下而上技术

D. 平衡四类指标的综合绩效衡量标准

186. External sources of new ideas include_____.

    A. tradeshows   B. suppliers and Partners

    C. focus group discussion   D. all of the above are right

186. 获取创意的外部途径包括_____。

    A. 贸易展会   B. 供应商以及合作伙伴

    C. 焦点小组讨论   D. 以上皆对

187. The house of quality is a tool to relate the VOC to_____.

    A. engineering design   B. new product developers

    C. lunching plan   D. marketing efforts

187. 质量屋是将客户之声与_____进行联系的工具。

    A. 工程设计   B. 新产品开发人员

    C. 上市计划   D. 营销工作

188. In order to implement the commitment to sustainability, the following aspects should be considered when developing incentive mechanisms, except for_____.

    A. examine the context of sustainability in business case

    B. take profitability as the primary objective

    C. attach awards to milestones as well as the end result due to uncertainty and lengthy timeframes

    D. structure the incentives to combine with leadership training and commitments for a supportive culture

188. 为了落实对可持续性的承诺,在制定激励机制时应该考虑以下哪些方面,除了_____。

    A. 检查商业论证中的可持续性内容

    B. 以盈利作为首要目标

    C. 由于不确定性及时间周期较长,因此不仅要对最终结果而且要对每个里程碑都进行激励

    D. 制定激励措施,将领导力培训与支持可持续性的文化结合起来

189. A high-risk project has adopted the Stage-gate process. How should the Stage-gate process be adjusted under this situation?

   A. Gather more information for decision making

   B. Reduce some stages and gates to mitigate risks

   C. Add some stages and gates to manage risks

   D. Conduct more market testing

189. 一个高风险项目采用了门径流程。在该情境下，应该如何调整门径流程？

   A. 获得更多决策信息   B. 缩减一些阶段和关口，以便减轻风险

   C. 增加一些阶段和关口，以便管理风险   D. 进行更多的市场测试

190. At which stage is the main goal of the product manager to get to product-market fit and adapt rapidly to new insight from customers and the market?

   A. Introduction   B. Growth   C. Maturity   D. Decline

190. 在以下哪个阶段，产品经理的主要目标是将产品和市场进行匹配，快速了解客户并顺应市场需求？

   A. 引入   B. 成长   C. 成熟   D. 衰退

191. In the product life cycle, which stage has the least capital input and the lowest financial risk?

   A. Evaluating ideas and early stage business analysis

   B. Opportunity identification and evaluation

   C. Pre-launch product and market testing

   D. Prototype and product use testing

191. 在产品生命周期中，哪个阶段投入的资金最少，财务风险最低？

   A. 创意评估与早期商业分析阶段   B. 机会识别与评估阶段

   C. 上市前产品与市场测试阶段   D. 原型与产品使用测试阶段

192. A leap in the application of a phased new product innovation process came in the early 1980s with the introduction of____.

   A. Booz, Hamilton, and Allen six stage process

B. the new product development trilogy

C. Cooper's process that uses stages and gates

D. NASA's phase review process

192. 在20世纪80年代初期，分阶段的产品创新流程应用的一个飞跃来自_____。

   A. 博思、艾伦和汉密尔顿的六阶段流程　　B. 新产品开发三部曲

   C. 库珀的门径流程　　D. NASA 的阶段评估流程

193. Home use testing is more effective for which of the following products?

   A. Commodity

   B. Food, beverage or beauty products

   C. Products used in sensitive or private situations

   D. All of the above are right

193. 家中使用测试对以下哪些产品较为有效？

   A. 日用品　　B. 食品、饮料或美容产品

   C. 在较为敏感或私密的情境下使用的产品　　D. 以上皆对

194. The cumulative costs increase dramatically throughout the product development process, especially during final prototyping and preparation for launch. To minimize the risks of failure in the latter stages of the process, market research should_____.

   A. be quick and easy to do　　B. provide clear information on customer needs

   C. be relatively inexpensive　　D. provide statistically reliable results

194. 在整个产品开发流程中，累积成本会大幅增加，尤其是在最后制作原型和上市准备阶段，更是如此。为了最小化后期的失败风险，市场调研应当_____。

   A. 又快又轻松地进行　　B. 提供关于客户需求的明确信息

   C. 相对便宜　　D. 提供可靠的统计结果

195. The variation studied in robust design does not include which of the following?

   A. Internal variation　　B. External variation

   C. Human emotion variation　　D. Variation between components

195. 稳健设计中所研究的变异不包括以下哪个？

   A. 内部变异
   B. 外部变异
   C. 与人情绪相关的变异
   D. 部件间变异

196. What can Life Cycle Assessment (LCA) provide?

   A. Quantitative data on the environmental impact of the product life cycle
   B. Return on investment in the product life cycle from creativity, concept, prototype, launching to end of life
   C. Technical evaluation of the product life cycle
   D. Assessment of market demand satisfaction throughout the product life cycle

196. 生命周期评估能提供什么？

   A. 产品整个生命周期对环境影响的定量数据
   B. 产品从创意、概念、原型、上市到退市整个生命周期的投资回报率
   C. 产品整个生命周期的技术评估
   D. 产品整个生命周期的市场需求满足情况评估

197. A product team is going to place an advertisement on a social media. The current budget is only enough to invite two bloggers. Now three bloggers meet the requirements. Here is the fans data:

   • 60% of users are Xiaohua's fans, and 25% are Xiaohua's and Xiaoming's common fans
   • 40% of the users are Xiaoming's fans, and Xiaoming and Xiaohong's fans are totally different
   • 30% of the users are fans of Xiaohong, and 5% are fans of Xiaohong and Xiaohua
   Please use TURF to analyze, which two bloggers can cover the most users?

   A. Xiaohua and Xiaoming
   B. Xiaohua and Xiaohong
   C. Xiaoming and Xiaohong
   D. All of the above are right

197. 一个产品团队准备在某社交媒体上投放广告。目前的预算只够邀请两位博主。现在有三位博主符合要求，他们的粉丝数据如下：

   • 有60%的用户是小华的粉丝，有25%的用户是小华和小明共同的粉丝
   • 有40%的用户是小明的粉丝，小明与小红没有共同的粉丝

- 有30%的用户是小红的粉丝，有5%的用户是小红和小华共同的粉丝

使用TURF分析，哪两位博主能够覆盖最多的用户？

A. 小华和小明 　　　　　　　　B. 小华和小红

C. 小明和小红 　　　　　　　　D. 以上皆对

198. What are the main differences between characteristics and benefits?

A. Features are specific product specifications, and benefits are advertising slogans

B. Features are the result of customer expectations, and benefits are designed by the company

C. Features are designed by the company, and the revenue is the result of customer expectations

D. Features are advertising slogans, and benefits are specific product specifications

198. 特性与收益的主要区别是什么？

A. 特性是具体的产品规格，收益是广告标语

B. 特性是客户期望的结果，收益由公司设计

C. 特性由公司设计，收益是客户期望的结果

D. 特性是广告标语，收益是具体的产品规格

199. Your company already has a majority of the market share of a profitable product for many years, during which time there is no clear reason to change the functionality of the product or make significant improvements to it, but currently a new competitor's product of the new technology has entered the market, but some features of the product do not meet the current products of your company. What should you do in the face of this situation?

A. Think of it as an example of a potentially disruptive innovation

B. You have a large market share and you can ignore competitors

C. Lower your product price

D. Consider a slight improvement in the functionality of your product

199. 你的公司已经占有某个盈利的产品的大部分市场份额很多年。在此期间，没有明确的理由需要改变产品的功能或对其进行重大改进，但是目前一个新的竞争对手通过使用新技术开发了一款新产品并进入了该市场，但该产品的某些功能不及你的公司当前的产品。面对这种情况，你应该怎么办？

A. 将其视为潜在的颠覆性创新

B. 因已有较大的市场份额，可以无视竞争对手

C. 降低自身产品价格

D. 考虑将自身产品功能稍加改进

200. A systematic and collaborative approach to identify and creatively solve problems is known as_____.

A. IPD
B. design thinking
C. Agile
D. Lean product innovation

200. 用来识别并创造性地解决问题的系统化、协作化方法被称作_____。

A. 集成产品开发
B. 设计思维
C. 敏捷
D. 精益产品创新

试题答案与解析

序号	答案	知识点	教材页码
1	B	创新管理/项目管理/产品创新中的项目管理/范围/产品范围/定义	P344 倒数第 3 行
2	C	文化/团队发展/塔克曼团队发展模型	P270 第 8 行
3	B	创新管理/项目管理/项目/定义	P343 第 5 行
4	C	流程/产品创新流程模型/敏捷方法/Scrum/特点	P122 倒数第 8 行
5	A	战略/创新支持战略/营销战略/分析现有产品组合/波士顿矩阵/瘦狗/特点	P39 图 1.21
6	C	战略/创新支持战略/产品平台战略	P28 倒数第 10 行和 P69 倒数第 9 行
7	A	创新管理/产品生命周期中的鸿沟/跨越鸿沟/早期采用者	P318 图 7.9 和 P454 倒数第 4 行
8	C	组合/平衡组合/气泡图	P79 第 8 行
9	A	市场调研/定性市场调研方法/客户现场访问/优点	P223 第 5 行
10	D	组合/平衡组合/气泡图/维度	P80 图 2.7、图 2.8 和图 2.9

序号	答案	知识点	教材页码
11	B	创新管理/产品路线图与技术路线图/产品路线图	P329 倒数第 10 行
12	C	创新管理/产品失败的两个主要原因	补充知识
13	D	战略/创新支持战略/营销战略/价值主张	P38 第 8 行和 P321 倒数第 1 行
14	A	市场调研/试销与市场测试/试销/定义	P242 第 7 行和 P413 第 2 行
15	C	组合/什么是产品组合/什么是组合管理/管道/定义	P430 倒数第 9 行
16	A	创新管理/项目管理/关键路径	P345 倒数第 5 行
17	C	创新管理/项目管理/进度压缩/赶工	P346 第 1 行
18	D	组合/组合与战略关系/组合与战略的连接方法/目标	P70 第 5 行
19	C	创新管理/需求与销售预测/工具/购买意向法/计算 80%×30%+20%×70%=38%	P335 倒数第 5 行
20	B	市场调研/定性市场调研方法/焦点小组/缺点	P219 倒数第 12 行
21	A	文化/团队发展/高绩效团队/成功因素	P269 图 6.7
22	D	工具/创意生成阶段/创意生成工具/头脑书写法/特点	P158 倒数第 10 行
23	B	市场调研/产品使用测试/目的	P240 第 9 行
24	D	工具/创意生成/创意来源	补充知识
25	B	组合/组合管理系统应用/组合管理准则/资源调整	P89 倒数第 10 行
26	C	战略/创新支持战略/知识产权战略/知识产权/定义	P33 第 7 行
27	A	市场调研/术语表/客户之声/定义	P436 倒数第 12 行
28	C	市场调研/一级与二级市场调研/二级市场调研/缺点	P214 倒数第 6 行
29	A	创新管理//风险管理/定义	P427 第 10 行
30	B	创新管理/产品创新成功率/关键因素	补充知识
31	C	流程/产品创新引论/价值	P101 图 3.2
32	B	战略/制定战略前的准备/SWOT/优势和劣势	P11 倒数第 4 行
33	A	文化/产品创新团队结构/轻量型团队/适用情境	P265 第 7 行
34	B	工具/概念设计阶段/TRIZ/内容	P167 第 10 行
35	C	战略/创新支持战略/技术战略/技术 S 曲线	P32 图 1.14
36	B	文化/团队发展/冲突管理/特点	P274 倒数第 10 行
37	A	组合/组合与战略的连接方法/自上而下法	P71 第 4 行
38	C	工具/制造与装配阶段/原型	P188 倒数第 10 行

序号	答案	知识点	教材页码
39	A	创新/产品生命周期/引论/产品生命周期变短/原因	P311 第 1 行
40	B	创新管理/度量指标与关键绩效指标/产品创新平衡计分卡/流程/组建跨职能团队	P357 第 3 行
41	D	战略/创新支持战略/营销战略/分析现有产品组合/波士顿矩阵/问题/特点	P39 图 1.21
42	C	战略/创新战略与战略框架/延续式与颠覆式产品创新	P25 第 6 行
43	D	市场调研/定性市场调研方法/定义	P215 第 8 行
44	B	市场调研/市场细分/定义	P445 第 10 行
45	A	流程/产品创新流程模型/博思、艾伦和汉密尔顿六个基本阶段	P107 倒数第 12 行
46	A	创新管理/术语/度量指标/定义	P425 第 9 行
47	B	创新管理/风险管理/什么是风险管理/减轻	P347 第 10 行
48	C	战略/创新战略与战略框架/波特竞争战略/差异化战略/特点	P21 倒数第 1 行
49	A	工具/设计流程引论/设计考虑因素	P156 第 3 行
50	C	组合/什么是组合管理/组合中的项目类型/衍生型项目	P69 倒数第 5 行
51	B	工具/创意生成阶段/创意生成工具/头脑风暴/特点	P157 倒数第 2 行
52	A	战略/开放式创新/开放式创新类型/参与者	P49 图 1.28
53	C	创新管理/财务成功/定义	P418 倒数第 5 行
54	A	文化/团队发展/冲突管理/折中/特点	P275 倒数第 9 行
55	B	流程/产品创新流程模型/系统工程/内容	P128 第 4 行
56	C	流程/产品创新流程模型/门径流程/关口/输出	P110 倒数第 10 行
57	B	流程/产品创新流程模型/门径流程/阶段/内容	P110 第 1 行和 P434 第 1 行
58	A	组合管理/责任者	补充知识
59	C	战略/开放式创新/开放式创新类型/关键成功因素与管理风格	P48 图 1.27
60	D	工具/概念设计阶段/概念工程/特点	P161 第 5 行
61	D	组合/新产品机会评估与选择/定性评估方法/新产品成功因素	P73 倒数第 5 行
62	A	工具/详细设计与规格阶段/质量功能展开/质量屋/特点	P181 倒数第 1 行和图 4.8

序号	答案	知识点	教材页码
63	B	工具/概念设计阶段/TRIZ/40 个发明原理/嵌套	P168 图 4.5
64	D	流程/产品创新章程/内容/总体目标与具体目标	P105 第 10 行
65	D	流程/产品创新流程模型/门径流程/商业论证/定义	P443 第 10 行
66	A	创新管理/项目管理/预算/估算方法/历史数据法	P346 第 9 行
67	B	战略/创新支持战略/营销战略/分析现有产品组合/波士顿矩阵/现金牛产品/现金流特点	P39 图 1.21
68	D	组合/新产品机会评估与选择/定性评估方法/评分法/使用场合	P75 倒数第 9 行
69	B	战略/创新支持战略/数字化战略/排序	P45 图 1.24
70	C	文化/产品创新团队结构/自治型团队/适用情境	P266 倒数第 4 行
71	D	文化/团队发展/高绩效团队/成功因素	P269 图 6.7
72	C	组合/项目组合/定义	P450 第 6 行
73	A	战略/创新战略与战略框架/迈尔斯和斯诺战略框架/探索者	P23 倒数第 3 行和图 1.10
74	B	战略/创新战略与战略框架/迈尔斯和斯诺战略框架/分析者	P24 倒数第 10 行
75	D	组合/组合管理系统应用/组合管理准则/资源调整	P89 倒数第 7 行
76	D	文化/产品创新团队结构/跨职能团队	P263 第 5 行
77	C	工具/概念设计阶段/卡诺模型/分析	P163 倒数第 10 行
78	D	流程/产品创新流程模型/门径流程/关口/构成部分	P110 第 10 行
79	B	流程/产品创新流程模型/门径流程/阶段/综合分析/参与者	P110 第 4 行
80	C	组合/组合与战略关系/组合与战略的连接方法/自下而上法/步骤和特点	P71 倒数第 2 行
81	C	创新管理/术语/风险管理/决策树/定义	P435 第 1 行
82	A	文化/团队结构/职能型团队/适用情境	P264 倒数第 7 行
83	D	战略/开放式创新/开放式创新类型/开放式创新的参与机制/开放者	P49 图 1.28
84	C	工具/详细设计与规格阶段/质量功能展开/特点	P180 倒数第 7 行
85	B	战略/经营战略与公司战略/公司战略/案例	P10 图 1.4
86	A	创新管理/需求与销售预测/工具/ATAR 和扩散模型	P334 倒数第 5 行

序号	答案	知识点	教材页码
87	B	工具/概念设计阶段/形态分析/应用情境	P164 第 2 行
88	C	战略/明确组织方向/愿景/案例	P7 第 4 行
89	B	文化/产品创新团队结构/重量型团队/适用情境	P266 第 5 行
90	A	流程/产品创新引论/管理新产品失败风险	P100 倒数第 4 行和图 3.2
91	C	战略/明确组织方向/使命/案例	P7 第 10 行
92	D	流程/产品创新章程/定义	P103 倒数第 3 行
93	C	创新管理/风险管理/内容	P346 倒数第 8 行
94	A	创新管理/度量指标与关键绩效指标/平衡计分卡	P351 图 7.39
95	C	流程/产品创新流程模型/精益产品创新方法/特点	P117 倒数第 1 行
96	B	战略/皮萨诺创新景观图/激进型	P27 图 1.12 和倒数第 4 行
97	C	流程/产品创新流程模型/敏捷方法/特点	P127 第 3 行
98	B	战略/创新支持战略/平台战略/衍生产品/定义	P28 倒数第 9 行
99	B	流程/产品创新流程模型/门径流程/阶段数量/决定因素	P109 第 7 行
100	C	组合/组合管理有效性/条件	补充知识
101	B	战略/制定战略前的准备/德尔菲技术	P13 倒数第 9 行
102	C	市场调研/一级与二级市场调研/二级市场调研方法/优点	P214 倒数第 10 行
103	C	流程/产品创新引论/PDMA 对流程的研究	P100 第 6 行
104	A	组合/什么是产品组合/什么是组合管理/内容	P68 第 3 行
105	B	流程/产品创新引论/在产品创新流程中"前端"的重要性/模糊前端	P103 第 3 行
106	A	流程/产品创新流程模型/瀑布模型/应用情境	P115 第 2 行
107	C	文化/管理职责/产品创造流程中的角色/流程经理	P262 第 4 行
108	D	流程/产品创新流程模型/精益创业/良好学习计划/特点	P135 第 5 行和倒数第 6 行
109	D	市场调研/市场调研引论/客户之声/客户细分	P212 第 1 行
110	B	工具/实体化设计阶段/联合分析/非补偿模型/示例	P173 第 9 行
111	B	市场调研/定性市场调研方法/焦点小组/人数	P218 第 7 行
112	C	创新管理/项目管理/总时差/定义	补充知识
113	A	创新管理/风险管理/产品创新项目风险管理/产品风险和项目风险/项目风险	P348 倒数第 8 行

序号	答案	知识点	教材页码
114	C	工具/基于问题的创意生成/定义	补充知识
115	A	工具/实体化设计阶段/功能分析/外部功能和内部功能	P174 倒数第 4 行
116	C	创新管理/财务分析/回收期/计算	P338 第 8 行
		回收期=4+1+（100000−10000）÷20000=9.5（月）	
117	B	创新管理/风险管理/决策树/作用	P349 第 7 行
118	D	工具/实体化设计阶段/功能分析/FAST 技术图	P175 第 2 行
119	A	创新管理/风险管理/风险减轻/定义	P427 倒数第 11 行
120	D	创新管理/风险管理/风险容限/定义	P427 倒数第 8 行
121	D	战略/创新战略与战略框架/迈尔斯和斯诺战略框架/探索者	P23 图 1.10 后倒数第 1 行
122	A	战略/创新支持战略/能力战略/关键职能	P40 倒数第 5 行
123	B	创新管理/可行性分析/可行性分析要素	P333 第 10 行
124	C	流程/产品创新流程模型/精益产品创新方法的理念	P118 图 3.9
125	C	战略/创新战略与战略框架/迈尔斯和斯诺战略框架/分析者	P24 第 13 行
126	C	战略/创新支持战略/技术战略/技术预测	P31 图 1.13
127	D	创新管理/产品生命周期/成熟阶段	P312 图 7.6
128	C	创新管理/产品创新关键成功因素/最佳公司在衡量上的最佳实践	P303 倒数第 3 行
129	D	创新管理/财务分析/衡量投资回报率指标	P337 倒数第 4 行
130	B	工具/实体化设计阶段/功能分析/逆向工程	P175 倒数第 7 行
131	A	战略/创新支持战略/营销战略/什么是产品/产品的三个层次/核心利益	P37 倒数第 2 行和 P169 第 9 行
132	D	工具/初始设计与规格阶段/可服务性设计/总成本构成	P180 第 8 行
133	B	组合/什么是产品组合/组合中的项目类型/突破型项目/特点	P69 第 12 行
134	A	创新管理/管理产品创新/产品管理的作用/经营	P304 倒数第 1 行
135	C	流程/产品创新引论/什么是产品创新/运用知识提升决策水平并减少不确定性	P102 第 1 行
136	D	创新管理/管理产品创新/产品管理的定义	P307 图 7.2
137	D	工具/详细设计与规格阶段/情感化设计/感性工学	P187 倒数第 11 行

序号	答案	知识点	教材页码
138	B	工具/制造与装配阶段/原型法/可体验原型法/服务行业应用	P190 倒数第 11 行
139	A	市场调研/市场调研中的度量指标与关键绩效指标	P249 第 4 行
140	B	战略/创新支持战略/营销战略/制定基础	P35 倒数第 8 行
141	D	市场调研/市场调研引论/目的	P210 第 3 行
142	A	创新管理/财务分析/成本/固定成本	P336 倒数第 8 行
143	C	流程/产品创新流程模型/敏捷方法/敏捷软件开发宣言/客户合作	P121 倒数第 10 行
144	A	工具/创意生成阶段/什么是创意生成/发散思维	P157 第 4 行
145	A	工具/创意生成阶段/什么是创意生成/收敛思维	P157 第 7 行
146	B	流程/产品创新流程模型/精益产品创新方法/浪费来源	P119 第 5 行
147	A	流程/产品创新流程模型/瀑布模型/特点	P115 第 1 行
148	A	战略/可持续创新/可持续产品创新/可持续性与战略/三重底线	P51 第 8 行
149	D	文化/创新文化与氛围/成功因素	P259 倒数第 6 行
150	D	文化/创新文化与氛围/创新环境	P258 倒数第 4 行
151	C	战略/制定战略前的准备/商业模式画布/核心资源	P16 图 1.8
152	B	文化/管理职责/产品创新流程中的角色/产品战略制定者	P261 第 4 行
153	A	战略/创新战略与战略框架/克里斯坦森颠覆式创新/特点	P26 倒数第 12 行
154	C	流程/产品创新流程模型/精益创业/转型/平台转型	P137 倒数第 7 行
155	A	流程/产品创新流程模型/系统工程/优点	P129 倒数第 9 行
156	A	战略/创新支持战略/营销战略/什么是产品/产品的三个层次/有形特性	P37 图 1.20
157	D	市场调研/定性市场调研方法/人种学方法/定义	P221 倒数第 10 行
158	D	战略/创新支持战略/营销战略/分析现有产品组合/波士顿矩阵/现金牛产品	P39 图 1.21
159	A	工具/创意生成阶段/创意生成工具/SCAMPER 法/去除	P157 倒数第 4 行
160	B	战略/创新支持战略/营销战略/营销组合	P36 第 7 行和 P37 图 1.19

序号	答案	知识点	教材页码
161	B	战略/创新支持战略/知识产权战略/知识产权管理优化方法	P33 第 10 行
162	C	工具/制造与装配阶段/六西格玛设计/IDOV 和 DMAIC /含义	P193 倒数第 10 行和 P194 第 3 行
163	D	战略/创新支持战略/知识产权战略/知识产权的价值	P35 图 1.17
164	D	工具/创意生成阶段/创意生成工具/六项思考帽/红色帽子	P159 第 1 行
165	B	工具/概念设计阶段/概念场景	P165 第 8 行
166	D	创新管理/产品生命周期/产品生命周期引论/产品生命周期缩短原因	P311 第 1 行
167	D	市场调研/多变量研究方法/多元回归分析/适用情境	P238 倒数第 4 行
168	B	组合/什么是产品组合/组合中的项目类型/平台型项目	P69 倒数第 9 行
169	A	战略/什么是战略/战略层级	P6 图 1.2 和补充知识
170	D	组合/组合绩效度量指标/选择	P89 倒数第 2 行
171	B	文化/团队发展/工作风格/DISC 工作风格评估工具/影响型/特点	P272 第 3 行
172	A	文化/团队发展/什么是高绩效团队	P268 倒数第 8 行
173	A	文化/团队发展/冲突管理/托马斯模型/回避/内容	P275 图 6.9
174	B	文化/虚拟团队/虚拟团队模式/会议/实践活动	P279 图 6.12
175	B	文化/团队与领导力中的度量指标/创新激励	P286 倒数第 8 行
176	D	创新管理/财务分析/净现值（NPV）/缺点	P339 倒数第 5 行和补充知识
177	D	战略/可持续创新/可持续产品创新/可持续性成熟度模型/领先级	P55 图 1.29
178	D	流程/产品创新流程模型/敏捷方法/定义	P120 倒数第 4 行
179	D	创新管理/产品生命周期/产品经理在产品生命周期中/成长阶段/角色	P315 图 7.8
180	D	工具/制造与装配阶段/可持续性设计/考虑要素	P195 倒数第 12 行
181	D	创新管理/需求与销售预测/工具/ATAR/计算 预计销量=1000000×40%×20%×40%×50%×1.5=24000	P335 图 7.28
182	D	创新管理/产品生命周期中的鸿沟/走向市场流程/价值	P321 倒数第 3 行

序号	答案	知识点	教材页码
		主张	
183	D	组合/组合与战略的连接方法/自上而下法	P71 第7行
184	D	组合/资源配置/资源配置工具	P84 图2.12和P85图2.13
185	A	创新管理/度量指标与关键绩效指标/对标与持续改进/对标/定义	P425 倒数第10行
186	D	市场调研/产品创新各阶段的市场调研/机会识别与评估/创意来源	P244 第6行
187	A	工具/详细设计与规格阶段/质量功能展开/质量屋/特点	P181 倒数第1行和图4.8
188	B	文化/团队与领导力中的可持续性/激励机制	P286 第5行
189	C	流程/产品创新流程模型/门径流程/决定阶段数量的因素	P109 第10行
190	A	创新管理/产品生命周期/产品经理在产品生命周期中/引入阶段/角色	P315 图7.8
191	B	市场调研/产品创新各阶段的市场调研/机会识别与评估	P246 图5.3
192	C	流程/产品创新流程模型/门径流程	P108 第12行
193	D	市场调研/产品使用测试/家中使用测试/适用情境	P240 第3行
194	D	市场调研/产品创新各阶段的市场调研/原型和上市前准备	P247 图5.3
195	C	工具/详细设计与规格阶段/稳健设计/特点	P186 第12行
196	A	工具/制造与装配阶段/可持续性分析工具/生命周期评估/内容	P197 倒数第1行
197	B	市场调研/多变量研究方法/TURF分析/计算	P239 第1行
		方案1：小华（60%）+小明（40%）−25%=75%； 方案2：小华（60%）+小红（30%）−5%=85%； 方案3：小明（40%）+小红（30%）=70%	
198	C	战略/创新支持战略/营销战略/什么是产品/产品的三个层次	P37 倒数第2行
199	A	战略/创新战略与战略框架/克里斯坦森颠覆式创新/特点	P26 第4行
200	B	流程/产品创新流程模型/设计思维/定义	P130 倒数第3行

考前冲刺试题二

说明：考试时间为 3.5 小时（9:00—12:30），共 200 题，均为单选题。答对 150 道（含）以上通过考试。

1. When using the top-down method for project selection and portfolio review, what is the first step?

    A. Bottom-up estimation

    B. Allocate resources

    C. Make budget

    D. Clearly define business strategies, strategic goals and priorities

1. 采用自上而下法进行项目选择和组合评审时，第一步是什么？

    A. 自下而上估算 　　　　　　　　　B. 配置资源

    C. 制定预算 　　　　　　　　　　　D. 明确定义经营战略、战略目标和优先级

2. Which type of Porter's Competitive strategy framework is suitable for choosing a strategy with "narrow market scope" rather than "broad market scope"?

    A. Cost leadership strategy 　　　　　B. Differentiation strategy

    C. Segmentation strategy 　　　　　　D. Defender strategy

2. 选择"窄市场范围"而非"宽市场范围"的战略，符合波特竞争战略框架中的哪种类型？

    A. 成本领先战略 　　　　　　　　　B. 差异化战略

    C. 细分市场战略 　　　　　　　　　D. 防御者战略

3. In the Ansoff Strategy Matrix, what strategies are applied for new products to enter new markets?

    A. Market penetration 　　　　　　　B. Market development

    C. Product development 　　　　　　D. Diversification

3. 在安索夫战略矩阵中，当新产品进入新市场时，应采用什么战略？

   A. 市场渗透　　　B. 市场开发　　　C. 产品开发　　　D. 多元化

4. Which of the following belongs to the types of product innovation project in a portfolio?

   A. Platform and technical service　　　B. Breakthrough and platform

   C. Breakthrough and technical service　　　D. Cost leadership and breakthrough

4. 以下哪个属于组合中的产品创新项目类型？

   A. 平台型和技术服务型　　　B. 突破型和平台型

   C. 突破型和技术服务型　　　D. 成本领先型和突破型

5. Knowledge will greatly affect decision-making. Where does knowledge come from in product innovation?

   A. Mainly from inside　　　B. Mainly from outside

   C. Combination of inside and outside　　　D. Mainly from stakeholders

5. 知识会极大地影响决策。在产品创新中，知识来源于哪里？

   A. 主要来源于内部　　　B. 主要来源于外部

   C. 来源于内部与外部的结合　　　D. 主要来源于相关方

6. What is the value of innovation strategy?

   A. Provide a framework for innovation decision-making

   B. Is used to prioritize innovative projects

   C. Use as a tool for product innovation and sustainable growth

   D. All of the above are right

6. 创新战略的价值是什么？

   A. 为创新决策提供框架

   B. 用于对创新项目进行排序

   C. 作为开展产品创新和实现持续增长的工具

   D. 以上皆对

7. Which of the following statements is incorrect about the ethnography and focus groups?

   A. Ethnography and focus groups are usually conducted in a special place set by researchers

   B. Ethnography and focus groups are both qualitative research methods

   C. Both ethnography and focus groups are primary market research methods

   D. Neither ethnography nor focus groups can draw statistical conclusions

7. 关于人种学方法与焦点小组方法，以下哪个说法不正确？

   A. 人种学方法与焦点小组通常由研究者设定一个专门场所进行群体调查

   B. 人种学方法与焦点小组都是定性研究方法

   C. 人种学方法与焦点小组都是一级市场调研方法

   D. 人种学方法与焦点小组都不能得出统计结论

8. Generally speaking, when the existing technology enters at what stage of the technology S-curve, will some companies introduce disruptive new technologies into the market?

   A. The embryonic stage   B. The maturity stage

   C. The decline stage   D. The growth stage

8. 通常而言，现有技术进入技术 S 曲线的什么阶段，就会有一些公司将颠覆性新技术引入市场？

   A. 引入阶段   B. 成熟阶段   C. 衰退阶段   D. 成长阶段

9. At the daily standup meeting, although team members may have arguments, they are all committed to reaching an agreed goal before the end of the meeting. What stage is the team at?

   A. Forming   B. Storming   C. Norming   D. Performing

9. 在每日站会上，虽然团队成员会有争论，但都能致力于在会议结束之前达成一致目标。该团队处于什么阶段？

   A. 形成   B. 震荡   C. 规范   D. 成熟

10. Which of the following statements is correct about customer site visits?

    A. Only for important issues or questions

    B. Helps to collect requirements in depth at the customer's site

C. Only lead by marketing personnel

D. There are no requirements for customers to attend

10. 关于客户现场访问，以下哪个说法是正确的？

   A. 仅用于重要议题或问题
   B. 有助于在现场深入收集客户需求
   C. 仅由营销人员主导
   D. 无需客户参加

11. In order to enter the smart wearable product market, focus groups are used first, and then surveys are used. Which of the following is the best description of this practice?

   A. Qualitative market research method
   B. Quantitative market research method
   C. Secondary market research method
   D. Mixed market research methods

11. 为了进入智能可穿戴产品市场，先使用焦点小组法，再使用问卷调查法。请问以下哪个是对该做法的最好描述？

   A. 定性市场调研方法
   B. 定量市场调研方法
   C. 二级市场调研
   D. 混合型市场调研方法

12. Test in the company's internal laboratory setting or regular operations to find and eliminate the most design defects or deficiencies. What test is this?

   A. Alpha test
   B. Gamma test
   C. Test marketing
   D. Beta test

12. 在公司内部的实验环境或常规环境下进行测试，目的是发现和消除明显的设计缺陷。这是什么测试？

   A. 阿尔法测试
   B. 伽马测试
   C. 试销
   D. 贝塔测试

13. This year's net profit margin is 25% higher than that of last year, and last year's net profit margin is 10%. So, what is the net profit margin this year?

   A. 25%　　　　B. 12.5%　　　　C. 35%　　　　D. 13.6%

13. 今年净利润率比去年增长25%，去年净利润率为10%。那么，今年净利润率为多少？

   A. 25%　　　　B. 12.5%　　　　C. 35%　　　　D. 13.6%

14. What methods do factor analysis, multidimensional scaling analysis and joint analysis belong to?
    A. Multivariate research method
    B. Regression method
    C. Qualitative analysis method
    D. Creativity generation tool

14. 因子分析、多维尺度分析、联合分析等都属于什么方法？
    A. 多变量研究方法
    B. 回归方法
    C. 定性分析方法
    D. 创意生成工具

15. A method is used to analyze all stakeholders in the product life cycle, as well as all cost related to products, processes and activities generated in the product life cycle. What is this method?
    A. R&D cost
    B. Operating cost
    C. Cost of capital
    D. Life cycle cost

15. 分析产品生命周期中所有相关方，以及在产品生命周期内产生的与产品、流程和活动相关的所有成本。这是什么方法？
    A. 研发成本
    B. 运营成本
    C. 资金成本
    D. 生命周期成本

16. What design tools are Microsoft Reaction Card and Emergent Emotions?
    A. Robust design
    B. Quality function deployment
    C. Design for assembly
    D. Emotional design

16. 微软反应卡和突发情绪法是什么设计工具？
    A. 稳健设计
    B. 质量功能展开
    C. 可装配性设计
    D. 情感化设计

17. IKEA is a furniture corporation that provides general-purpose and low-cost products. It has a foothold in the market by producing furniture in low-cost countries and providing consumers with basic services. What is the best description of the strategy?
    A. Cost leadership
    B. Differentiation
    C. Analyzer
    D. Reactor

17. 宜家是一家提供普通且低价产品的家具企业。它通过在低成本国家生产家具，并给消费者提供基本服务的方法在市场立足。对该战略的最佳描述是什么？

    A. 成本领先　　　　　　　　　　　　B. 差异化
    C. 分析者　　　　　　　　　　　　　D. 回应者

18. Jack is responsible for product innovation in a company. He will find the products and ideas needed by the market. Which thinking cap should Jack use?

    A. Blue　　　　B. White　　　　C. Red　　　　D. Green

18. 杰克在一家公司负责产品创新工作。他要找出市场所需的产品和创意。杰克应该使用哪项思考帽？

    A. 蓝色　　　　B. 白色　　　　C. 红色　　　　D. 绿色

19. Which of the following methods can best understand the choices consumers make for various attribute combinations of product or service?

    A. Multiple regression analysis　　　　B. Multidimensional scaling analysis
    C. Conjoint analysis　　　　　　　　　D. Focus groups

19. 通过以下哪个方法，最能了解消费者对产品或服务的各种属性组合所做出的选择？

    A. 多元回归分析　　　　　　　　　　B. 多维尺度分析
    C. 联合分析　　　　　　　　　　　　D. 焦点小组

20. Where does Design for Six Sigma originate?

    A. Supply Chain Management　　　　　B. Quality management
    C. Operation engineering　　　　　　D. Product Management

20. 六西格玛设计起源于哪个领域？

    A. 供应链管理　　　　　　　　　　　B. 质量管理
    C. 运营工程　　　　　　　　　　　　D. 产品管理

21. In the product innovation life cycle, which stage has the highest cumulative cost, the lowest uncertainty and the highest investor confidence?

    A. Idea generation　　　　　　　　　B. Prototype development

C. Scale-up to commercialization D. Product launch

21. 在产品创新生命周期中，哪个阶段累积成本最高、不确定性最低、投资者信心最高？

    A. 创意生成 B. 原型开发
    C. 规模化和商业化 D. 产品上市

22. Which is the best description of product innovation process governance?

    A. Ensure the overall effectiveness of the product innovation process
    B. Focus on specific process management
    C. Administrative management, emphasizing documents and process records
    D. It is the work of the product owner, not the work of the management

22. 对产品创新流程治理的正确描述是哪个？

    A. 确保产品创新流程的整体有效性 B. 专注于具体的流程管理
    C. 行政管理，强调文件和记录 D. 是产品负责人的工作而不是管理层的工作

23. Which is the best description of idea generation?

    A. Test and validate concepts
    B. New product launch
    C. Prototyping
    D. It is a creative process of generating, developing and communicating new ideas

23. 对创意生成的最佳描述是哪个？

    A. 测试并确认概念 B. 新产品上市
    C. 制作原型 D. 是生成、开发和交流新创意的创造性过程

24. Which of the following does not belong to the principles of circular economy?

    A. Control commodity stocks and balance the flow of renewable resources to protect and increase natural resources
    B. Recycle products, parts and raw materials to optimize resource output and maximize utilization in the technological and biological cycle
    C. Provide free products and values to the society
    D. Improve system efficiency by exposing and eliminating negative external influences

24. 以下哪个不属于循环经济的原则?

    A. 控制库存商品以及平衡可再生资源的流动,保护并增加自然资源

    B. 循环利用产品、零部件和原材料,实现资源产出的优化,在技术和生物周期中保持利用率最大化

    C. 给社会提供免费产品和价值

    D. 通过揭露和消除负面的外部影响来提升系统效率

25. Which of the following decisions was made at the gate in Stage-Gate process?

    A. Go/Kill   B. Go/Kill/Hold

    C. Go/Kill/Hold/Rework   D. Go/Conditional Go/Kill/Hold/Rework

25. 在门径流程中,关口处做出的决策是以下哪个?

    A. 通过/否决   B. 通过/否决/搁置

    C. 通过/否决/搁置/重做   D. 通过/有条件通过/否决/搁置/重做

26. Which of the following is correct about vision and mission?

    Statement 1: Kickstarter - help you bring creative projects into life

    Statement 2: Tesla - Accelerating the transformation of the world to sustainable energy

    Statement 3: Southwest Airlines - the most popular, efficient and profitable airline in the world

    Statement 4: Alibaba – a company that has lived for 102 years

    A. Statement 1 and 3 are vision, and Statement 2 and 4 are mission

    B. Statement 1 and 2 are vision, and Statement 3 and 4 are mission

    C. Statement 3 and 4 are vision, and Statement 1 and 2 are mission

    D. Statement 2 and 4 are vision, and Statement 1 and 3 are mission

26. 关于愿景和使命,以下哪个选项正确?

    描述 1:Kickstarter——帮助你将创意项目带入生活

    描述 2:特斯拉——加速世界向可持续能源的转变

    描述 3:西南航空——成为世界上最受欢迎、最高效、最赚钱的航空公司

    描述 4:阿里巴巴——成为一家活 102 年的企业

    A. 描述 1 和 3 是愿景,描述 2 和 4 是使命

    B. 描述 1 和 2 是愿景,描述 3 和 4 是使命

C. 描述 3 和 4 是愿景，描述 1 和 2 是使命

D. 描述 2 和 4 是愿景，描述 1 和 3 是使命

27. Which of the following participants participate in open innovation through auction or partnership?

    A. Seeker   B. Provider

    C. Intermediary   D. Opener

27. 以下哪类参与者采用拍卖或合伙等方式参与开放式创新？

    A. 寻求者   B. 提供者   C. 中介者   D. 开放者

28. In the Stage-Gate process, what are the tasks of the business case stage?

    A. Conduct in-depth technical, marketing and business feasibility analysis

    B. Testing all aspects of new products and commercialization

    C. Quickly understand market opportunities, technical requirements and available functions

    D. Improve product design, prototype making, manufacturing design, manufacturing preparation and launch plan

28. 在门径流程中，商业论证阶段的任务是什么？

    A. 进行深入的技术、市场和商业可行性分析

    B. 测试新产品及其商业化计划的所有方面

    C. 快速了解市场机会、技术需求及可用功能

    D. 完善产品设计、原型制作、制造设计、制造准备和上市计划

29. Which is not the content of big data 3V?

    A. Velocity   B. Value   C. Volume   D. Variety

29. 哪个不是大数据 3V 的内容？

    A. 高速   B. 价值   C. 大量   D. 多样

30. Which of the following is not a financial performance metrics?

    A. Warranty costs   B. Revenue generated

    C. Gross profit margin   D. Return on investment

30. 以下哪个不是财务绩效指标？

   A. 保修费　　　　B. 产生的收入　　　C. 毛利率　　　　D. 投资回报率

31. There is already a successful product on the market. Now, what ideation tools should the team use to find a better substitute?

   A. SWOT analysis　　　　　　　　B. PESTLE analysis
   C. Delphi technique　　　　　　　D. SCAMPER method

31. 市场上已有一款成功的产品。现在，团队要找一个更优的替代品，应该采用以下哪个创意工具？

   A. SWOT 分析　　　　　　　　　B. PESTLE 分析
   C. 德尔菲技术　　　　　　　　　D. SCAMPER 法

32. Dajiang UAV has been popular in North America for several years, and now it is ready to enter the commercial UAV field, but it is found that there are many competitors. The market competition is very fierce, and the price is low, so we can know what stage the commercial UAV field is in the product life cycle?

   A. Introduction　　B. Growth　　　C. Maturity　　　D. Decline

32. 大疆无人机在北美已经畅销了几年，现在准备进军商用领域。公司发现该市场有非常多的竞争对手，竞争非常激烈，价格也较低。由此可以得知商用无人机领域处于产品生命周期的哪个阶段？

   A. 引入　　　　　B. 成长　　　　C. 成熟　　　　D. 衰退

33. A company deeply understands the needs of its target customers and provides them with products with unique functions. Which of the following strategies has the company adopted?

   A. Differentiation　　B. Cost leadership　　C. Target market　　D. First to market

33. 一家公司深入理解目标客户的需求，为他们提供具备独特功能的产品。该公司采用了以下哪个战略？

   A. 差异化　　　　B. 成本领先　　　C. 目标市场　　　D. 率先上市

34. A musician has created a new popular song and wants to protect his rights. So, what type of intellectual property should he apply for the new song?

   A. Patent　　　B. Trademarks　　　C. Copyright　　　D. Trade secrets

34. 一位音乐家创作了一首新的流行歌曲，他想保护自己的权益。他应该为他的新歌曲申请什么类型的知识产权？

   A. 专利　　　B. 版权　　　C. 商标　　　D. 商业秘密

35. Which of the following is the value of feasibility analysis?

   A. Reduce risk

   B. Estimate project success probability

   C. Identify gaps between existing and required capabilities

   D. All of the above are right

35. 可行性分析的价值是以下哪个？

   A. 降低风险　　　　　　　　　　　B. 预估项目成功概率
   C. 识别现有能力与所需能力之间的差距　　D. 以上皆对

36. Many organizations are undergoing digital transformation. Which of the following statements is correct about digital transformation?

   A. It means upgrading information technology, such as hardware, software or digital platforms

   B. It is to collect, analyze and use big data

   C. Transform the heart of business processes not only with information technology, but also with digital capabilities

   D. All reports need to be data-based

36. 许多组织都在进行数字化转型。关于数字化转型，以下哪个说法是正确的？

   A. 就是将信息技术进行升级，如硬件、软件或数字平台

   B. 就是收集、分析和利用大数据

   C. 不仅利用信息技术，而且利用数字化能力对经营流程核心进行转型

   D. 所有的报告都需要用数据说话

37. Which of the following is the sunk cost?

   A. Cost already invested in product development

   B. Factory construction cost

   C. Salary of R&D personnel

   D. Outsourcing costs spent on failed projects

37. 以下哪个是沉没成本？

   A. 在产品开发中已经投入的成本   B. 工厂建设成本

   C. 研发人员工资   D. 在失败项目上花费的外包费用

38. Which of the following statements is wrong about the product roadmap and technology roadmap?

   A. Product roadmap is a plan that matches the specific solutions of product innovation with short-term and long-term business objectives to achieve these objectives. The technology roadmap is an important supplement to the product roadmap

   B. The purpose of a product roadmap is to communicate direction and progress to internal teams and external stakeholders. Technology roadmaps are an important complement to the product roadmap in aligning technology planning and development to overall planning for the launch of a single product or a range of products.

   C. The product roadmap must be prepared before the technical roadmap

   D. The development of product roadmap is a continuous process throughout the product life cycle. The technology roadmap is particularly important for companies that strategically attach great importance to innovation and the technologies needed for product innovation

38. 关于产品路线图和技术路线图，以下哪个说法是错误的？

   A. 产品路线图是将产品创新的具体解决方案与短期、长期经营目标相匹配以实现这些目标的计划。技术路线图是对产品路线图的重要补充

   B. 产品路线图目的是向团队内、外部相关方就产品方向和进展进行沟通。技术路线图是产品路线图的重要补充，它将技术规划和开发与单个产品或一系列产品发布的总体规划协调起来

   C. 产品路线图一定要先于技术路线图制定

   D. 制定产品路线图是贯穿产品生命周期的持续过程。对战略上极为重视创新以及产品创新所需技术的公司而言，技术路线图尤为重要

39. In product management, the BCG growth-share matrix can be used to analyze the product portfolio. What two dimensions does it consist of?

   A. Market and products
   B. Market share and total market growth
   C. Technology and risk
   D. Technology and business model

39. 在产品管理中,可以用波士顿矩阵来分析产品组合。波士顿矩阵由哪两个维度组成?

   A. 市场和产品
   B. 市场份额和市场增长率
   C. 技术和风险
   D. 技术和商业模式

40. Select 30-40 customers and investigate their brand familiarity and preference for a specific product category. Distribute promotional materials to these customers, give them a small sum of money, and then invite them to the store. There, they can buy any product. This method is used to test the effectiveness of promotional materials. This is an example of which of the following methods?

   A. Sales wave research
   B. Simulated test marketing
   C. Controlled test marketing
   D. Brand promotion

40. 选出30~40位客户,调查他们对某个特定产品类别的品牌熟悉度和偏好。将产品促销材料发放给这些客户,给他们一小笔钱,然后邀请他们前往商店。在那里,他们可以购买任何产品。该方法用于测试促销材料的有效性。这是以下什么方法的例子?

   A. 销售波调研
   B. 模拟试销
   C. 受控试销
   D. 品牌推广

41. Which of the following is not a key success factor of product innovation?

   A. Strong market orientation
   B. Senior management support
   C. Making full use of core competencies
   D. Lightweight team structure

41. 以下哪个不是产品创新关键成功因素?

   A. 强烈的市场导向
   B. 高级管理层的支持
   C. 核心能力的充分利用
   D. 轻量型团队结构

42. In an organization, who is responsible for establishing the product innovation process and training of new staff members and talent development to support innovation?

   A. Process manager
   B. Process owner

C. Process champion　　　　　　D. Scrum master

42. 在一个组织中,谁负责建立产品创新流程、培训新员工和培养创新人才以支持创新？

　　A. 流程经理　　B. 流程负责人　　C. 流程倡导者　　D. 敏捷教练

43. Which method is based on functional analysis?

　　A. PESTLE analysis　　　　　　B. Empathy analysis
　　C. Value analysis　　　　　　　D. Portfolio analysis

43. 哪种方法以功能分析为基础？

　　A. PESTLE 分析　　B. 移情分析　　C. 价值分析　　D. 组合分析

44. What is the most important job of the product manager?

　　A. Product development　　　　B. Marketing
　　C. Integration management　　　D. Technical research

44. 产品经理最重要的工作是什么？

　　A. 产品开发　　B. 市场营销　　C. 统筹管理　　D. 技术研究

45. With more and more attention being paid to sustainability, some organizations evaluate their performance from the three dimensions of financial, social and environmental. What is this called?

　　A. Triple bottom line　　　　　B. Balanced scorecard
　　C. Product strategy triangle　　D. Triple constraint

45. 随着可持续性越来越得到重视,一些企业从财务、社会和环境三个维度评估企业绩效,这被称作什么？

　　A. 三重底线　　　　　　B. 平衡计分卡
　　C. 产品战略三角　　　　D. 三重约束

46. Why should the time value of money be considered in the financial analysis of product innovation projects?

　　A. It allows the team to calculate the sales required for return on investment

B. A dollar that you invest today will bring you more than a dollar next year—having the dollar now provides you with an investment opportunity

C. The concept of time value of capital enables corporations to discover the final opportunity cost of projects

D. Help to consider various direct expenses and variable costs related to new products waiting to be launched

46. 在产品创新项目的财务分析中，为什么要考虑资金的时间价值？

A. 它允许团队计算投资回报率所需的销售额

B. 今天投资 1 美元，明年得到的回报会比 1 美元更多。也就是说，现在的钱可以提供投资机会

C. 资金时间价值的理念可以让企业发现项目的最终机会成本

D. 帮助考虑新产品等待上市相关的各种直接支出和可变成本

47. A pet product development team is developing product design specifications. What are the characteristics of product design specifications?

A. Provide quantitative and objective standards

B. From customer demand

C. Challenging

D. Both A and B

47. 一个宠物用品开发团队正在制定产品设计规格。产品设计规格有何特点？

A. 提供量化与客观的标准 B. 来自客户需求

C. 具有挑战性 D. A 和 B 选项

48. What is the most used tool in the project evaluation tools used by companies?

A. Scoring methods B. Option pricing

C. Quality Function Deployment D. Payback periods

48. 在企业所采用的项目评估工具中，用得最多的是什么工具？

A. 评分法 B. 期权定价

C. 质量功能展开 D. 投资回收期

49. According to the suggestions of Miles and Snow, what strategies should corporations that dare to take risks and are eager to explore new opportunities adopt?

    A. Analyzer   B. Reactor   C. Defender   D. Prospector

49. 根据迈尔斯和斯诺的建议，敢于承担风险并渴求探索新机会的企业应采用什么策略？

    A. 分析者   B. 回应者   C. 防御者   D. 探索者

50. Integrating new technologies and business models to form architectural innovation helps organizations develop strong competitiveness. This approach is mainly inspired by which strategy framework?

    A. Pisano innovation landscape map   B. Porter's competitive strategy
    C. Ansoff matrix   D. Miles and Snow strategy framework

50. 将新技术和新商业模式进行结合，形成架构型创新，帮助组织形成强大的竞争力。该做法主要受到了以下哪个战略框架的启发？

    A. 皮萨诺创新景观图   B. 波特竞争战略
    C. 安索夫矩阵   D. 迈尔斯和斯诺战略框架

51. ABC Company needs to develop a plan for the maintenance and development of technologies that supports the future growth of the organization and aids the achievement of its strategic goals. What is this strategy?

    A. Corporate strategy   B. Technology strategy
    C. Platform strategy   D. Business strategy

51. ABC 公司需要制定一份有关技术开发和技术维护的计划，能够支持组织的未来发展，有助于组织战略目标的实现。这是什么战略？

    A. 公司战略   B. 技术战略   C. 平台战略   D. 经营战略

52. Social media is increasingly valued and applied by product manager and marketing professionals. What advantages of social media for market research?

    A. Provides direct and immediate contact with current and potential markets
    B. If selected carefully, specific social media allows targeting to a very narrow audience

C. Provides the opportunity to engage with a loyal following of supporters or lead users

D. All of the above are right

52. 社交媒体越来越受到产品管理者和市场营销人士的重视和应用。当社交媒体被用于市场调研时，其有什么优点？

　　A. 可以与现有及潜在市场进行直接、即时的联系

　　B. 通过甄选，某些特定的社交媒体可用来与某些特定的客户建立联系

　　C. 有机会与忠诚的支持者或领先用户进行互动

　　D. 以上皆对

53. The product team of Gox pays close attention to the following aspects, including individuals and interactions, working software, customer collaboration and responding to change. These are the core elements in which of the following processes?

　　A. Stage-Gate　　　　　　　　　B. Integrated Product Development

　　C. Agile　　　　　　　　　　　　D. Waterfall model

53. Gox 公司的产品团队非常关注以下几个方面，包括个体和交互、可运行的软件、客户合作和拥抱变化。这些是以下哪个流程中的核心要素？

　　A. 门径流程　　　　　　　　　　B. 集成产品开发

　　C. 敏捷方法　　　　　　　　　　D. 瀑布模型

54. Jerry is the marketing director of a company and he is ready to develop a marketing strategy. What is the basis for guiding the formulation of marketing strategy and requiring it to be consistent with it?

　　A. Product innovation process

　　B. Instructions of the Chief Executive Officer

　　C. Product Innovation charter

　　D. Business objectives of the organization

54. 杰瑞是一家公司的营销负责人，他准备制定营销战略。指导营销战略制定并要求与其保持一致的基础是什么？

　　A. 产品创新流程　　　　　　　　B. 首席执行官的指示

　　C. 产品创新章程　　　　　　　　D. 组织经营目标

55. A company develops a new product. The life cycle of the product is 5 years. It is estimated that 5000 units will be sold every year. The R&D and development cost is $60000, the single unit cost is $5, and the delisting cost at the end of the product life cycle is $15000. So, what is the life cycle cost of each product?

   A. $5   B. $5.5   C. $7.5   D. $8

55. 一家公司开发一款新产品。该产品生命周期为5年，预计每年销售5000台，研发和开发成本60000美元，每台成本5美元，产品生命周期末期退市成本15000美元。那么，每台产品的生命周期成本为多少？

   A. 5美元   B. 5.5美元   C. 7.5美元   D. 8美元

56. Corporate strategy is the core of leading an organization, and what can it be defined as?

   A. How to launch new products to the market and sell them for the first time
   B. Vision of the organization
   C. The company's business field and the company's primary plan on how to compete and win the competitive advantage
   D. Implementation mode of innovation process

56. 公司战略是引领组织的核心，它可以被定义成什么？

   A. 向市场推出新产品并进行首次销售的方法
   B. 组织的愿景
   C. 公司所在的业务领域以及公司如何进行竞争并赢得竞争优势的首要计划
   D. 创新流程的实施方式

57. A team uses Agile methods to develop software. Which of the following roles is responsible for sorting the priorities and requirements of the product backlog?

   A. Product manager   B. Project manager
   C. Product owner   D. Product leader

57. 一个团队采用敏捷方法开发软件，以下哪个角色负责对产品待办列表的优先级和需求进行排序？

   A. 产品经理   B. 项目经理
   C. 产品负责人   D. 产品领导者

58. In portfolio management, there are usually four types of projects. What are the characteristics of breakthrough projects?

   A. Expanded the scope of product application

   B. Projects derived from existing products

   C. Significantly different from existing products

   D. Product development projects that optimize processes and reduce prices

58. 在组合管理中，通常有四种类型的项目。其中，突破型项目有何特点？

   A. 扩大了产品应用范围　　　　　　B. 在现有产品基础上衍生的项目

   C. 与现有产品有着显著的不同　　　D. 优化流程、降低价格的产品开发项目

59. What is the strategic bucket method in portfolio management?

   A. A top-down approach to ensure that the allocation of each project type reflects the business strategy

   B. A method for visualizing portfolio balance

   C. A bottom-up approach to creating a list of project priorities aligning with strategy

   D. A financial method used to replace NPV or discounted cash flow

59. 项目组合管理中的战略桶方法是指什么？

   A. 一种自上而下法，以确保在各个项目类型上的分配能够反映经营战略

   B. 一种用于将组合平衡可视化的方法

   C. 一种自下而上法，以创建一个与战略相关的项目优先级列表

   D. 一种用于替代净现值或折现现金流的财务方法

60. YOY expects to improve the organizational product innovation performance. The consultant suggested that the company should adopt benchmarking to improve pertinently. What are the advantages of benchmarking?

   A. Limited applicability

   B. Clear goals and strong operability

   C. Neglecting one's own characteristics and advantages

   D. Difficulty in obtaining comprehensive information

60. YOY 公司期望能够提高组织产品创新绩效。顾问建议公司采用对标方法进行有针对性的提升。对标的优点是什么？

   A. 适用范围有限 B. 目标明确，操作性强
   C. 忽视了自身的特点和优势 D. 难以获得全面信息

61. XP Company has entered the emerging aircar market and is now preparing to develop a new product. Which role does the company belong to in the innovation strategy of Miles and Snow?

   A. Prospector B. Analyzer C. Defender D. Reactor

61. XP 公司进入了新兴的飞行汽车市场，目前准备开发一款全新的飞行汽车产品。请问公司属于迈尔斯和斯诺创新战略中的哪个角色？

   A. 探索者 B. 分析者 C. 防御者 D. 回应者

62. MK Company has operated a certain product for many years, with a high market share and substantial income. Since this year, the market has grown rapidly. The company is ready to purchase more equipment to expand production and gain more market share. Where is this product in the BCG growth-share matrix?

   A. Low market share, low market growth rate
   B. High market share, low market growth rate
   C. High market share, high market growth rate
   D. Low market share, high market growth rate

62. MK 公司经营某产品多年，市场份额较高，收益颇丰。今年以来，市场快速增长。公司准备购买更多设备扩大生产并获得更多市场份额。该产品处于波士顿矩阵中的什么位置？

   A. 低市场份额，低市场增长率 B. 高市场份额，低市场增长率
   C. 高市场份额，高市场增长率 D. 低市场份额，高市场增长率

63. What is the innovation mode that can lead to significant changes in product functions and ultimately lead to the demise of a certain type of product?

   A. Iterative innovation B. Continuous innovation
   C. Disruptive innovation D. Risk-based innovation

63. 能够导致产品功能发生显著改变，并最终导致当前某类产品消亡的创新方式是什么？

    A. 迭代式创新 B. 延续式创新
    C. 颠覆式创新 D. 风险式创新

64. Who is responsible for developing the business strategy?

    A. Process management department B. Executive team of business unit
    C. Shareholders D. Consultants

64. 谁负责制定经营战略？

    A. 流程管理部门 B. 事业部的高级管理层
    C. 股东 D. 顾问

65. Product innovation performance metrics are divided into two categories: measuring the process of product innovation and measuring the outcomes of product innovation. Which of the following is metrics of product innovation outcomes?

    A. Number of commercialized products per year
    B. Accuracy of achieving milestones in product innovation projects
    C. Time to market
    D. Duration of particular process stages

65. 产品创新度量指标分为度量产品创新过程和度量产品创新结果两类。以下哪个属于度量产品创新结果的指标？

    A. 每年商业化产品数量 B. 产品创新项目中的里程碑到达准确率
    C. 上市时间 D. 某一阶段的持续时间

66. Cooper believes that in product innovation, investment should be closely related to risk. What are the rules he proposes?

    A. As risks decrease then reduce investment B. Both C and D
    C. As risks decrease then increase investment D. As risks increase then reduce investment

66. 库珀认为，在产品创新中，投资应与风险密切相关，他建议的规则是什么？

    A. 风险降低，投资下降 B. C 和 D 选项

C. 风险降低，投资增加 D. 风险加大，投资下降

67. Which of the following is the limitation of the Stage-Gate process?

   A. Provide guidelines and constraints for product innovation

   B. Emphasize quality decision-making

   C. May become overly bureaucratic

   D. Applicable to many types of organizations

67. 以下哪个是门径流程的局限性？

   A. 为产品创新提供准则和约束   B. 强调高质量的决策

   C. 有可能变得过度官僚化   D. 适用于多种类型的组织

68. When the sales and profit of the product increase, the number of customers and competitors increases, and the cost per customer decreases, what stage is the product life cycle in?

   A. Introduction stage   B. Growth stage

   C. Maturity stage   D. Decline stage

68. 当产品的销量和利润上升，客户数量增加，竞争对手也越来越多，单位客户成本下降时，说明处于产品生命周期的什么阶段？

   A. 引入阶段   B. 成长阶段   C. 成熟阶段   D. 衰退阶段

69. What industries and fields can the House of Quality be used for?

   A. Multiple industries   B. Manufacturing industry

   C. Software industry   D. Service industry

69. 质量屋可用于什么行业和领域？

   A. 多个行业   B. 制造业   C. 软件业   D. 服务业

70. What is the main purpose of the product roadmap?

   A. To illustrate that over time, a product or service can bring profits to the corporation throughout the product life cycle

   B. Used to describe the current status of the product when it is introduced to the public

   C. Explain the direction and progress of product development and marketing to internal and external interested parties

D. Demonstrate the full technology of the product or service, marketing and strategic objectives

70. 制定产品路线图的主要目的是什么？

   A. 为了说明随时间推移，一种产品或服务在整个产品生命周期可以为企业带来利润

   B. 在产品向公众推出时用来描述产品的当前状态

   C. 向内部和外部相关方说明产品开发与上市的方向和进度

   D. 展示产品或服务的全部技术、营销以及战略目标

71. What should a product manager do after the product is launched?

   A. Track the progress, monitor whether the product establish its position in the market, analyze product sales data and customer feedback, and help improving marketing strategy

   B. Transfer the after-launch work to the sales department

   C. Quit from this product project in order to take over another new product innovation project

   D. All of the above are wrong

71. 产品上市后，产品经理应该如何做？

   A. 跟踪进展，监督产品是否在市场中立足，分析产品销售数据和客户反馈，帮助优化营销战略

   B. 将上市后的工作移交给销售部门

   C. 从该产品项目中退出，以便接手另一个新产品创新项目

   D. 以上皆错

72. David used a bubble diagram when reporting the company's product portfolio to senior management. What does bubble diagram help senior management know?

   A. Market share of the company

   B. Feasibility of the projects

   C. Alignment of the portfolio with the organization's overall strategy with respect to risk

   D. Comparison with competitors

72. 在向高管层汇报公司产品组合情况时，大卫采用了气泡图。气泡图有助于管理层了解什么？

   A. 公司的市场份额

   B. 项目的可行性

C. 在考虑风险的基础上，快速了解组合与总体战略的一致性

D. 与竞争对手的比较

73. A company needs to do market research on UAVs. The method they adopted was to let third-party market research institutions select several people from several companies, and then conduct one-to-one interviews, mainly to understand how they use and manage UAVs. What type of market research method is this?

    A. In-depth interviews　　　　　　　　B. Quantitative research
    C. Focus groups　　　　　　　　　　　D. Secondary market research

73. 一家公司要做无人机的市场调研。他们采用的方法是让第三方市场调研机构选择几家公司中的几个人，然后进行一对一的谈话，主要目的是了解他们如何使用和管理无人机。这是什么类型的市场调研方法？

    A. 深度访谈　　　　　　　　　　B. 定量研究
    C. 焦点小组　　　　　　　　　　D. 二级市场调研

74. The new energy automobile development team uses the Kano model to classify the product quality elements. The team found that the longer the battery life, the higher the customer satisfaction. What quality element does this belong to?

    A. Attractive quality elements　　　　　　B. One-dimension quality elements
    C. Must-be quality elements　　　　　　　D. Indifferent quality elements

74. 新能源汽车开发团队用卡诺模型对产品属性进行分类。团队发现电池寿命越长，消费者的满意度越高。电池寿命属于什么质量属性？

    A. 魅力属性　　　B. 期望属性　　　C. 必备属性　　　D. 无差异属性

75. Which of the following statements is correct about the lightweight team in product innovation?

    A. The skill level of team members is not important, they are just full-time equivalent
    B. Resources do not belong exclusively to the project team, and functional work has higher priority than project work
    C. Since time to market is critical to success, the team must move forward at a high speed
    D. The project manager formally guides the work of team members, with high resource concentration

75. 关于产品创新中的轻量型团队，以下哪个说法是正确的？

　　A. 团队成员的技能水平并不重要，他们只是全职人力工时数

　　B. 资源并非专属于项目团队，职能工作比项目工作的优先级更高

　　C. 由于上市时间对成功而言至关重要，因此团队必须高速前进

　　D. 项目经理正式指导团队成员的工作，资源集中度高

76. What is the core competencies?

　　A. The ability to provide one or more competitive advantages to the organization in the process of creating and delivering value for customers

　　B. Existing competencies in the team or organization

　　C. All functions of new products to meet customer needs

　　D. Personnel provided by one company for other companies

76. 核心竞争力是什么？

　　A. 在为客户创造和交付价值的过程中，为组织提供一个或多个竞争优势的能力

　　B. 团队或组织中已有的能力

　　C. 新产品满足客户需要的全部功能

　　D. 一家公司为其他公司提供的人员

77. What aspect of the corporate culture does Agile better reflect?

　　A. Competition　　　B. Empathy　　　C. Collaboration　　　D. Freedom

77. 敏捷方法较好地体现了企业文化中的哪个方面？

　　A. 竞争　　　B. 移情　　　C. 协作　　　D. 自由

78. Dennis found that the competition for resources among the company's projects was serious. As the portfolio management leader, what should he use as the basis for decision-making when resources compete?

　　A. Willingness of interested parties　　　B. CEO's preference

　　C. Degree of competing resources　　　D. Innovation strategy and goals

78. 丹尼斯发现公司项目间争夺资源的情况很严重。作为组合管理负责人，当发生资源争夺时，他应该将什么作为决策依据？

   A. 相关方的意愿　　　　　　　　　B. CEO 的偏好
   C. 资源争夺的程度　　　　　　　　D. 创新战略和目标

79. Which stage in the product life cycle does skimming pricing apply to?

   A. Introduction stage　　　　　　B. Growth stage
   C. Maturity stage　　　　　　　　D. Decline stage

79. 撇脂定价法适用于产品生命周期中的哪个阶段？

   A. 引入阶段　　B. 成长阶段　　C. 成熟阶段　　D. 衰退阶段

80. The general reasons for the failure of portfolio management are as follows?

   A. Too many breakthrough projects
   B. Less derivative projects
   C. Lack of support, too few resources
   D. More platform projects, less derivative projects

80. 项目组合管理失败的一般原因是什么？

   A. 突破型项目太多　　　　　　　　B. 衍生型项目较少
   C. 缺乏支持，资源太少　　　　　　D. 平台型项目多，衍生型项目少

81. A company attaches great importance to the work efficiency of its employees, and requires that the email should be replied on the same day, even if it is midnight. Otherwise, it will receive feedback that the email response is not timely. What aspect of the company does this reflect?

   A. Culture　　B. Climate　　C. Strategy　　D. Values

81. 一家企业非常注重公司员工的工作效率，要求当天邮件当天回复，即使半夜发出的邮件也要当天得到回复，否则就会收到邮件回复不及时的反馈。这体现了公司的哪个方面？

   A. 文化　　B. 氛围　　C. 战略　　D. 价值观

82. A company is already in the stage of product introduction. What stage will it usually go through before reaching the early mass market?
    A. Fuzzy front end   B. Innovator's dilemma
    C. Crossing the chasm   D. Go to market

82. 一家公司已经处于产品引入阶段，在进入早期大众市场前，通常会经历什么阶段？
    A. 模糊前端   B. 创新者窘境   C. 跨越鸿沟   D. 走向市场

83. S company focuses on building shared beliefs among the employees and attaches great importance to talent incentive and emphasizes to provide an environment for talents to succeed together with the company. Which aspect does this belong to?
    A. Culture   B. Climate   C. Strategy   D. Vision

83. S 公司强调在公司员工中建立共同信念，同时非常重视人才激励，强调给人才提供和企业一起走向成功的环境，这属于以下哪个方面？
    A. 文化   B. 氛围   C. 战略   D. 愿景

84. A company developed an artificial intelligence software for the medical industry, but it is not clear what negative impact the voice function will have on patients. The market prospect of this product is very broad, and the company also hopes to obtain a higher market share in this field. In the BCG growth-share matrix, which category does this product belong to?
    A. Cash cows   B. Question marks   C. Stars   D. Dogs

84. 一家公司开发一款人工智能软件，应用于医疗行业，但尚不清楚语音功能对病人会产生什么负面影响。该产品的市场前景非常广阔，公司也有希望在该领域获得较高的市场份额。在波士顿矩阵中，该产品会属于哪一类？
    A. 现金牛   B. 问题   C. 明星   D. 瘦狗

85. DMAIC is the acronym of the five phases of Six Sigma. What does A stand for?
    A. Adapt   B. Analyze   C. Achieve   D. Adjust

85. DMAIC 是六西格玛五个阶段的首字母缩略词，其中的 A 代表什么？

   A. 改造　　　　　B. 分析　　　　　C. 实现　　　　　D. 调整

86. What is the recommended method for project portfolio management if you want to get more product ideas and projects from employees?

   A. Top-down approach　　　　　　B. Strategic bucket
   C. Middle expansion approach　　　D. Bottom-up approach

86. 在开展项目组合管理时，如果希望从员工身上获得更多的产品创意和项目，推荐采用什么方法？

   A. 自上而下法　　　　　B. 战略桶
   C. 中间展开法　　　　　D. 自下而上法

87. After adopting the product platform strategy, Volkswagen has significantly reduced the model of parts, shortened the development duration of new products, and saved the development cost. In addition, what major advantages can the product platform strategy bring?

   A. Change the value proposition of the product
   B. Expand new markets
   C. Based on the product platform, quickly and continuously launch a series of derivative products
   D. Closer customer relationship

87. 大众汽车公司采用了产品平台战略后，显著减少了零部件型号，缩短了新产品开发周期，节约了开发成本。此外，产品平台战略还能带来什么主要优势？

   A. 改变产品的价值主张
   B. 拓展新的市场
   C. 基于产品平台，快速、连续地推出一系列衍生产品
   D. 客户关系更为密切

88. What is the difference between the new school approach and the old school approach of go-to-market?

   A. The new school approach is to make products first, and then consider how to sell the linear process
   B. The new school approach is no different from the old one

C. The new school approach is an iterative process that comprehensively considers "where", "who", "what", "how" and other elements

D. The old school approach is an iterative process in which "where", "who", "what", "how" and other elements are considered as a whole

88. 关于走向市场战略，新式做法与老式做法的区别在哪里？

A. 新式做法是先做出产品，然后再考虑如何出售产品的线性化流程

B. 新式做法和老式做法没有什么区别

C. 新式做法是将"哪里""谁""什么""如何"等要素进行统筹考虑的迭代式流程

D. 老式做法是将"哪里""谁""什么""如何"等要素进行统筹考虑的迭代式流程

89. Nestle "takes the values based on respect as guidance, cooperates with partners and interested parties, creates shared value in all activities of the company, contributes to the society and ensures the long-term success of the company's business." What is this practice?

A. Integrate sustainability into product innovation

B. Incorporate benefits into product innovation

C. Incorporate win-win thinking into product innovation

D. Crowdsourcing

89. 雀巢公司"以基于尊重的价值观为指导，与合作方和相关方进行合作，在公司的所有活动中创造共享价值，为社会做出贡献的同时确保公司业务长期成功"。该做法体现了什么？

A. 将可持续发展纳入产品创新中　　B. 将收益纳入产品创新中

C. 将共赢思维纳入产品创新中　　　D. 众包

90. Cathy is doing demand and sales forecasting. Which of the following tools can she use, except for_____.

A. Bass model　　　　　　　　　　B. ATAR model

C. Purchase intention methods　　　D. Simulated test marketing

90. 凯西在开展需求与销售预测工作，她可以采用以下这些工具，除了_____。

A. 巴斯模型　　　B. ATAR 模型　　　C. 购买意向法　　　D. 模拟试销

91. What does the product strategy triangle contain?

   A. Business, user experience and technology

   B. Technology, product and market

   C. Scope, time and cost

   D. Market needs, business needs and value proposition

91. 产品战略三角包含什么？

   A. 经营、用户体验和技术   B. 技术、产品和市场

   C. 范围、进度和成本   D. 市场需求、经营需求和价值主张

92. The CEO of IDEO, Tim Brown, introduced a people-centered innovation method, which draws inspiration from the designer's tool library and combines human needs, technical possibilities and requirements for commercial success. What is this innovative approach?

   A. Kansei engineering   B. Emotional analysis

   C. Design thinking   D. Emotional design

92. IDEO 公司 CEO 蒂姆·布朗介绍了一种以人为中心的创新方法，该方法从设计者的工具库中汲取灵感，将人的需求、技术可能性和商业成功要求结合起来。这是什么创新方法？

   A. 感性工学   B. 情感分析   C. 设计思维   D. 情感化设计

93. In the portfolio evaluation criteria, which of the following is the highest level?

   A. NPV, payback period and revenue

   B. Risk, finance and strategy

   C. Technical risk, product risk and market risk

   D. Growth potential, strategic direction and positioning

93. 在组合评估标准中，以下哪个是最高阶标准？

   A. 净现值、投资回收期和收入   B. 风险、财务和战略

   C. 技术风险、产品风险、市场风险   D. 增长潜力、战略方向、定位

94. An ice cream company with a long history, strong technology and manufacturing capacity should carry out a simple product line extension project. The development complexity of

this project is very low and the probability of success is high. The company is going to adopt a Stage-Gate process. As a product manager, which of the following do you suggest?

　　A. Simplified 4-stage gate process　　B. Typical 5-stage gate process
　　C. More detailed 10-stage gate process　　D. Extended 8-stage gate process

94. 一家历史悠久、技术和制造能力都较强的冰激凌公司要进行一个简单的产品线延伸项目。该产品开发复杂度很低，成功概率较高。该公司准备采用门径流程，作为产品经理，你的建议是以下哪个？

　　A. 简化的 4 阶段门径流程　　B. 典型的 5 阶段门径流程
　　C. 更为详尽的 10 阶段门径流程　　D. 扩展的 8 阶段门径流程

95. Jim is going to formulate the company strategy. He considers the macro elements through PESTLE analysis. What are these macro elements?

　　A. Product, economy, society, technology, law and environment
　　B. Politics, economy, society, technology, law and environment
　　C. Politics, economy, strategy, technology, law and environment
　　D. Politics, economy, society, technology, logistics and environment

95. 吉姆准备制定公司战略，他通过 PESTLE 分析来考虑宏观要素。这些宏观要素都包含什么？

　　A. 产品、经济、社会、技术、法律和环境
　　B. 政治、经济、社会、技术、法律和环境
　　C. 政治、经济、战略、技术、法律和环境
　　D. 政治、经济、社会、技术、物流和环境

96. In the balanced scorecard, which dimension does the employee turnover rate, employee core competence, employee satisfaction and other indicators belong to?

　　A. Finance　　B. Customer
　　C. Internal processes　　D. Learning and growth

96. 在平衡计分卡中，员工流失率、员工核心能力、员工满意度等指标属于哪个维度？

　　A. 财务　　B. 客户　　C. 内部流程　　D. 学习与成长

97. Which of the objectives of portfolio management is to maximize portfolio value by allocating resources?

   A. Value maximization
   B. Project balance
   C. Strategic alignment
   D. Pipeline balance

97. 通过配置资源实现组合价值最大化，这属于组合管理目标中的哪一个？

   A. 价值最大
   B. 项目平衡
   C. 战略一致
   D. 管道平衡

98. The quantification level in the portfolio scoring rules is conducive to better selection of items and consistency of scoring. Which of the following scoring rules has the highest degree of quantification?

   A. Sales high and low
   B. Sales very high, high, medium, low, very low
   C. 10 represents the sales of 1 million pcs; 9 represents the sales of 900,000 pcs; and so on
   D. Sales high, medium and low

98. 组合评分规则中的量化水平有助于更好地对项目进行选择和评分。以下哪个评分规则量化程度最高？

   A. 销量高、低
   B. 销量非常高、高、中、低、非常低
   C. 10分代表销量100万台，9分代表销量90万台，以此类推
   D. 销量高、中、低

99. Sam plans to use systems engineering in the development of a large and complex product. He needs to understand the advantages and disadvantages of this method. Which of the following is the disadvantage of systems engineering?

   A. Decisions related to design are very detailed and can be made in advance with the deep participation of customers
   B. There are learning opportunities early in the project and knowledge can be disseminated to all interested parties
   C. Easily identify and manage upcoming changes
   D. Long term planning and/or development risks can also cause solutions to become obsolete

99. 山姆准备在一款大型复杂产品开发中采用系统工程，他要了解该方法的优缺点。以下哪个是系统工程的缺点？

   A. 与设计相关的决策非常详细，并可在客户深度参与下提前做出决策

   B. 在项目早期就有学习机会，可将知识传播给所有相关方

   C. 容易识别和管理即将发生的变化

   D. 长期计划或开发风险会造成解决方案过时

100. What to do during the stage of embodiment design?

   A. Provide more aesthetics, form and function details

   B. Transforming qualitative design concepts into quantitative specifications

   C. More detailed initial design specifications

   D. Provide detailed specifications for large-scale, mass production and marketing of products

100. 实体化设计阶段做什么？

   A. 提供更多的外观、形态和功能细节

   B. 将定性设计概念转化为定量规格

   C. 将初始设计规格更为详细化

   D. 为产品规模化、批量生产和上市提供详细的规格

101. Several students from Stanford University School of Design want to start up a business together. They are going to draw a business model canvas. They considered customer segments, channels, customer relationships, revenue streams, key activities, key resources, key partners, and cost structure, but what element did they miss?

   A. Target market   B. Value propositions
   C. Market potential   D. Product pricing

101. 斯坦福大学设计学院的几个学生想一起创业。他们准备一起绘制商业模式画布。他们考虑了客户细分、渠道通路、客户关系、收入来源、关键业务、核心资源、重要合作、成本结构，但是他们遗漏了什么要素？

   A. 目标市场   B. 价值主张   C. 市场潜力   D. 产品定价

102. Why should sprints be used in the Agile product innovation approach?

   A. Continuous and infinite changeability

B. Team response to unpredictability through incremental and iterative work cadences

C. Integrated product development

D. Part of the Lean product innovation process

102. 在敏捷产品创新方法中，为什么要采用冲刺？

   A. 连续和无限的可变性

   B. 通过增量和迭代的工作，团队可以应对不可预知性

   C. 集成产品开发

   D. 是精益产品创新方法的一部分

103. What is a unit of work small enough to be completed by the team in one sprint iteration called?

   A. Product backlog item　　　　　B. Scrum

   C. Concept evaluation　　　　　　D. TPS

103. 在一个冲刺中，由团队完成的足够小的工作单位被称作什么？

   A. 产品待办项　　　　　　　　　B. Scrum

   C. 概念评估　　　　　　　　　　D. 丰田生产方式

104. Jack has been assigned to a product innovation project that is in the early stages of idea generation. How can Jack apply TRIZ to this project?

   A. Use resource allocation tools to allocate cross functional resources to each aspect of the problem

   B. Use the new customer first principle to find new markets for existing products

   C. Use the voice of customers to actively listen to their needs

   D. Using the segmentation principle to divide an object into independent parts

104. 杰克被分配到一个在早期构思阶段的产品创新项目中。杰克如何在该项目中应用发明问题解决理论（TRIZ）？

   A. 使用资源配置工具，将跨功能资源分配到问题的每个方面

   B. 使用新客户优先原则，为现有产品寻找新的市场

   C. 使用客户之声，积极地倾听客户的需求

   D. 用分割原理将一个物体分成多个独立部分

105. Carl is preparing to manage a product development project. He learned that a project typically involves five process groups, which of the following is correct?

   A. Initiating, planning, executing, monitoring & controlling, and closing
   B. Define, measure, analyze, improve, and control
   C. Empathize, define, ideate, prototype, and test
   D. Forming, storming, norming, performing, and adjourning

105. 卡尔准备管理一个产品开发项目。他了解到，一个项目通常包括五个过程组，以下哪个是正确的？

   A. 启动、规划、执行、监控、收尾
   B. 定义、测量、分析、改进、控制
   C. 移情、定义、创意、原型、测试
   D. 形成、震荡、规范、成熟、解散

106. Martin Eriksson defined the intersection between the following three as the scope of product management, namely user experience, technology and what?

   A. Function   B. Business   C. Market   D. Benefits

106. 马丁·埃里克森将以下三者之间的交汇点定义为产品管理的范围，分别是用户体验、技术和什么？

   A. 功能   B. 经营   C. 市场   D. 收益

107. What is the method to pivot the deodorizing materials in the cat litter into a total deodorizing cat litter product?

   A. Zoom-in pivot
   B. Zoom-out pivot
   C. Value capture pivot
   D. Business architecture pivot

107. 将猫砂中的除臭材料转型为完全除臭型猫砂产品，采用的是什么转型方式？

   A. 放大式转型
   B. 缩小式转型
   C. 价值获取转型
   D. 商业架构转型

108. According to 2011 Sustainability and Innovation Global Executive Study (Haanaes et al., 2012), what the percentage of the surveyed organizations included sustainability permanently on the management agenda and invest in it?

   A. 50%   B. 70%   C. 30%   D. 10%

108. 根据2011年全球可持续性和创新研究（汉拿斯等人，2012年），有多大比例的受访组织将可持续性永久列入管理日程并对其进行投资？

   A. 50% B. 70% C. 30% D. 10%

109. Bob asks the design team to reduce variation in the product without eliminating the causes of the variation or make the product or process insensitive to variation. What kind of design method should the team use?

   A. Robust design B. Quality function deployment
   C. Emotional design D. Design for functionality

109. 鲍勃要求设计团队要在不消除变异原因的情况下减少产品质量的波动。或者使产品或流程对变异不敏感。团队应该采用什么设计方法？

   A. 稳健设计 B. 质量功能展开
   C. 情感化设计 D. 功能性设计

110. Jessica applies Kansei engineering to product design. She focuses on users' subjective feelings about products, such as product color, size and shape, because these factors determine users' preferences. What is the typical feature of this method?

   A. Emphasize quantitative analysis B. Emphasize rational logic
   C. To identify kansei words D. Emphasize product quality

110. 杰西卡应用感性工学进行产品设计。她关注用户对产品的主观感受，诸如产品颜色、大小和形状等，因为这些要素决定了用户偏好。该方法还有一个典型特点是什么？

   A. 强调量化分析 B. 强调理性逻辑
   C. 要识别感性词语 D. 强调产品质量

111. What factors should be considered comprehensively in the design cycle and product life cycle for sustainable design?

   A. Environment B. Society
   C. Economy D. All of the above are right

111. 可持续性设计要求在设计周期和产品生命周期中，综合考虑什么因素？

   A. 环境 B. 社会 C. 经济 D. 以上皆对

112. What is the SPSD framework in the sustainability approach?
    A. Sustainable product and service development. By realizing the sustainable development of products and services in the product life cycle, the provision of products will be transformed into the provision of services to reduce manufacturing
    B. Analyze, report, sort and improve. Advocate ecological design, including environmental assessment, analysis and report, rank relevant factors and propose improvement measures
    C. Guiding principles on materials, design and ecology. Emphasize material selection and its impact on product method, functional design, market demand, price and environment
    D. All of the above are wrong

112. 可持续性方法中的 SPSD 框架是什么？
    A. 可持续产品和服务开发。通过在产品生命周期中实现产品和服务的可持续开发，将提供产品转化为提供服务，以减少制造
    B. 分析、报告、排序和改进。提倡开展生态设计，包括对环境进行评估、分析和报告，对相关因素进行排序并提出改进措施
    C. 关于材料、设计和生态的指导原则。强调材料选择及其对产品方法、功能设计、市场需求、价格和环境的影响
    D. 以上皆错

113. The team structure where the team leader is most like a chief executive officer is?
    A. Heavyweight team   B. Autonomous team
    C. Lightweight team   D. Functional team

113. 在什么类型的团队中，团队领导者最像一个首席执行官？
    A. 重量型团队   B. 自治型团队   C. 轻量型团队   D. 职能型团队

114. What types of market research methods are concept testing and concept classification?
    A. Qualitative market research methods
    B. Quantitative market research methods
    C. Neither qualitative nor quantitative methods
    D. Secondary market research

114. 概念测试与概念分类是什么类型的市场调研方法？

    A. 定性市场调研方法   B. 定量市场调研方法

    C. 既非定性方法，又非定量方法   D. 二级市场调研方法

115. Which of the following statements is correct about the Triangle test and the Duo-Trio test?

    A. A duo-trio test, includes three samples, including two that are identical and one that is different. Triangle tests compare two samples to a reference. One of the samples is identical to the reference

    B. Triangle tests, include three samples, including two that are identical and one that is different. A duo-trio test compares two samples to a reference. One of the samples is identical to the reference.

    C. Duo-trio test is to conduct two times triangle test

    D. Triangle test is a simplified approach of duo-trio test

115. 关于三点检验和二三点检验，以下哪个说法是正确的？

    A. 三点检验是将两个样本与一个对照样本进行比较，找出与对照样本相同的那一个。二三点检验则是三个样本中有两个是相同的，要找出不同的那一个

    B. 三点检验是三个样本中的两个是相同的，要找出不同的那一个。二三点检验则是将两个样本与一个对照样本进行比较，找出与对照样本相同的那一个

    C. 二三点检验就是做两次三点检验

    D. 三点检验是简化版的二三点检验

116. Which of the following is not a feature of systems engineering?

    A. Interdisciplinary

    B. Define the "problem" from general analysis to specific analysis

    C. Complexity management

    D. Eliminate waste

116. 以下哪个不是系统工程的特点？

    A. 跨学科   B. 通过从一般分析到具体分析来界定"问题"

    C. 复杂度管理   D. 消除浪费

117. What is the purpose of design for assembly?

   A. Consider component assembly, production cost and quality. Simplify product design and reduce assembly costs in the manufacturing process

   B. Consider the ability to inspect, repair, and restore the system in the event of product failure

   C. Minimize product cost and production time while ensuring quality standards

   D. Determine the final performance of the product

117. 可装配性设计的目的是什么？

   A. 考虑零部件组装、生产成本及质量。简化产品设计，降低制造流程中的装配成本

   B. 考虑产品发生故障时，检查、维修和复原系统的能力

   C. 在确保质量标准的同时，尽量减少产品成本和生产时间

   D. 决定产品的最终性能

118. Can control emotional impulses and convert bad emotions into positive energy. Better cope with changes and build a team atmosphere with trust, respect and fairness. Which element of EQ is this?

   A. Self-awareness　　B. Self-regulation　　C. Motivation　　D. Empathy

118. 能够控制情绪冲动和将不良情绪转化为正能量，更好地应对变化，并用信任、尊重和公平来营造团队氛围。这是情商中的哪个要素？

   A. 自我认知　　B. 自我调节　　C. 激励　　D. 移情

119. What is the pivot of a manufacturer producing beverage packaging equipment from the original equipment cost plus profit model to the model of free equipment but charging for packaging materials?

   A. Value capture pivot　　　　B. Engine of growth pivot
   C. Channel pivot　　　　　　　D. Technology pivot

119. 一家生产饮料包装设备的制造商将原来的设备成本加成模式转为设备免费但包装材料收费的模式，这属于什么转型？

   A. 价值获取转型　　　　B. 增长引擎转型
   C. 渠道转型　　　　　　D. 技术转型

120. During the COVID-19 epidemic, many temporary inspection rooms were added at the exit of expressway and railway station. These temporary houses are made of containers. Which of the SCAMPER is used?

   A. E (Eliminate)　　　　　　　　　　B. R (Reverse)
   C. M (Modify)　　　　　　　　　　　D. P (Put to another use)

120. 在新冠疫情期间，在高速路出口和火车站出口处增加了很多临时检查房。这些临时检查房都是用集装箱制作的。这是采用了 SCAMPER 法中的哪个？

   A. R（去除）　　　　　　　　　　　B. B（逆向操作）
   C. M（调整）　　　　　　　　　　　D. D（改变用途）

121. Among the six thinking hats, what is the hat that emphasizes objectivity, facts, data and information?

   A. White　　　　B. Yellow　　　　C. Green　　　　D. Red

121. 在六项思考帽中，强调客观、事实、数据和信息的是什么帽子？

   A. 白色　　　　B. 黄色　　　　C. 绿色　　　　D. 红色

122. What questions should answer when analyzing from left to right when using FAST technical diagram?

   A. Is this a basic function　　　　　B. How is this function carried out
   C. Why do we need this function　　D. Is this function a secondary function

122. 使用 FAST 技术图时，当从左到右进行分析时，要回答什么问题？

   A. 该功能是基本功能吗　　　　　　B. 该功能是如何实现的
   C. 为什么需要该功能　　　　　　　D. 该功能是次要功能吗

123. SK team wants to reduce the product development time in the concept design stage. As the product manager, Joe decides to use the concept scenarios. Which of the following activities can be reduced in the concept scenarios to reduce the product development life cycle?

   A. Identify critical customer requirements
   B. Introduce product functions in user experience

C. Communicate new product features and provide guidance for concept testing

D. All of the above are right

123. SK 团队希望在概念设计阶段缩短产品开发时间。产品经理乔选择了概念场景技术。概念场景可以减少下述哪些活动上所耗费的时间，从而缩短产品开发生命周期？

　　A. 识别关键客户需求　　　　　　　B. 介绍用户体验中的产品功能
　　C. 交流新产品特性及为概念测试提供指导　　D. 以上皆对

124. Which statement is inappropriate about the portfolio performance measurement?

A. The criteria used to assess the project can also be used as portfolio performance metrics

B. The more portfolio performance metrics the better, because they help to comprehensively measure the effectiveness of portfolio management

C. Portfolio performance metrics are used to achieve portfolio balance and effectiveness

D. Portfolio performance metrics are used to promote consistency and balance between portfolio and strategy

124. 关于组合绩效度量，以下哪个说法是不恰当的？

A. 用于评估项目的标准也可以用作绩效度量指标

B. 组合绩效度量指标多多益善，因为有助于全面衡量组合管理的有效性

C. 组合绩效度量指标用于实现组合平衡和有效性

D. 组合绩效度量指标用于促进组合与战略保持一致和平衡

125. What are the characteristics of steady people in the DISC work assessment tool?

A. Non emotional, keen on precise and meticulous work, and rational decisions can be made only on the basis of evaluating complete data

B. Energetic and very talkative, easy to establish social relations, and like to meet new people

C. Even-tempered and calm, valuable traits, more accommodating than many other people and will easily show empathy for others

D. Like fast paced work, making decisions quickly, demanding, action oriented

125. 在 DISC 工作评估工具中，稳健型的人有何特点？

A. 非感性，热衷于精确和细致的工作，在评估完整数据的基础上才会做出理性决策

B. 精力充沛且非常健谈，很容易建立社会关系，并喜欢接触新人

C. 平和、冷静、有价值，比其他人更容易适应环境，也更容易表现出对他人的理解

D. 喜欢快节奏的工作，做决策很快，要求也很高，以行动为导向

126. What are the characteristics of the creator in the Z model for innovation?

   A. Enjoy brainstorming ideas and are energized by considering lots of different ideas

   B. Develop business and project plans, analyze and coordinate all aspects of work

   C. Transform creativity into action, be detail oriented, and focus on delivering the milestones set in the project plan

   D. Develop strategies and implement creativity, and publicize the importance of innovation projects to key stakeholders

126. 在创新Z模型中，开创者有何特点？

   A. 喜欢集思广益，充满活力并生成许多不同的创意

   B. 制定经营和项目计划，对工作的方方面面进行分析和协同

   C. 将创意转化为行动，以细节为导向，专注于交付项目计划设定的里程碑

   D. 制定战略并落实创意，并向关键相关方宣传创新项目的重要性

127. Product development teams often use Beta prototype to test products with component manufacturers and product assemblers to evaluate product reliability. What is the Beta prototype?

   A. Incomplete functional version products for testing purposes

   B. The full functional version of the product is used to evaluate the product before the preproduction stage

   C. Final product. Confirm assembly and manufacturing design, and confirm detailed production process, assembly time, parts outsourcing and integration, production line balance and production improvement

   D. All of the above are wrong

127. 产品开发团队经常会采用贝塔原型与零部件制造方、产品装配方一起测试产品，从而评估产品的可靠性。贝塔原型是什么？

   A. 用于测试目的的非完整功能版本产品

   B. 完整功能版本产品，用于在试生产阶段之前对产品进行评估

   C. 最终版产品，用于确认装配和制造设计，并确认详细的生产工艺、装配时间、零部件外购

与集成、产线平衡和生产改善

D. 以上皆错

128. Ethnography is more effective for which of the following products?

A. Software

B. Industrial products

C. Products used in sensitive or private situations

D. All of the above are right

128. 人种学方法对以下哪些产品较为有效？

A. 软件

B. 工业品

C. 在较为敏感或私密的情境下使用的产品

D. 以上皆对

129. Company A has initiated a new architecture development project. On this architecture, other different components can be integrated to form a series of new products. What kind of project is this?

A. Platform projects   B. Breakthrough projects
C. Support projects   D. Derivative projects

129. A 公司发起了一个新架构开发项目。在该架构上，可以集成其他不同的组件，从而形成一系列新产品。这是什么类型的项目？

A. 平台型项目   B. 突破型项目   C. 支持型项目   D. 衍生型项目

130. Which one is not a quantitative market research method?

A. Sensory testing   B. Eye tracking
C. Biometric feedback   D. Customer site visit

130. 以下哪个不是定量市场调研方法？

A. 感官检验   B. 眼动追踪
C. 生物特征反馈   D. 客户现场访问

131. The product manager and the supplier signed a performance guarantee contract. The supplier will be fined for each day of delay in delivery. What kind of risk response strategy does the product manager use?

    A. Avoid   B. Mitigate   C. Accept   D. Transfer

131. 产品经理和供应商签订了履约保证书。保证书上规定，供应商每延期一天交付就会被处以相应罚金。请问产品经理用了哪种风险应对策略？

    A. 回避   B. 减轻   C. 接受   D. 转移

132. In the heavy-weight team structure, who has more power Compared to the project manager and functional manager?

    A. Just the same   B. Functional manager

    C. Project manager   D. All of the above are wrong

132. 在重量型团队结构中，项目经理和职能经理相比，谁的权力更高？

    A. 一样   B. 职能经理   C. 项目经理   D. 以上皆错

133. The general manager held an important meeting. The meeting invited heads of relevant departments. In the meeting, participants discussed how to promote the company's product innovation by purchasing technology. What strategy are they discussing?

    A. Sales strategy   B. Human resources strategy

    C. Marketing strategy   D. Technology strategy

133. 总经理召开了一次重要会议。该会议邀请了相关部门的负责人。在会议中，与会者讨论如何通过购买技术来推进公司的产品创新。他们讨论的是什么战略？

    A. 销售战略   B. 人力资源战略

    C. 营销战略   D. 技术战略

134. What does the focus area in the product innovation charter cover?

    A. Target market

    B. Key technologies and marketing methods

    C. The strengths and weaknesses of competitors

    D. All of the above are right

134. 产品创新章程中，聚焦领域包含的是什么？

   A. 目标市场
   B. 关键技术和营销方法
   C. 竞争对手的优劣势
   D. 以上皆对

135. What should we do when defining a value proposition?

   A. Focus on benefits rather than features
   B. Focus on features rather than benefits
   C. Focus on price rather than function
   D. Focus on quality rather than price

135. 定义价值主张时，我们应该如何做？

   A. 注重利益而非特性
   B. 注重特性而非利益
   C. 注重价格而非功能
   D. 注重品质而非价格

136. In order to strengthen the innovation work of the company, the senior management initiated the innovation health assessment of the company. What can the innovation health assessment provide for senior management and the team?

   A. Senior manager's decision-making preference
   B. Internal and external benchmarks to identify innovation improvement areas
   C. Information from competitors
   D. Best practices of high-performance companies

136. 为了加强公司的创新工作，高级管理层发起了对企业自身的创新健康状况评估。创新健康状况评估能为管理层和团队提供什么？

   A. 高级管理层的决策偏好
   B. 内部和外部基准，识别创新改进领域
   C. 竞争对手的情况
   D. 高绩效企业的最佳实践

137. Which scenario is the multiple regression analysis widely used?

   A. Predicting, optimizing, supporting, or validating decisions
   B. Avoid risks or prevent mistakes
   C. Provide new insight into the implicit relationship in the studied product variables
   D. All of the above are right

137. 多元回归分析被广泛应用于以下哪个情境？

   A. 预测、优化、支持或验证决策

B. 避免风险或预防错误

C. 为所研究的产品变量中的隐性关系提供新洞察

D. 以上皆对

138. Product innovation is affected by various conditions and factors, some of which are controllable and some of which are uncontrollable. Which of the following is controllable factor?

    A. Competitors   B. Corporate strategy
    C. Government policy   D. International environment

138. 产品创新受到各种条件和因素的影响，有些是可控因素，有些是不可控因素，以下哪个是可控因素？

    A. 竞争对手   B. 公司战略   C. 政府政策   D. 国际环境

139. Jeffrey wants to be a successful product manager. As a consultant, you suggest that he focus on creating a vision, develop a plan, guide product development and what?

    A. Commercialize the products   B. Technical research
    C. Complete specific project work package D. Negotiate with customers

139. 杰弗里希望成为一个成功的产品经理。作为顾问，你会建议他专注于树立愿景、制订计划、指导产品开发以及哪个方面？

    A. 将产品商业化   B. 技术研究
    C. 完成具体的项目工作包   D. 和客户进行谈判

140. Which group should we focus on when crossing the chasm?

    A. Innovators   B. Early adopters and early majority
    C. Laggards   D. Late majority

140. 跨越鸿沟时应重点关注哪个群体？

    A. 创新者   B. 早期采用者和早期大众
    C. 落后者   D. 后期大众

141. What are the core benefits of a product?

    A. Those benefits that truly drive a person to purchase and re purchase a product

B. The basic technology of the product

C. How the product works

D. The length of the product's life cycle

141. 产品的核心利益是什么？

A. 那些真正驱使人们购买和重新购买某种产品的收益

B. 产品的基本技术

C. 产品的工作原理

D. 产品生命周期的长度

142. When Steve used the scoring criteria to assess the projects, he found that the most promising project had the lowest score. What should he do now?

A. Review whether the scoring criteria are complete

B. Review whether the project has lost its original value

C. Both A and B

D. Kill this project

142. 史蒂夫在采用评分标准给项目打分时，发现有个最被看好的项目得分却最低。此时，他应该怎么办？

A. 重新审视评分标准是否完整

B. 重新审视该项目是否已经失去了原有价值

C. A 和 B 选项

D. 淘汰该项目

143. What strategy would normally best use for a "Dogs" product in the BCG's Matrix?

A. Promote the product more widely

B. Put a lot of R&D investment into improving the product

C. Divest or focus on changing the value proposition

D. Reduce the price

143. 在波士顿矩阵中，什么样的策略最适合"瘦狗"产品？

A. 加大产品推销力度   B. 投入大量的研发资金来改进产品

C. 放弃或改变价值主张   D. 降低产品价格

144. Which of the following belongs to disruptive innovation?

   A. iPhone with new screen

   B. More fuel-efficient car engines

   C. More secure cloud technology

   D. Intelligent agricultural machinery equipment that replaces manual operations

144. 以下哪个属于颠覆式创新?

   A. 换了新屏幕的 iPhone 手机　　B. 更节油的汽车发动机

   C. 更加安全的云技术　　D. 取代了人工作业的智能化农业机械设备

145. What is an example of Herman Miller's use of degradable materials and disassembly design in product design?

   A. Design for production　　B. Circular economy

   C. Design for assembly　　D. Design for maintenance

145. 赫曼米勒公司在进行产品设计时采用了可降解材料和可拆解设计。这是一个什么的例子?

   A. 可生产性设计　　B. 循环经济

   C. 可装配性设计　　D. 可维护性设计

146. In the classic Waterfall process, what can be the requirement phase described as?

   A. Actual code is mitten according to project requirements

   B. Ensuring the product meets customer expectations

   C. Use of the customer to identify shortcomings of the product

   D. Understanding what is required to design the product: function, purpose, user needs, etc.

146. 在经典瀑布流程中,需求阶段可以被描述成什么?

   A. 根据项目需求编写实际代码

   B. 确保产品符合客户的期望

   C. 通过客户来识别产品缺点

   D. 了解产品设计所需的功能、目的、用户需求等

147. Some companies like Nike take sustainability as an important part in corporate strategy. Why do they do this?

   A. Integrating sustainability into operations can bring competitive advantages to companies

   B. It just is a "greenwashing" activity

   C. Mandatory requirements of laws and regulations

   D. Sustainability costs a lot and generates few benefits

147. 一些企业，如耐克公司，在制定公司战略时，将可持续性作为其中的重要组成部分。他们为什么这么做？

   A. 将可持续性纳入运营中能够给企业带来竞争优势

   B. 只是一种"漂绿"行为

   C. 法律法规的强制性要求

   D. 可持续性要花费很多成本，很少能产生收益

148. What is a sign of a mature product innovation process within an organization?

   A. Include and integrate stakeholders and senior management it throughout the product innovation process

   B. Use iterative and risk limiting steps to facilitate effective and efficient product innovation

   C. Continuously fill the pipeline with new products

   D. Develop its own best practices from the various process models and experiences

148. 以下哪个是一个组织具有成熟的产品创新流程的标志？

   A. 将相关方和高级管理层结合在整个产品创新流程中

   B. 使用迭代和风险限制步骤去促进有效和高效的产品创新

   C. 持续地在管道中引入新产品

   D. 基于各种产品创新流程模型和经验来开发自己的最佳实践

149. Which of the following is incorrect about the key characteristics of portfolio management?

   A. At the beginning, it is necessary to do a good job in portfolio management and decision-making, because after decision-making, it is no longer possible to continuously review the portfolio

   B. In the portfolio, projects are at different stages of completion

   C. Portfolio management is used to increase the overall odds of success across the full range of projects or products.

D. The resources for product innovation and product management are limited, and resources are often shared with functional departments. Therefore, organizations need to allocate resources to achieve best returns

149. 关于组合管理的关键特征，以下哪个是错误的？

   A. 一开始时就要做好组合管理和决策，因为决策后就无法持续评审组合了
   B. 组合中的项目处于不同的完成阶段
   C. 组合管理旨在提高组合中项目或产品的总体成功率
   D. 产品创新和产品管理的资源有限，常常要与职能部门共享资源。因此组织需要配置好资源，以实现最大回报

150. Tencent advocates integrity, proactive, collaboration and innovation. What does this statement stand for?

   A. Strategy   B. Vision   C. Mission   D. Values

150. 腾讯公司提倡"正直、进取、协作、创造"。该说法代表了公司哪方面的内容？

   A. 战略   B. 愿景   C. 使命   D. 价值观

151. What is the pattern in TRIZ problem-solving matrix?

   A. Identify the specific problem first, test a solution with a targeted customer group, generate more prototypes, select specific solution
   B. Identify the specific problem first, then the general problem and identify a general solution before a specific solution, finally produce the specific solution
   C. First use a general problem with general solution, then select the specific problem to solve
   D. Identify a cross-functional team that can test various product solutions with customers and select the best solution

151. TRIZ 问题解决矩阵的模式是什么？

   A. 首先确定具体问题，然后在一个目标客户群体中测试解决方案，从而生成更多原型，最后选择具体解决方案
   B. 首先确定具体问题，然后是通用问题，在解决具体问题前先解决通用问题，最后产生具体解决方案

C. 首先用通用解决方案解决通用问题，然后选择要解决的具体问题

D. 建立跨职能团队，和客户一起测试各种产品解决方案，最后选择最优解决方案

152. Which of the following is a product risk?

    A. Failure to meet the project funding needs

    B. Core personnel may quit

    C. Unreliable information required for decision-making

    D. Does not meet customer expectations, such as aesthetics, features, functionality, or price

152. 以下哪个是产品风险？

    A. 未能满足项目资金需求

    B. 核心人员可能离职

    C. 决策所需信息不可靠

    D. 未满足客户期望，如外观、特性、功能或价格

153. Within a project, risk management is typically focused on which of the following?

    A. Project cost
    B. Project scope
    C. Project duration
    D. Project uncertainty

153. 项目风险管理通常侧重于以下哪个？

    A. 项目成本
    B. 项目范围
    C. 项目进度
    D. 项目不确定性

154. Your product team has developed multiple product prototypes, thus providing customers with different versions of solutions. What is the value of product prototypes in the product innovation process?

    A. As development costs continue to increase in the development phases, product prototypes allow you to obtain valuable customer feedback on the concept before investing more resources

    B. Including multiple product prototypes allows customers to evaluate these products simultaneously in market testing

    C. The product prototype is not a full and accurate representation of the solution, and has no effect on determining the final form and function of the product

    D. The product prototype method is used in the past. Secondary market research methods are the best choice to test the user experience

154. 产品团队开发了多个产品原型，为客户提供了不同的解决方案。在产品创新流程中，产品原型有何价值？

　　A. 随着开发成本在开发阶段不断增加，产品原型允许你在投入更多资源之前获得客户对产品概念的有价值反馈

　　B. 如果有多个产品原型的话，客户就可以在市场测试中同时评估这些产品

　　C. 产品原型不能充分、准确地表达解决方案，对于确定产品最终形式和功能没有影响

　　D. 以往习惯使用产品原型方法，二级市场调研方法才是测试用户体验的最佳选择

155. David is leading the team to create a user journey map. Different from other methods, what should be highlighted in the user journey map?

　　A. User segmentation

　　B. The emotions triggered as the experience evolves when experience the product or service

　　C. Demographic data of target users

　　D. Differentiation of products or services

155. 大卫正在带领团队一起制作用户体验地图。不同于其他一些方法，用户体验地图要重点突出什么？

　　A. 用户细分

　　B. 用户在体验产品或服务过程中产生的情绪

　　C. 目标用户的人口统计学数据

　　D. 产品或服务的差异化

156. Why should quantitative research be considered after qualitative research?

　　A. As the project cost and risk are increasing, the quantitative research is reasonable

　　B. Quantitative research allows the establishment of a theory of customer problems

　　C. Qualitative research creates a verifiable quantitative statistical model

　　D. Only consider quantitative research when conducting questionnaire survey on customers

156. 在进行定性研究之后，为什么还应考虑定量研究？

　　A. 由于项目成本和风险都在不断增加，所以定量研究是必要的

　　B. 定量研究允许建立一种关于客户问题的理论

C. 定性研究创建了可验证的量化统计模型

D. 仅在对客户进行问卷调查时考虑定量研究

157. Eric is the product manager of a consumer packaging company with a global customer base. He is currently responsible for designing and marketing a new type of derivative that is very popular in Asia, and the product features meet the needs of the Western European market. The company's standard practice is to develop a complete product innovation charter for each new product project. What are the two parts of Eric's product innovation charter?

    A. Business demonstration and project schedule

    B. Background and focus areas

    C. Regulatory constraints and project deliverables

    D. Project charter and market objectives

157. 艾瑞克是一家拥有全球客户群的消费品包装公司的产品经理。他目前负责设计和营销一种在亚洲非常受欢迎的新型衍生产品，该产品特性符合西欧市场的需求。公司的标准做法是为每个新产品项目制定产品创新章程。艾瑞克要撰写的产品创新章程应至少包含哪两个部分？

    A. 商业论证和项目进度表　　B. 背景与聚焦领域

    C. 法规限制和项目可交付成果　　D. 项目章程和市场目标

158. Under what circumstances is convergent thinking a good tool for ideation?

    A. Generate a lot of ideas in a short time

    B. Organize and evaluate ideas and make decisions

    C. Find a group of people to agree with an idea that has already been thought about in advance

    D. All of the above are wrong

158. 在什么情况下，收敛思维是一个非常好的创意生成工具？

    A. 在短时间内产生大量创意

    B. 组织和评估创意并做出决策

    C. 找一群人对已经事先想好的创意表示同意

    D. 以上皆错

159. A project is expected to generate $7.5 million in the next five years, with no cash flow and a known discount rate of 10%. What is the cumulative net present value of the project?

   A. $6.82 million
   B. $5.00 million
   C. $4.66 million
   D. $12.08 million

159. 某项目预计将在第五年产生 750 万美元的现金流，中间年份的现金流为零。已知折现率为 10%。那么，该项目的累计净现值是多少？

   A. 682 万美元
   B. 500 万美元
   C. 466 万美元
   D. 1208 万美元

160. what does the range and proportion of new product opportunities depend on?

   A. Corporate strategy or business strategy, and align with innovation strategy
   B. CEO's instructions
   C. Whether the risk is the lowest
   D. Is anyone willing to do it

160. 新产品机会的范围和比例取决于什么？

   A. 公司战略或经营战略，并与创新战略保持一致
   B. CEO 的指示
   C. 是否风险最低
   D. 是否有人愿意去做

161. Company B produces high-volume, low-cost products. In the past decades, the products have hardly changed. Since the product was put into production, the company has not fully considered the optimization of production site layout, and workers are forced to shuttle around the entire site every day. Which of the following methods is most suitable for improving the current production situation?

   A. Agile
   B. Lean
   C. Stage-Gate
   D. Waterfall model

161. B 公司生产大批量、低成本产品。在过去数十年中，产品几乎未做任何改变。自产品投产以来，公司就未充分考虑生产现场布局的优化，员工被迫每天都围着整个现场折返忙碌。以下哪种方法最适合用于改进当前生产状况？

   A. 敏捷方法
   B. 精益方法
   C. 门径流程
   D. 瀑布模型

162. What is the financial analysis method that sets the net present value to zero and then calculates the rate of return?

   A. Payback period   B. ROI   C. IRR   D. NPV

162. 将净现值设为零，然后计算收益率的财务分析方法被称作什么？

   A. 投资回收期   B. 投资回报率
   C. 内部收益率   D. 净现值

163. What should Peter consider as the first step in leading the team to develop a go-to-market strategy?

   A. Value proposition   B. Whole solution
   C. Market segmentation   D. Beachhead strategy

163. 皮特带领团队制定走向市场战略，第一步应该考虑什么？

   A. 价值主张   B. 整体解决方案
   C. 市场细分   D. 抢滩战略

164. What are the characteristics of the advancer in the Z-model for innovation?

   A. Like to brainstorm, be energetic and generate many different ideas
   B. Formulate business and project plans, analyze and coordinate all aspects of work
   C. Transform creativity into action, be detail oriented, and focus on delivering the milestones set in the project plan
   D. Work on broad strategies to implement the idea and communicate the importance of the innovation project to key stakeholders

164. 在创新 Z 模型中，推进者有何特点？

   A. 喜欢集思广益，充满活力并生成许多不同的创意
   B. 制订经营和项目计划，对工作的方方面面进行分析和协同
   C. 将创意转化为行动，以细节为导向，专注于交付项目计划设定的里程碑
   D. 制定战略并落实创意，并向关键相关方宣传创新项目的重要性

165. Bill is allocating resources. He found several resources whose utilization rate exceeded 100%. What actions should he take at this time?

   A. Add resources
   B. Reduce project scope
   C. Choose smaller projects
   D. All of the above are right

165. 比尔正在进行资源配置。他发现了几个利用率超过100%的资源。这时，他应采取什么措施？

   A. 增加资源
   B. 缩小项目范围
   C. 选择更小的项目
   D. 以上皆对

166. A company that produces agricultural machinery recently adopted an active sustainability strategy. The technical department of the company is responsible for evaluating the impact on environment during the product life cycle. Which of the following is the most appropriate method for the product manager?

   A. Product Feature Analysis (PFA)
   B. Product Processing Analysis (PDA)
   C. Life Cycle Assessment (LCA)
   D. Product Composition Analysis (PCA)

166. 一家生产农业机械的公司最近采用了积极的可持续性战略。公司技术部门负责评估公司每种产品在其生命周期中对环境的影响，产品经理应采取以下哪个最恰当的方法？

   A. 产品特性分析
   B. 产品处理分析
   C. 生命周期评估
   D. 产品成分分析

167. In order to estimate the project cost, Sam collected some project parameters and built an estimation model. Then he referred to some data of past product development projects, and also learned some of the latest industry standard data. Finally, he put these data into the model to calculate the project cost. What estimation method did Sam use?

   A. Bottom-up
   B. Parametric
   C. Historical data
   D. Company-specific methods

167. 为了估算项目成本，山姆收集了一些项目参数，还构建了一个估算模型。随后他参考了过往产品开发项目的一些数据，也了解了一些行业最新标准数据。最终，他将这些数据代入模型中，估算出了项目成本。山姆使用了什么估算方法？

    A. 自下而上法   B. 参数法

    C. 历史数据法   D. 公司特有方法

168. Walmart is collecting biometric feedback from sensors on shopping cart handles for monitoring consumer biometrics like pulse, temperature, and stress, and comparing against a baseline. Then they can better understand the shopping process and behavior of consumers. What is this market research method?

    A. Eye tracking   B. Sensory testing

    C. Biometric feedback   D. Virtual reality

168. 沃尔玛公司通过在购物车把手上安装传感器来采集购物者的生命体征参数，如脉搏、体温和血压等，并将采集到的实际值与基准值进行对比，从而更好地了解购物者的购物过程和行为。这是什么市场调研方法？

    A. 眼动追踪   B. 感官检验

    C. 生物特征反馈   D. 虚拟现实

169. What is the top organizational practice level based on the IPD system?

    A. Knowledge, skills and innovation   B. Basic tools

    C. Strategy and portfolio   D. Focus on customers

169. 在集成产品开发体系的组织实践等级中，最高等级是以下哪个？

    A. 知识、技能和创新   B. 基本工具

    C. 战略和组合   D. 聚焦客户

170. What are the characteristics of the competing strategy in Thomas-Kilmann' conflict management model?

    A. Low level of cooperativeness and low level of assertiveness

    B. High level of cooperativeness and low level of assertiveness

    C. Both cooperativeness level and assertiveness level are in the middle

    D. Low level of cooperativeness and high level of assertiveness

170. 在托马斯冲突管理模型中，竞争策略有何特点？

    A. 合作水平和自信水平都低
    B. 合作水平高和自信水平低
    C. 合作水平和自信水平都居中
    D. 合作水平低和自信水平高

171. Mary is a product development engineer of an auto parts supplier. Her boss has been complaining about the long lead time for new products to come into the market recently, and thinks that the iterative improvement born in most new products can be more efficient. What type of product innovation process would you recommend Mary to her boss to shorten the time to market?

    A. Waterfall model
    B. Integrated Product Development
    C. Agile
    D. Stage-Gate

171. 玛丽是某汽车配件供应商的产品开发工程师，她的上司最近一直在抱怨新产品上市时间太长，并认为大部分新产品的迭代性改进可以做得更高效。你会建议玛丽向上司推荐何种产品创新流程，从而缩短上市时间？

    A. 瀑布模型
    B. 集成产品开发
    C. 敏捷方法
    D. 门径流程

172. Which of the following is incorrect about the description of a sustainable business?

    A. Greenwashing
    B. An enterprise that has minimal negative impact on the global or local environment, community, society, or economy
    C. A business that strives to meet the triple bottom line
    D. A green business

172. 关于可持续性经营的描述，以下哪个是错误的？

    A. 漂绿
    B. 对全球或当地环境、社区、社会或经济的负面影响最小的企业实践
    C. 企业设法达到"三重底线"的要求
    D. 绿色经营

173. In product innovation, what does formal phase completion mean?

    A. Has been completed at this stage and sometimes includes authorization to proceed to the next stage

B. It has been completed at this stage and always includes authorization to proceed to the next stage

C. It has been completed in this stage but never includes authorization to proceed the next stage

D. All phases have been completed

173. 在产品创新中，阶段正式完成意味着什么？

A. 在该阶段已经完成，可能得到授权进入下一阶段

B. 在该阶段已经完成，并直接得到授权进入下一阶段

C. 在该阶段已经完成，无法得到授权进入下一阶段

D. 全部阶段都已完成

174. How would you describe the business strategy of a technology-based company focusing on purchasing business that is closing its purchasing business and integrating its products from purchasing business into its product line?

A. Merge & acquisition strategy　　B. Technology strategy

C. Marketing strategy　　D. Corporate strategy

174. 一家聚焦于收购的技术型公司，在收购完相关产品后，就将收购到的产品整合到自己的产品线中。你会如何描述这种类型的经营战略？

A. 并购战略　　B. 技术战略　　C. 营销战略　　D. 公司战略

175. In order to gain advantages in the global market competition, HUAWEI took the lead in launching 5G technology. At what stage is the technology on the technology S-curve at that year?

A. Growth stage　　B. Embryonic phase

C. Maturity stage　　D. Decline stage

175. 为了在全球市场竞争中获得优势，华为公司率先推出了5G技术。在推出的当年，该技术在技术S曲线上处于哪个阶段？

A. 成长阶段　　B. 引入阶段　　C. 成熟阶段　　D. 衰退阶段

176. Recently, Sam was employed by company A as a product innovation consultant to optimize the product innovation process. Company A has already delayed the release of several products. In the initial study, Sam found that due to the lack of early

coordination between the design and manufacturing teams, rework is required, which leads to delays. What is Sam's best choice to improve this situation?

A. Replacement of project manager

B. Introduce additional decision stages in the product development process

C. Establish a cross functional product development team

D. Add more documents to improve communication

176. 最近，山姆被 A 公司聘为产品创新顾问，负责优化产品创新流程。A 公司已经有多个产品被延迟发布。在初步调研中，山姆发现由于设计和制造团队之间缺乏早期协调，导致返工和延误。要改善这种状况，山姆的最佳做法是什么？

A. 更换项目经理
B. 在产品开发流程中增加额外的决策阶段
C. 组建跨职能产品开发团队
D. 增加更多的文档来改善沟通

177. Dennis is about to develop a digital strategy. After clarifying the vision, mission, values and supporting strategies, he decides to adopt the structured process of digital strategy development. Now that the identifying and prioritizing work has been completed, what will Dennis do next?

A. Identify　　　B. Design　　　C. Implement　　　D. Refine

177. 丹尼斯着手制定数字化战略。在明确愿景、使命、价值观及支持战略后，他决定采用结构化流程来制定数字化战略。现在已经完成了识别和排序工作，接下来山姆要开展什么工作？

A. 识别　　　B. 设计　　　C. 实施　　　D. 改进

178. As a product manager, Frank knows that team performance is affected by many factors. In order to improve team performance, he should focus on the construction of many elements. Which of the following practices is not appropriate?

A. Encourage high performance values and behaviors

B. Does not spend time on collaborating with functional teams and other teams

C. Let team members fully demonstrate their skills and abilities, and give recognition and encouragement in a timely manner

D. Leadership involvement and support at all levels

178. 作为产品经理，弗兰克深知团队绩效受到很多要素的影响。为了提高团队绩效，他应该将工作重点放在很多要素的构建上。以下做法中不恰当的是哪个？

   A. 鼓励高绩效的价值观和行为

   B. 不花时间与职能部门和其他团队协作

   C. 让团队成员充分展现其技能和能力，并及时给予认可和激励

   D. 争取各级领导者的参与和支持

179. Gloria rarely considers sustainability in setting new product goals and specifications, and rarely uses sustainability metrics in product design. At what level is the company in the Sustainability Maturity Model?

   A. Succeeding   B. Improving   C. Beginning   D. Leading

179. 格洛丽亚公司在制定新产品目标和规格中很少考虑可持续性，在产品设计中也很少采用可持续性指标。该公司处于可持续性成熟度模型中的什么级别？

   A. 成功级   B. 改进级   C. 初始级   D. 领先级

180. Company X hopes to conduct consumer research through a sufficiently large consumer sample, so as to obtain statistically reliable results that can be used for target market prediction. The company wants to understand consumers' reactions to the three developed product concepts and the possibility of purchasing. What should the company do?

   A. Well trained interviewers use open-ended questions to investigate samples randomly selected from the target market

   B. Interview shoppers outside selected retail stores

   C. Internal test and interview of employees

   D. Select people from local sports clubs to form focus groups

180. X 公司希望采集足够大的消费者样本进行消费者研究，从而得到可用于目标市场中可预测、统计上可靠的结果。该公司希望了解消费者对三个已经开发好的产品概念的反馈以及购买的可能性。X 公司应该如何做？

   A. 由经过良好训练的采访者使用开放式问题对从目标市场上随机抽取的样本进行调查

   B. 在选定的零售店外面采访购物者

   C. 在公司内部进行测试并对公司员工进行采访

D. 从当地的运动俱乐部中选取人员组成焦点小组

181. Jack is a consultant who is good at Lean product innovation methodology. He is reviewing the product innovation process of a new car company. The audit results show that there are a lot of rework in multiple stages of the product innovation process. What advice should he give to the CEO?

   A. Reduce the number of ongoing product designs
   B. Formulate product innovation articles
   C. Standardize tasks to improve product innovation processes
   D. Hire more staff to handle rework

181. 杰克是一名熟谙精益产品创新方法的顾问。他正在审核一家新汽车公司的产品创新流程。审计结果显示，在产品创新流程的多个阶段都存在大量的返工。他应对首席执行官提出何种建议？

   A. 减少正在进行的产品设计数量
   B. 制定产品创新章程
   C. 将任务标准化，并改进产品创新流程
   D. 雇用更多工作人员来处理返工

182. Leaders are confident and have a deep understanding of their emotions, strengths, weaknesses and needs. Their decision is consistent with its value system, and can be adjusted between honesty and reality to finally find a balance point. Which element of EQ is this?

   A. Self-regulation   B. Self-awareness
   C. Motivation   D. Empathy

182. 领导者通常很自信，对自己的情绪、长处、短处和需求都有深刻的理解。他们的决策与其价值体系相吻合，并能在坦诚和现实之间进行调整，最终找到平衡点。这是情商中的哪一个要素？

   A. 自我调节   B. 自我认知   C. 激励   D. 移情

183. A company has completed the development of a product and is producing the product in the final form and performance. According to the company's previous experience with

such products, quick launch is absolutely the first priority. The company's management believes that the risk of product failure is relatively low. Which of the following steps should be included in the company's project plan?

A. Conduct product pre-release testing for at least 12 months in multiple test markets with high BDI

B. Purchase product failure insurance to minimize the risk of financial loss

C. Carry out beta test or enter the comprehensive listing plan because the company has rich experience and the risk of product failure has been determined to be low

D. Review the product design specifications again, and add some secondary or even tertiary product attributes that may improve user satisfaction

183. 一家公司完成了某款产品的开发，正以最终商品形式和性能生产该产品。根据公司以往对此类产品的经验，快速上市绝对是首要优先级，公司管理层分析认为产品失败风险相对较低。该公司的项目计划应该包括以下哪个步骤？

A. 在品牌发展指数较高的多个测试市场进行至少 12 个月的产品预发布测试

B. 购买产品失败保险，将财务损失风险最小化

C. 因为公司拥有丰富经验并且产品失败风险较低，所以可以直接进行贝塔测试，或开始全面上市策划

D. 重新审查产品设计规格，添加一些能够提升用户满意度的二级甚至三级产品属性

184. What scenarios are eye tracking often used in?

A. Software, retail product packaging, marketing and advertising

B. Food and cosmetics

C. Military industry and national defense

D. Aviation and aerospace

184. 眼动追踪经常用于哪些情境？

A. 软件产品、零售产品包装、营销和广告

B. 食品和化妆品

C. 军工和国防

D. 航空和航天

185. John is a product manager of JAT company. After participating in a PDMA seminar on product innovation performance indicators, he decided to use an indicator framework to

promote the company to become a real learning organization in product innovation. Which method would you suggest John use to achieve the goal?

A. Develop a set of indicators that can be used for regular reporting to senior executives and the board of directors

B. Develop a set of lagging, leading and synchronization indicators according to the company's own weaknesses, so as to report these indicators to senior executives regularly to make decisions on improvement actions

C. Appoint a consulting firm to help develop a performance indicator framework

D. Implement a set of vitality indicators for the profitability of new products developed in the past five years

185. 约翰是 JAT 公司的产品经理，在参加了一个关于产品创新绩效指标的 PDMA 研讨班之后，他决定通过运用一个指标框架来促使公司在产品创新方面成为真正的学习型组织。你会建议约翰采用以下哪个方法来实现该目标？

A. 开发一整套可用于定期向高管和董事会进行汇报的指标

B. 根据公司自身的薄弱环节，开发一整套滞后指标、领先指标以及同步指标，定期向高管报告这些指标，以做出改进行动的决策

C. 雇用咨询公司来帮助制定绩效指标框架

D. 针对过去 5 年所开发的新产品的盈利能力，制定一套活力指标

186. Allan serves as a process champion for an intelligent equipment company. The company has both hardware and software development. He suggests that the company's product innovation adopt an Agile-Stage-Gate-Hybrid process. Why does he do so?

A. Because the company is afraid of falling behind its competitors in order to keep up with the trend

B. Due to the universal applicability of an Agile-Stage-Gate-Hybrid process, all companies should use it

C. Because he wants to leave a good impression on the board of directors

D. Due to the integration of the advantages of both Stage-gate process and Agile approach in Agile-Stage-Gate-Hybrid process, including the focus, structure, and control of Stage-gate process, as well as the speed, agility, and productivity of Agile approach

186. 艾伦出任一家智能化设备公司的流程倡导者。该公司既有硬件开发又有软件开发。他建议公司的产品创新采用敏捷门径混合型流程。他为什么会这么做？

   A. 因为该公司为了赶时髦，生怕落在竞争对手的后面
   B. 因敏捷门径混合型流程具有普遍适用性，所有公司都应该使用该流程
   C. 因为他希望给董事会留下一个良好印象
   D. 因敏捷门径混合型流程综合了门径流程和敏捷方法的优点，包括门径流程的聚焦、结构化和控制，以及敏捷方法的速度、灵敏性和生产率

187. In the virtual team model, what practical activities are included in the elements of knowledge management?

   A. Use email, language, customs and encourage diversity
   B. Meeting form, strict plan and quality standard
   C. Task oriented, on-site visit and 80/20 listening
   D. Systems engineering, collaboration tools and lessons learned

187. 在虚拟团队模式中，知识管理要素包含了哪些实践活动？

   A. 使用电子邮件、语言、习俗和鼓励多元化
   B. 会议形式、严格的计划和质量标准
   C. 任务导向、现场访问和 80/20 倾听
   D. 系统工程、协作工具和经验教训

188. We know that IDOV is a specific design for six sigma method used for the design of new products and services, which aims to meet the six sigma standard. What does "O" stand for in IDOV?

   A. Observe   B. Open
   C. Optimize   D. Opportunity

188. IDOV 是一种用于新产品和服务设计的六西格玛设计方法，目的在于满足六西格玛标准。IDOV 中的 "O" 代表什么？

   A. 发现   B. 开放   C. 优化   D. 机会

189. Christine and Tom are the product managers of the company. Christine is doing feasibility analysis, considering more about market potential, marketing ability, financial potential and investment requirements. Tom gives more consideration to technical capability, manufacturing capability and intellectual property. What key elements have they missed?

  A. Team members   B. Vision
  C. Mission   D. Regulatory impact

189. 克瑞斯汀和汤姆是公司的产品经理，克瑞斯汀在做可行性分析，考虑较多的是市场潜力、营销能力、财务潜力和投资需求。汤姆则更多地考虑技术能力、制造能力和知识产权。他们遗漏了什么关键要素？

  A. 团队成员   B. 公司愿景   C. 公司使命   D. 法规影响

190. The project has experienced delays and requires the use of schedule compression methods. Which of the following is not a crashing method?

  A. Add human resources   B. Change tasks from serial to parallel
  C. Increase physical resources   D. Work overtime

190. 项目出现了延误，需要采用进度压缩方法。以下哪个不是赶工方法？

  A. 增加人员   B. 将任务由串行改为并行
  C. 增加物质资源   D. 加班

191. Jane calculated the annual revenue according to the unit price and quantity of the product, and subtracted the total cost from the revenue. What is Jane calculating?

  A. Annual cash flow   B. Net profit
  C. ROI   D. Profit margin

191. 简根据产品单价和年度销售数量算出了年度总销售收入，并用总收入减去总成本，得出一个值。她在计算什么指标？

  A. 年度现金流   B. 净利润
  C. 投资回报率   D. 利润率

192. What model inspires Geoffrey Moore to build Cross-the-Chasm model?

　　A. Porter's Competitive Strategy　　B. Kotler's Marketing Theory

　　C. Rogers' Diffusion of Technology　　D. Christensen's Disruptive Innovation

192. 杰弗里·摩尔的跨越鸿沟模型受到了以下哪个模型的启发？

　　A. 波特的竞争战略　　B. 科特勒的营销理论

　　C. 罗杰斯的技术扩散曲线　　D. 克里斯坦森的颠覆式创新

193. Balanced scorecard is a comprehensive performance measurement method. Which four performance dimensions does it cover?

　　A. Management, development, operation, financial

　　B. A great idea, 2-3 new customer value propositions, well-executing and product launch

　　C. Product champion, project sponsors, project leaders and process owners

　　D. Customer, internal processes, learning and growth, financial

193. 平衡计分卡是一种综合绩效测量方法，它包含哪四个绩效维度？

　　A. 管理、开发、运营、财务

　　B. 1个杰出的创意、2~3个新的客户价值主张、良好的执行力、产品上市

　　C. 产品推动者、项目发起人、项目领导者、流程负责人

　　D. 客户、内部流程、学习与成长、财务

194. Which of the following is not suitable about the effectiveness of virtual teams?

　　A. Compared with offline co-location, virtual team is an expedient

　　B. Anywhere connectivity allows virtual teams to drive project goals with generalist-specialist skills

　　C. Virtual teams support new product innovation by reducing cycle time in uncertain environments

　　D. Team members for virtual teams are selected for their motivation and shared purpose for the project mission. This leads to better and quicker decisions

194. 关于虚拟团队的有效性，以下哪个说法是不合适的？

　　A. 与线下集中办公相比，虚拟团队只是权宜之计

　　B. 随时随地的连接可以使虚拟团队利用通才和专才结合的技能实现项目目标

　　C. 虚拟团队通过缩短不确定环境中的开发周期来支持产品创新

D. 通过激励并用项目使命及共同目标的方式遴选虚拟团队成员，这么做可以制定更好、更快的决策

195. You are assigned to a new product development project. There is no such product in the market. What should you focus on in your feasibility study?

   A. Is this product available in the market

   B. Are consumers willing to buy this product

   C. How can the salesperson make the current buyer buy the new product instead

   D. Will distributors increase costs

195. 你被指派到一个全新的产品开发项目中。市场上还没有这种产品，此时，你的可行性研究重点应该是什么？

   A. 市场有这种产品吗

   B. 消费者愿意购买该产品吗

   C. 销售人员如何让现有客户购买该新产品

   D. 分销商会增加成本吗

196. What is the best description of the process map?

   A. A project plan that decomposes each process stage into multiple tasks

   B. Guidelines for tasks and deliverables for each process phase

   C. Work flow chart with horizontal axis representing process time and vertical axis representing participants and tasks

   D. Icons describing input-throughput-output in new product design

196. 对流程地图的最佳描述是以下哪个？

   A. 将每个流程阶段分解为多个任务的项目计划

   B. 每个流程阶段任务与可交付成果的指南

   C. 用横轴表示流程时间、纵轴表示参与者和任务的工作流程图

   D. 描述新产品设计中输入—产量—输出的图标

197. What role should the product manager play in the mature stage of the product life cycle?

   A. Subject expert　　　　　　　　　B. Growth hacker

   C. Solution seeker　　　　　　　　D. Retention strategist

197. 在产品生命周期的成熟阶段，产品经理应该担任什么角色？

   A. 洞察专家　　　　B. 增长黑客　　　　C. 方案达人　　　　D. 留存大师

198. As research shows, how many projects do engineers assign in at the same time, their productivity will begin to decrease?

   A. One project　　　B. Three projects　　C. Two projects　　D. Five projects

198. 研究表明，工程人员被同时分配到多少个项目中时，其生产率会就开始下降？

   A. 1个项目　　　　B. 3个项目　　　　C. 2个项目　　　　D. 5个项目

199. Which of the following is the best practice of sustainability in teams and leadership?

   A. Leverage sustainability to drive innovation success and competitive advantage and gain commitment from senior management
   B. Integrate sustainability into existing innovation projects and processes, and make relevant organizations responsible for measurable results
   C. Invest in building sustainable innovation and resource capabilities and make full use of existing capabilities
   D. All of the above are right

199. 在团队与领导力的可持续性中，推荐采用以下哪些最佳实践？

   A. 利用可持续性推动创新成功和竞争优势，获得高级管理层的承诺
   B. 将可持续性纳入现有的创新项目和创新流程中，让相关组织对可测量的结果负责
   C. 在构建可持续创新和资源能力上进行投资，并充分利用现有能力
   D. 以上皆对

200. Mary knows that it is not easy to conduct a portfolio management system into the company. She hopes to adopt a more stable strategy. As a consultant, what would you suggest?

   A. With the support of the senior management, it is carried out in a comprehensive and high standard within the company
   B. Punish those people who do not accept management change
   C. According to the current situation of the company and the user's acceptance, gradually increase the complexity

D. Focus only on supporters and ignore opponents

200. 玛丽知道推荐组合管理系统并不是一件易事。她希望采取一个较为稳妥的策略。作为顾问，你会建议她如何做？

    A. 在高管层的支持下，在公司范围内全面、高标准地展开

    B. 对不接受管理变革的人进行处罚

    C. 根据公司现状和使用者接受程度，循序渐进，逐渐增加复杂度

    D. 只关注支持者，忽略那些不支持者或反对者

试题答案与解析

序号	答案	知识点	教材页码
1	D	组合/组合与战略关系/组合与战略的连接方法/自上而下法/步骤/第一步/内容	P71 第7行
2	C	战略/创新战略与战略框架/波特竞争战略/细分市场战略/窄市场范围	P22 倒数第6行
3	D	战略/创新战略与战略框架/安索夫矩阵/多元化	补充知识
4	B	组合/什么是产品组合/组合中的项目类型/突破型和平台型	P69 第10行
5	C	流程/产品创新引论/运用知识提升决策水平并减少不确定性	P102 第1行
6	D	战略/创新战略/价值	P3 倒数第3行
7	A	市场调研/定性市场调研方法/人种学方法与焦点小组/特点	P221 倒数第8行和 P218 第8行
8	B	战略/创新支持战略/技术战略/技术S曲线/成熟阶段	P32 图1.15
9	C	文化/团队发展/团队发展阶段/塔克曼团队发展模型/规范阶段	P270 倒数第3行
10	B	市场调研/定性市场调研方法/客户现场访问/特点	P223 第4行
11	D	市场调研/定性市场调研方法和定量市场调研方法/结合	P218 第6行和P227 倒数第10行

序号	答案	知识点	教材页码
12	A	市场调研/产品使用测试/阿尔法测试和贝塔测试/阿尔法测试/内容	P240 倒数第 4 行和 P417 倒数第 5 行
13	B	创新管理/财务分析/计算 10%×（1+25%）=12.5%	P335
14	A	市场调研/多变量研究方法/种类	P235 倒数第 7 行
15	D	工具/制造与装配阶段/可持续性分析工具/生命周期成本/内容	P199 倒数第 3 行
16	D	工具/详细设计与规格阶段/情感化设计/微软反应卡和突发情绪法	P186 倒数第 4 行
17	A	战略/创新战略与战略框架/波特竞争战略/成本领先战略/特点	P21 第 5 行
18	D	工具/创意生成阶段/创意生成工具/六顶思考帽/绿色帽子	P159 第 2 行
19	C	市场调研/多变量研究方法/联合分析/内容	P237 第 2 行
20	B	工具/制造与装配阶段/六西格玛设计/六西格玛 DFSS 和 DMAIC	P193 第 4 行
21	D	流程/管理新产品失败风险/产品创新生命期中的不确定性和成本	P101 图 3.2
22	A	流程/产品创新流程控制/产品创新流程治理	P141 第 9 行
23	D	工具/创意生成阶段/什么是创意生成/定义	P156 倒数第 2 行
24	C	战略/可持续性创新/可持续性产品创新/循环经济与创新/循环经济/内容	P56 第 8 行
25	C	流程/产品创新流程模型/门径流程/关口/决策/结果	P110 倒数第 10 行
26	C	战略/明确组织方向/愿景和使命	P7 第 4 行和第 10 行
27	C	战略/开发式创新/开放式创新类型/开放式创新的参与机制/中介者	P49 图 1.28
28	A	流程/产品创新流程模型/门径流程/商业论证阶段/内容	P108 倒数第 2 行
29	B	市场调研/定量市场调研方法/大数据/内容	P232 倒数第 6 行
30	A	创新管理/质量指标与关键绩效指标/平衡计分卡/财务	P351 图 7.40
31	D	工具/创意生成阶段/创意生成工具/SCAMPER 法/替代	P157 倒数第 9 行
32	C	创新管理/产品生命周期/管理产品生命周期/成熟阶段	P313 第 12 行

序号	答案	知识点	教材页码
33	A	战略/创新战略与战略框架/波特竞争战略/差异化战略/特点	P21 倒数第 1 行
34	B	战略/创新支持战略/知识产权战略/知识产权类型/版权	P33 倒数第 6 行
35	D	创新管理/可行性分析/价值	P332 第 6 行
36	C	战略/创新支持战略/数字化战略/数字化转型/特点	P42 第 6 行
37	D	创新管理/财务分析/沉没成本/定义	补充知识
38	C	创新管理/产品路线图和技术路线图	P33 第 1 行，P39 倒数第 4 行，P329 第 1 行
39	B	战略/创新支持战略/营销战略/分析现有产品组合/波士顿矩阵/两个维度	P39 图 1.21
40	B	市场调研/试销与市场测试/模拟试销	P242 倒数第 4 行
41	D	创新管理/产品创新关键成功因素	P300 倒数第 4 行和倒数第 1 行，P301 第 9 和第 12 行
42	C	文化/管理职责/产品创新流程中的角色/流程倡导者/职责	P261 倒数第 3 行
43	C	工具/实体化设计阶段/功能分析/特点	P174 第 8 行
44	C	创新管理/管理产品创新/产品管理的作用/统筹管理	P306 倒数第 5 行
45	A	战略/可持续创新/可持续性与战略/三重底线	P51 倒数第 11 行
46	B	创新管理/财务分析/资金的时间价值	P339 第 2 行
47	D	工具/初始设计与规格阶段/产品设计规格/特点	P176 第 5 行
48	D	组合/新产品机会评估与选择/项目评估工具/最常用工具/投资回收期	P73 图 2.2
49	D	战略/创新战略与战略框架/迈尔斯和斯诺战略/探索者	P23 倒数第 2 行
50	A	战略/创新战略与战略框架/皮萨诺创新景观图	P27 图 1.12
51	B	战略/创新支持战略/技术战略	P30 第 4 行
52	D	市场调研/定性市场调研方法/社交媒体/优点	P226 第 2 行
53	C	流程/产品创新流程模型/敏捷产品创新方法/价值声明	P121 第 6 行
54	D	战略/创新支持战略/营销战略/制定基础	P35 倒数第 9 行和 P36 图 1.18

序号	答案	知识点	教材页码
55	D	工具/制造与装配阶段/可持续性分析工具/生命周期成本/计算	P199 倒数第 2 行
		LCC=5+(60000+15000)/(5×5000)=8（美元）	
56	C	战略/经营战略与公司战略/公司战略	P9 倒数第 1 行
57	C	流程/产品创新流程模型/敏捷产品创新方法/产品负责人/职责	P123 倒数第 4 行
58	C	组合/什么是产品组合/组合中的项目类型/突破型项目/特点	P69 第 12 行
59	A	组合/组合与战略的关系/组合与战略的连接方法/自上而下法（战略桶）	P71 第 4 行
60	B	创新管理/度量指标与关键绩效指标/对标与持续改进/对标/内容	P358 第 2 行
61	A	战略/创新战略与战略框架/迈尔斯和斯诺战略/探索者	P23 图 1.10
62	C	战略/创新支持战略/营销战略/分析现有产品组合/波士顿矩阵/明星产品	P38 倒数第 2 行和 P39 图 1.21
63	C	战略/创新战略与战略框架/克里斯坦森颠覆式创新/特点	P26 倒数第 12 行
64	B	文化/管理职层/产品创新战略中的角色/高级管理层/职责	P260 倒数第 7 行
65	A	创新管理/度量指标与关键绩效指标/产品创新度量指标	P352 第 3 行
66	B	流程/产品创新引论/产品创新是"风险与回报"过程	P99 倒数第 5 行
67	C	流程/产品创新流程模型/门径流程/缺点	P111 第 2 行
68	B	创新管理/产品生命周期/管理产品生命周期/成长阶段/特点	P312 图 7.8
69	A	工具/详细设计与规格阶段/质量功能展开/质量屋/应用领域	P181 图 4.9
70	C	创新管理/产品路线图和技术路线图/产品路线图/目的	P329 倒数第 10 行
71	A	创新管理/管理产品创新/产品管理战略/商业化阶段	P310 第 7 行
72	C	组合/平衡组合/将产品组合可视化/气泡图/作用	P79 倒数第 2 行
73	A	市场调研/定性市场调研方法/深度访谈/特点	P220 第 1 行
74	B	工具/概念设计阶段/卡诺模型/期望属性	P163 第 5 行

序号	答案	知识点	教材页码
75	B	文化/产品创新团队结构/轻量型团队/特点	P265 倒数第 7 行
76	A	战略/创新支持战略/能力战略/核心竞争力	P40 第 7 行
77	C	流程/产品创新流程模型/敏捷产品创新方法/12 条关键原则/协作	P125 倒数第 1 行
78	D	组合/资源配置/资源配置工具/资源争夺/决策依据	P85 第 3 行
79	A	创新管理/产品生命周期/管理产品生命周期/引入阶段/价格策略	P313 第 2 行
80	C	组合/资源配置/组合管理有效性	P81 第 3 行
81	B	文化/创新文化和氛围/氛围/内容	P258 第 8 行
82	C	创新管理/产品生命周期中的鸿沟/跨越鸿沟	P318 图 7.9
83	A	文化/创新文化和氛围/文化/内容	P258 第 2 行
84	C	战略/创新支持战略/营销战略/分析现有产品组合/波士顿矩阵/明星产品	P38 倒数第 2 行和 P39 图 1.21
85	B	工具/制造与装配阶段/六西格玛设计/六西格玛/DMAIC/分析	P193 倒数第 7 行
86	D	组合/组合与战略的连接方法/自下而上法/应用情境	P71 倒数第 5 行
87	C	战略/创新支持战略/产品平台战略/优势	P28 倒数第 1 行
88	C	创新管理/产品生命周期中的鸿沟/走向市场流程/新式和老式走向市场战略	P320 图 7.10 和图 7.11
89	A	流程/产品创新流程模型/集成产品开发/在集成产品开发中纳入可持续性	P117 倒数第 8 行
90	D	创新管理/需求与销售预测/工具	P334 第 2 行
91	D	创新管理/管理产品创新/产品管理战略/产品战略三角	P309 图 7.3
92	C	流程/产品创新流程模型/设计思维/定义	P131 第 3 行
93	B	组合/组合评估标准/最高阶标准	P88 图 2.15
94	A	流程/产品创新流程模型/门径流程/决定阶段数量的因素	P109 第 6 行
95	B	战略/制定战略前的准备/PESTLE 分析	P13 图 1.7
96	D	创新管理/度量指标与关键绩效指标/平衡计分卡/员工满意度/内容	P351 图 7.40
97	A	组合/什么是组合管理/组合管理五个目标/价值最大	P67 倒数第 9 行

序号	答案	知识点	教材页码
98	C	组合/组合管理系统应用/组合管理准则/评分规则/量化程度	P87 倒数第 6 行
99	D	流程/产品创新流程模型/系统工程/缺点	P129 倒数第 1 行
100	A	工具/实体化设计阶段/特点	P155 一览图，左侧第 3 个方框
101	B	战略/制定战略前的准备/商业模式画布/内容	P15 第 12 行
102	B	流程/产品创新流程模型/敏捷产品创新方法/冲刺/原因	P120 倒数第 3 行
103	A	流程/产品创新流程模型/敏捷产品创新方法/产品待办列表/产品待办项	P122 第 8 行
104	D	工具/概念设计阶段/TRIZ/TRIZ 方法/40 个发明原理/分割	P168 图 4.5
105	A	创新管理/项目管理/五个过程组	P343 倒数第 8 行
106	B	创新管理/管理产品创新/产品管理的作用/产品管理——三者交叉点	P304 图 7.1
107	A	流程/产品创新流程模型/精益创业/转型/放大式转型	P137 第 10 行
108	B	战略/可持续创新/可持续产品创新/可持续性对产品创新的重要性	P54 第 5 行
109	A	工具/详细设计与规格阶段/稳健设计/特点	P186 第 11 行
110	C	工具/详细设计与规格阶段/感性工学/特点	P187 倒数第 11 行
111	D	工具/制造与装配阶段/可持续性设计/考虑要素	P195 第 3 行
112	A	工具/制造与装配阶段/可持续性方法/SPSD	P196 第 4 行
113	B	文化/产品创新团队结构/自治型团队/特点	P267 第 2 行
114	B	市场调研/定量市场调研方法/概念测试和概念分类/特点	P230 第 2 行
115	B	市场调研/定量市场调研方法/感官检验/三点检验和二三点检验/内容	P230 倒数第 9 行
116	D	流程/产品创新流程模型/系统工程/特点	P128 倒数第 4 行
117	A	工具/初始设计与规格阶段/可装配性设计/目的	P177 第 6 行
118	B	文化/领导力/情商/自我调节/内容	P278 第 8 行
119	A	流程/产品创新流程模型/精益创业/转型/价值获取转型	P137 倒数第 3 行
120	D	工具/创意生成阶段/创意生成工具/SCAMPER 法/改变用途	P157 倒数第 5 行

序号	答案	知识点	教材页码
121	A	工具/创意生成阶段/创意生成工具/六项思考帽/白色帽子	P158 倒数第 3 行
122	B	工具/实体化设计阶段/FAST 技术图/特点	P175 第 6 行
123	D	工具/概念设计阶段/概念场景/特点	P165 倒数第 10 行
124	B	组合/组合绩效度量指标/选择	P89 倒数第 4 行
125	C	文化/团队发展/工作风格/DISC 工作风格评估工具/稳健型/特点	P272 第 7 行
126	A	文化/团队发展/项目团队生命周期/创新 Z 模型/开创者/特点	P273 第 1 行
127	B	工具/制造与装配阶段/原型法/贝塔原型/定义	P191 第 2 行
128	C	市场调研/定性市场调研方法/人种学方法/适用情境	P222 倒数第 10 行
129	A	组合/什么是产品组合/组合中的项目类型/平台型项目/特点	P69 倒数第 9 行
130	D	市场调研/定性市场调研方法和定量市场调研方法	P223 第 5 行
131.	D	创新管理/风险管理/什么是风险管理/风险应对措施/转移	P347 第 10 行
132	C	文化/产品创新团队结构/重量型团队/特点	P266 第 1 行
133	D	战略/创新支持战略/技术战略	P30 第 3 行
134	D	流程/产品创新章程/聚焦领域/内容	P105 第 3 行
135	A	战略/创新支持战略/营销战略/价值主张	P38 第 9 行和 P321 倒数第 1 行
136	B	文化/团队与领导力中的度量指标/创新健康状况评估/价值	P289 第 4 行
137	D	市场调研/多变量研究方法/多元回归分析/适用情境	P238 倒数第 2 行
138	B	创新管理/引论/可控因素	P300 第 7 行
139	A	创新管理/管理产品创新/产品管理战略/四个关键方面	P308 第 2 行
140	B	创新管理/产品生命周期中的鸿沟/跨越鸿沟	P318 图 7.9
141	A	战略/创新支持战略/营销战略/什么是产品/产品的三个层次/核心利益	P37 倒数第 2 行
142	C	组合/组合管理系统应用/组合管理准则/意外结果/对策	P87 第 4 行

序号	答案	知识点	教材页码
143	C	战略/创新支持战略/营销战略/分析现有产品组合/波士顿矩阵/瘦狗产品	P39 图1.21
144	D	战略/创新战略与战略框架/延续式与颠覆式产品创新/颠覆式创新示例	P26 第12行
145	B	战略/可持续性创新/可持续性产品创新/循环经济与创新	P56 图1.30
146	D	流程/产品创新流程模型/瀑布模型/需求阶段/内容	P115 第2行
147	A	战略/可持续创新/可持续产品创新/可持续性与战略	P54 倒数第11行
148	D	流程/产品创新流程模型比较/成熟产品创新流程的标志	P141 第3行
149	A	组合/什么是产品组合/组合管理的关键特征	P68 倒数第1行
150	D	战略/明确组织方向/价值观	P7 倒数第7行
151	B	工具/概念设计阶段/TRIZ/TRIZ问题解决矩阵	P166 图4.3
152	D	创新管理/风险管理/产品创新项目风险管理/产品风险和项目风险/产品风险	P349 第2行
153	D	创新管理/风险管理/什么是风险管理	P346 倒数第6行
154	A	工具/制造与装配阶段/原型法/价值	P188 倒数第10行
155	B	工具/创意生成阶段/创意生成工具/用户体验地图	P160 第5行
156	A	市场调研/定性市场调研方法和定量市场调研方法/结合	P215 倒数第2行
157	B	流程/产品创新章程/内容	P104 第8行
158	B	工具/创意生成阶段/什么是创意生成/收敛思维	P157 第7行
159	C	创新管理/财务分析/净现值（NPV）/计算 $NPV=0+0+0+0+750\div(1+10\%)^5 \approx 466$	P339 倒数第4行
160	A	组合/平衡组合/新产品机会的范围和比例的决定因素	P78 第7行
161	B	流程/产品创新流程模型/精益产品创新方法/特点和应用情境	P118 第7行
162	C	创新管理/财务分析/内部收益率（IRR）/定义	P341 第2行
163	A	创新管理/产品生命周期中的鸿沟/走向市场流程/制定走向市场战略的八个步骤	P328 图7.24
164	D	文化/项目团队生命周期/创新Z模型/推进者/特点	P273 第4行
165	D	组合/资源配置/资源配置工具/资源过载/对策	P85 第2行

序号	答案	知识点	教材页码
166	C	工具/制造与装配阶段/可持续性分析工具/生命周期评估/内容	P198 第 1 行
167	B	创新管理/项目管理/预算/估算方法/参数法	P346 第 7 行
168	C	市场调研/定量市场调研方法/生物特征反馈/应用	P231 倒数第 8 行
169	A	流程/产品创新流程模型/集成产品开发/集成产品开发实践等级/最高等级（第 5 级）	P116 图 3.8
170	D	文化/团队发展/冲突管理/托马斯模型/竞争/内容	P275 倒数第 6 行和图 6.9
171	C	流程/产品创新流程模型/敏捷产品创新方法/12 条关键原则/尽快交付	P125 倒数第 2 行
172	A	战略/可持续创新/什么是可持续经营/定义	P50 第 3 行和 P440 倒数第 8 行
173	A	流程/产品创新流程模型/门径流程/阶段/内容	P110 第 8 和第 13 行
174	A	战略/开放式创新/开放式创新类型/开放式创新的参与机制/开放者	P49 图 1.28
175	B	战略/创新支持战略/技术战略/技术 S 曲线/引入阶段	P32 第 1 行和图 1.14
176	C	文化/产品创新团队结构/理想的跨职能团队/特征	P263 第 5 行和 P355 第 1 行
177	B	战略/创新支持战略/数字化战略/数字化战略框架/数字化战略制定流程	P45 图 1.24
178	B	文化/领导力/组织沟通/团队绩效/影响因素	P277 第 2 行
179	C	战略/可持续创新/可持续产品创新/可持续性成熟度模型/初始级	P55 图 1.29
180	A	市场调研/定量市场调研方法/问卷调查/应用	P227 倒数第 6 行
181	C	流程/产品创新流程模型/精益产品创新方法/13 项精益原则	P119 倒数第 8 行
182	B	文化/领导力/情商/自我认知/内容	P278 第 3 行
183	C	市场调研/产品使用测试/阿尔法测试和贝塔测试/贝塔测试/适用情境	P241 第 3 行
184	A	市场调研/定量市场调研方法/眼动追踪	P231 第 6 行
185	B	创新管理/度量指标与关键绩效指标/产品创新度量指标	P355 图 7.42

序号	答案	知识点	教材页码
186	D	流程/产品创新流程模型/门径流程/敏捷门径混合型流程	P112 第 1 行
187	D	文化/虚拟团队/虚拟团队模式/知识管理/实践活动	P279 图 6.12
188	C	工具/制造与装配阶段/六西格玛设计/IDOV/内容	P194 第 4 行
189	D	创新管理/可行性分析/内容	P333 倒数第 8 行
190	B	创新管理/项目管理/进度压缩/赶工和快速跟进	P346 第 1 行
191	A	创新管理/财务分析/现金流/算法	P336 图 7.29
192	C	创新管理/产品生命周期中的鸿沟/跨越鸿沟/罗杰斯技术扩散曲线	P318 第 5 行
193	D	创新管理/度量指标与关键绩效指标/平衡计分卡/四个维度	P351 图 7.39
194	A	文化/虚拟团队/有效性	P279 第 6 行
195	B	创新管理/可行性分析/内容	P332 第 10 行
196	C	流程/流程地图	补充知识
197	D	创新管理/产品生命周期/产品经理在产品生命周期中/成熟阶段/角色	P315 图 7.8
198	B	组合/资源配置/工程人员生产率与项目数量的关系	补充知识
199	D	文化/团队与领导力中的可持续性/最佳实践	P284 倒数第 2 行
200	C	组合/组合管理系统应用/组合管理的复杂性/对策	P86 第 9 行

作者介绍

楼政

《产品经理认证（NPDP）知识体系指南（第 2 版）》编委和译者。业内知名的产品管理、项目管理、创新方法培训师和咨询顾问。金指南管理咨询（中国国际人才交流基金会优秀授权合作机构）创办人。全国项目管理标准技术委员会专家。国家创新方法研究会技术创新方法专业委员会理事。科技部创新方法新系统课题负责人。《项目管理知识体系指南》、《项目集管理标准》等国际标准的编审参与者。中国国际人才交流基金会特聘产品经理（NPDP）师资班培训师（国内首位）。产品经理（NPDP）、项目集管理（PgMP）、项目管理（PMP）授权培训师。六西格黑带和 TRIZ 专家。专业著译作近 20 部。

从事一线项目实践 20 余年，领导和交付了数十个大型复杂项目。从事培训、咨询工作 20 年，辅导了数百家企业，培训了数万名专业人士。首创了实战演习和全真项目实战培训方法，并创立了产品、管理和经营"三者融合"咨询方法，个人、团队和组织"三位一体"咨询方法，帮助企业实现收益倍增，受到企业推崇。

楼政老师历时 8 年，倾力打造《金指南产品管理实战培训》精品课程，成为后 NPDP（参加 NPDP 认证培训之后）和产品管理从业者必修的实训课程。在该实训中，学员组成团队，置身真实的应用情境，运用专业方法，共同开发产品（分为指定产品和自选产品），产出专利并进行成果转化。该课程线上和线下同步进行，不受地域限制。

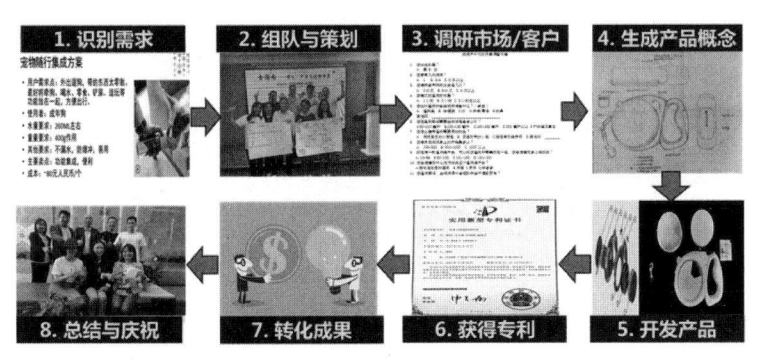

图 1 "金指南产品管理实训"核心内容

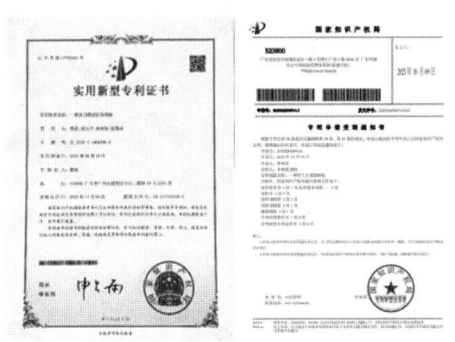

图 2 金指南学员在实训中产生的专利

金指南颠覆传统培训方法，推出培训 7.0 版，为客户实现最高的培训投资回报率。

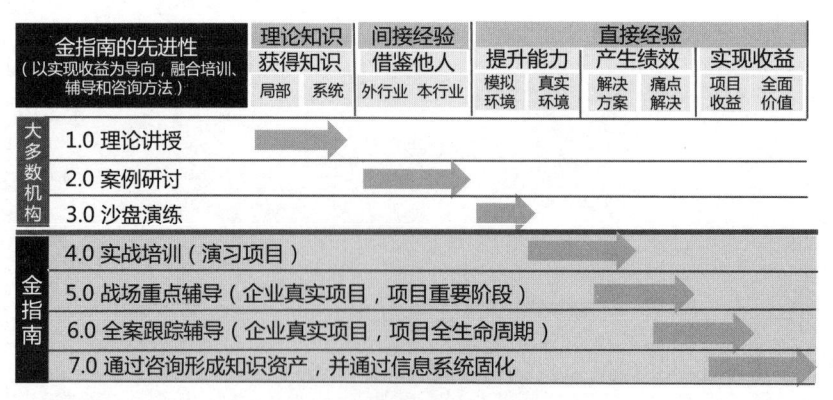

图 3　金指南培训 7.0 版

图 4　金指南培训、辅导与咨询服务一览图

推荐阅读： 产品管理、项目管理、创新类图书。

图 5　金指南楼政老师的著作和译作

欢迎广大读者致电楼政老师交流阅读感受，联系电话：18029169969（微信同步）。亦可登录金指南官网或联系俞老师（18681113109）咨询产品管理（NPDP）、项目管理（PMP）、敏捷项目管理（ACP）、信息系统项目管理师（软考高项）、中国标准化项目管理专业人员（CSPM）等的学习、认证考试和实战应用问题。